North of Normal

North of Normal

A Memoir of My Wilderness Childhood, My Unusual Family, and How I Survived Both

CEA SUNRISE PERSON

HARPER

NEW YORK . LONDON . TORONTO . SYDNEY

HARPER

A hardcover edition of this book was published in 2014 by HarperCollins Publishers.

HarperCollins books may be purchased for educational, business, or sales promotional use. For information please e-mail the Special Markets Department at SPsales@harpercollins.com.

All photographs are courtesy of the author except where noted.

FIRST HARPER PAPERBACK EDITION PUBLISHED 2015.

Library of Congress Cataloging-in-Publication Data has been applied for.

ISBN 978-0-06-228987-2 (pbk.)

HB 11.30.2022

For Mom, who taught me to focus on the positive and banish fear to the dungeon of useless emotions

November's winds
are keen and cold
As Brownies know
who roam the world
And have no home
to which to run
When they have had
their night of fun
But cunning hands
are never slow
To build a fire
of ruddy glow.

PALMER COX,
Brownie Year Book

Author's Note

This is the story of my life. Most of the memories depicted here are my own, but I have also drawn on the memories of my mother, grandparents, aunts and father. My early life was a complicated jumble of events that was difficult to put into order, even for my family, but I have done my best. Timelines may not be exact, and dialogue and settings have obviously been re-created in the interest of storytelling. I have also omitted certain events in my life that were not significant to this memoir. Some names, distinguishing features and locations have been changed to protect certain individuals.

Prologue

I rolled over in bed, reaching for the warmth of my mother under the bearskin blanket. She wrapped her arms around me, and I pulled Suzie Doll into my chest so we were three spoons. The birds were just starting to call. Through the tipi poles above, I could see a patch of lightening sky. Any moment now, our canvas walls would begin to turn from gray to orange. It was the time of day I liked best, because it was the start of everything.

"Mommy," I whispered.

"Shh . . . still sleeping."

I turned to look at her, then placed a finger on each eyelid and pulled them up. "Mommy. Is this the day Papa Dick gets back from hunting?"

"Maybe," she mumbled, batting my hand away. "Now go back to sleep."

I lay quietly beside her, but I was too excited to keep still. It had been a long winter, the meat from my grandfather's last big hunt had run out long ago, and he had promised he would try to get a bear, my favorite. My feet jiggled back and forth under the covers. I finally got them to stop, but then my fingers started to twitch. I drummed them on Mom's hip. "Mm-mm," she said, putting her hand on top of mine. "Cea, if you can't sleep, why don't you go start the fire? Heat up the footstone for me—it's cold this morning."

I lifted the bearskin and reached for the heavy rock. Wrapped in one of my grandfather's old wool shirts, it smelled like smoke and pine needles. I set it down beside the stove and pulled my clothes on: turtleneck, sweater, cords and leather moccasins. The summer before, one of the visitors' daughters had shown me something called underwear. They had tiny rainbows on them, and they were the most beautiful things I'd ever seen. Mom said I could have a pair one day, probably when I was five. But right now, I was still just four.

Mom was snoring lightly. I crept across our fir-needle floor, lifted the canvas door flap and stepped outside. It was no colder out here than it was in the tipi, but a breeze made goose bumps pop up on my skin. I hurried across the meadow to the shit pit and dropped my pants, peering down at the massive pile of poop beneath me as I peed. After zipping my pants, I slid the cover back over the pit and skipped over to my grandparents' tipi, stood quietly outside. I could tell by Grandma Jeanne's breathing she was still asleep, but there was another sound coming from my aunts' tipi a little farther down. I walked toward it, my moccasins skimming over the dewy grass, and peeked inside. My Aunt Jessie was asleep in her bed with her mouth wide open, but across from her, my Aunt Jan was doing the screwing with the guy visitor. She was sitting on top of him, her long blond hair hanging over her breasts in sweaty strings. I gazed at them curiously, wondering where the visitor's woman was. Mom said it usually wasn't a good idea to do the screwing with a visitor who had a woman, but my aunts didn't seem to mind. Maybe the woman was looking for her cat, which had disappeared yesterday. Anyway, Grandma Jeanne said that lady was awfully silly for bringing her city cat all the way to the wilderness like that.

I was starting to shiver. In the distance I could hear the rush of the river, finally set free from its winter freeze. The sun was peeking over the top of the highest mountain now, flooding our meadow with orange light. I headed toward the woodpile, thinking that I would build the fire and then ask Mom to make hot porridge with prunes for breakfast. I picked up a log, but was distracted by the sight of one of my stick horses propped against the sawhorse along with my bow and arrow.

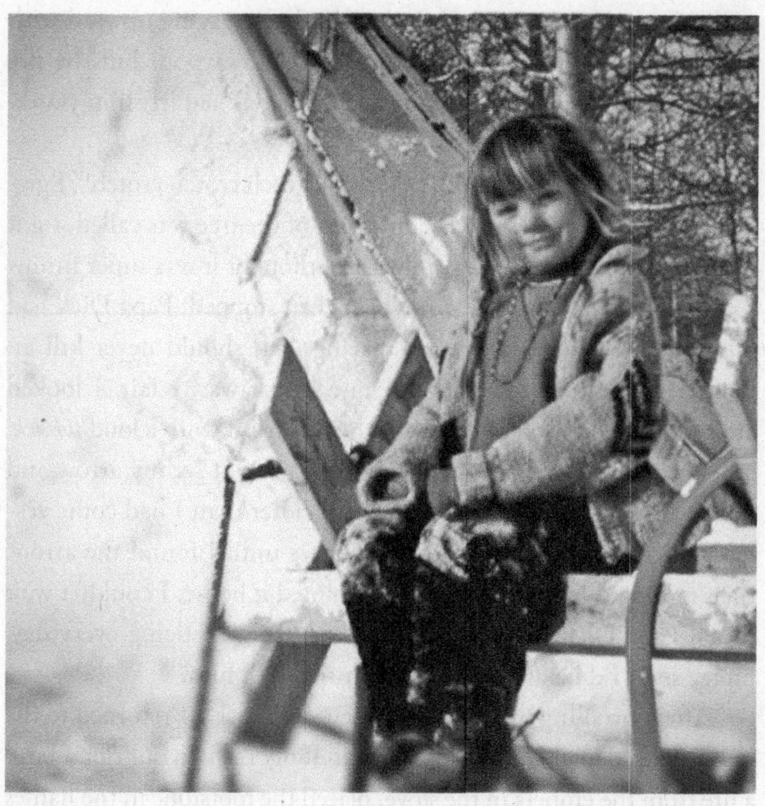

Me in front of our tipi in Kootenay Plains, sitting on the sawhorse that we used to cut our firewood.

Dropping the log back onto the woodpile, I mounted my horse, threw my bow over my shoulder and galloped across the meadow. "Giddyap! Giddyap, Apache!" I yelled, whipping the leather rein behind me. Randall, the Indian chief who lived across the river, had told me that word meant "go really fast" in horse language, and my horse always listened. He circled me around the meadow and then headed for the forest, almost bucking me off. Branches tugged at my sleeves, snagging my sweater as we ran, but my horse wouldn't stop. He kept going until we got to Porcupine Tree. I pulled back the reins and slipped off his back, gazing upward with my hand shading my eyes. It was dark in the woods but the sky was bright. And porcupine was exactly where I had left him yesterday, snoozing high up on a branch.

"Crotch," I said to myself quietly. "Crotch crotch crotch!" I giggled. Mom said that was what that part of the tree was called, right where the branch met the trunk, and I thought it was super funny. I reached for my bow and arrow, but then stopped. Papa Dick had told me that unless you were starving, you should never kill an animal when it was sleeping because it just wasn't fair. I looked around for a rock and pitched it at the tree trunk with a loud *whack*. The porcupine shook and snapped its head up. I set my arrow and pulled back my bow. It was a miss, but closer than I had come yesterday. I scrounged around in the bushes until I found the arrow, then mounted my horse again and pointed it home. I couldn't wait to tell Papa Dick. He had said that if I kept practicing every day, pretty soon I'd be allowed to go hunting with him.

After corralling my horse with a circle of rocks, I returned to the woodpile and loaded my arms with kindling. Back in our tipi, I built a fire from the embers in the stove, placed the footstone in the flames and waited for it to heat up. Then I carefully pulled it out with oven mitts, wrapped it up in the wool shirt and rolled it over to the bed.

"Thank you, sweetheart," Mom said with her eyes still closed, and opened her arms for me.

I snuggled into her naked body and she kissed my hair. After a little while, I decided to stop being so excited about Papa Dick maybe coming home, tucked my head under Mom's chin and fell fast asleep.

THE SUN WAS JUST starting to hide behind the tipi when I saw him. I was playing in the dirt, mixing it with water to paint on rocks, when I spotted Papa Dick across the meadow. I jumped up and ran full-speed until I slammed into his arms.

"Peanut!" he cried, spinning me around in circles.

I laughed and buried my face in his bushy hair. My eyes fell to the wheeled sled he was pulling behind him, brimming with chunks of bloody meat wrapped in wax paper.

"Did you get a bear? Did you get a bear?"

"Aha! Now that's a surprise. What do you say we get Grandma Jeanne to cook some up and see if you can guess what it is."

"Hooray!" I squirmed out of his arms and bolted for my grandparents' tipi, calling for my grandmother. "Grandma Jeanne! Papa got meat! Let's cook some up!"

She came out of the tipi, smiling, and ran to my grandfather. They hugged and kissed, Grandma Jeanne so happy she had tears running down her cheeks. My Aunt Jessie and Aunt Jan came out of their tipi and then Mom, and we were all hugging and laughing.

"Geez, you'd think I'd been gone a month instead of just a few days," Papa Dick said, but I could tell he was pleased.

The late-afternoon sun was warm on my head, the birds were singing, and Grandma Jeanne was in such a good mood that she put Van Morrison on the tape deck, even though Papa Dick said there was only a bit of juice left in the battery. We all boogied in the meadow to "Moondance," Mom rolled a joint and passed it around, and my grandmother heated up the iron skillet and fried up some of the meat in caribou fat. I took one bite, then jumped up to give my grandfather a hug.

"It's bear! It's bear! Oh, thank you, Papa Dick!"

When I went to bed that night, I was so full and happy that I didn't even care when Mom and Randall woke me up later. I rolled to the edge of the bed and faced the tipi wall, pretending the grunts and groans were just part of a dream and that really it was just Mom and me lying in bed, snuggled up all warm in the dying light of the kerosene lantern.

Part One

Dream

Chapter One

The story that is the life I now reflect on began with my grandfather Richard Abel Person. His history is likely even more interesting than my own, but I only know tidbits of it. Born in Duluth, Minnesota, to Swedish immigrant parents, he seemed to come into this world knowing his passion. When he was just a boy, he began taking to the woods behind his family's house to practice building campfires and setting handmade snares that brought down rabbits for his family's dinner. By the time he was sixteen, he had memorized nearly every edible plant in North America and had taught himself how to climb, fish and hunt with both rifle and bow and arrow. He could build a weatherproof shelter from tree branches and twine and paddle through stormy waters with a coffee mug clenched between his knees. Even early on, he knew he wasn't long for the urban life. When he walked the streets of his hometown, the concrete beneath his feet offended him. Sometimes he dreamed of escaping to a much different world altogether. But then he met my grandmother, and she gave him reason to stay.

Jeanne was nineteen years old when she first met Dick, who was three years younger. She was sitting on the grass at the local pool where she worked as a lifeguard, eating lunch with a girlfriend. His moccasined feet stopped in front of her, she lifted her eyes to meet his, and that was it. For my grandmother, meeting Dick wasn't just finding a kindred spirit, it was also a welcome distraction from reality. Her parents had divorced when she was eleven, and not much later Jeanne's mother had suffered a stroke that left half her body paralyzed. It fell to Jeanne, the only child, to run her family's bakery. She would wake each morning before sunrise, go to the bakery to work, walk the three miles to school, return to the bakery to help her mother until closing time, and fall into bed each night exhausted. And now that she was finished with school, between her bakery and lifeguard jobs her days seemed an endless cycle of work. When she could get away she would go to the forest to walk alone, sometimes wishing to get lost among the hills and valleys.

My grandparents courted for three years before marrying, and both of them were certain that there was no other love quite like theirs in the world. It was a love affair not just with each other, but with the rivers and trees and animals of the wild. Nature fed their souls and gave them purpose. On the day of their wedding, Jeanne was walking to city hall to meet Dick when she got her period. Dismayed when it left an unsightly stain on the back of her fancy tweed skirt, she returned home and changed into a pair of jeans. And this was how she was dressed an hour later, when she stood in front of her mother, stepfather and Dick's parents to exchange vows. Her mother despaired at her lack of formality, but Jeanne secretly thought it was the perfect outfit for the occasion and a true symbol of her relationship with her husband. They spent their honeymoon fishing and hiking around Lake Superior. My grandfather helped steady Jeanne's hands on the rifle as she fired her first bullet at a moose, felling it with one clean shot to the head.

My grandparents discussed ways they might live close to nature and still earn a living, and Dick decided on a career in forestry. He

Where it all began: my grandparents Dick and Jeanne Person, photographed in Duluth, Minnesota, in 1945.

joined the army to get a free university education, but a war was raging in Korea, and within a year he found himself fighting in the trenches of Incheon. He wrote letters home to Jeanne, telling of his anger with the U.S. government—here he was battling against communism, he lamented, when he wasn't even sure he believed in capitalism—along with his unexpected enjoyment of an existence that challenged the most basic elements of human nature. He was sleeping in the rain and eating live crickets right off the ground, things that his fellow soldiers loathed but that made Dick feel strangely alive, as if he were actually thriving in such an environment rather than merely surviving. He had long debates about the state of the American psyche with his comrades. "Folks don't own houses," he loved to say. "Houses own folks. Once you're beholden to an institute of finance, you may as well just put yourself in prison and throw away the key for good." Dick's friends listened to his rants, but he understood that most of his words fell on deaf ears. And that was okay, because he had his wife back at home, the woman who he knew would stay up knitting wool socks for him while he talked to her about everything that mattered.

After he returned from Korea, disillusioned with American values but otherwise unharmed, Dick completed his university degree and took a job as a forest ranger. It was an occupation that kept my grandparents broke and rootless, sending them from Minnesota to Washington and Missouri all within the span of a year, but neither of them really minded. They lived simply and were able to unpack their belongings at each new home within a few hours. Before long, the babies came—Jan, Michelle, Dane and then Jessie. Shortly after Jessie's birth she was proclaimed mentally retarded, but by that time, my grandmother was in such a state of depression that it barely seemed to register. She complained of migraines and spent hours in bed, and sometimes when Dick came home from work he would find her sitting in the dark while the kids ran wild around her. The truth was, he didn't blame her much. He loved his children, though between Jessie's mental challenges, Michelle's slowness, Dane's oddness—he seemed to live completely within his own world—and Jan's rages, they were a deeply mysterious handful of trouble. But Dick kept his concerns to himself. After all, this wasn't a subject he was about to bring up with his wife, who was teetering at the edge of an abyss he hardly dared to contemplate.

By the time the kids reached their teens, my family had moved to Jackson Hole and Jeanne's mental health had improved. Privately, though, Papa Dick felt as if his wife's years of depression had stolen a piece of her for good. She seemed more fragile than he remembered, and less confident. But perhaps my grandmother knew this about herself, because in 1966, she discovered something that made her realize happiness didn't necessarily need to come from within: marijuana. Within a few months, her occasional toke had evolved into a daily habit. The pot numbed her guilt and relieved her of the worries about her children that had plagued her for years. Even more than that, it helped her bond with them. After being introduced to it by a friend, Jeanne started offering it to her three oldest kids when Dane was twelve, Michelle thirteen and Jan fifteen. But the one thing her friend had neglected to tell her was that marijuana was a drug, and it was illegal. And so it was that in that very same year, the Persons had the distinction of being the subject of Wyoming State's very first pot bust.

It all started with Jan and Michelle riding in the back of a car. Mom's boyfriend was in the front passenger seat, and Jan's boyfriend, who owned the vehicle, was driving. The car blew through a stop sign, and the police pulled it over. When Jan's boyfriend rolled the window down, a cloud of pot smoke billowed into the officer's face. It only took a few minutes for Michelle to admit that her drug suppliers were also her parents. Their cabin was raided, Dick and Jeanne went to jail, and the children were dispersed to foster families. Dick eventually managed to convince the judge to let them go, and by that evening the family was in stitches around the dinner table over the whole episode. That was the night, Mom said, when the family decided to move to northern California. And that's when all hell broke loose.

Chapter Two

After years of living as misfits, coming to California felt like coming into their own to my family. People here actually seemed to care about things like freedom, healthy eating, and what was going on in the rest of the world. My grandparents rented a ramshackle old house ten miles south of San Jose on the outskirts of Los Gatos, and dedicated their days to pot smoking, nude cookouts, and philosophical discussions with the friends my grandfather made at his new job as a climbing instructor. The kids, left to their own devices, dropped out of school one by one. By the time my future mother Michelle was fifteen, all four of them were spending their days smoking at home and their evenings with various love interests. Dane's primary affair seemed to be with LSD, but the girls made the most of their sexual freedom. They brought home guys, scruffy-looking characters with matted hair and rambling political opinions that no one listened to, who spent the night and then sat at the breakfast table with Grandma Jeanne the next morning with their dingdongs in full view. Before long, the Person residence became known to many as the coolest place in town to hang out; the music was hip, the drugs were in good supply, the two older daughters were pretty and willing, and the parents were always totally groovy with it all.

One afternoon, my grandfather came home from work to find his wife having sex with another man. The couple was huddled under a sleeping bag on the living room floor, but the noises coming from within were unmistakable. Papa Dick stared down at the scene before him, his expression hard. It wasn't that he was angry; he and my grandmother had had an open marriage almost since they arrived in California. It's just that until that day, the arrangement had been strictly one-sided. While my grandfather brought women home to their bed, Jeanne had preferred to numb her evenings away with pot. Now panic gripped my grandfather's heart. He turned away before his wife could notice him, and went to the backyard to sit with his head in his hands. At that moment, he admitted the truth to himself: this latest development was just another tear in the thin fabric that was barely holding his family together. His children were in crisis. Jan had taken up with a Hells Angels leader, and often came home drugged out on acid and beaten blue. Michelle was rarely seen without a joint in her hand, and didn't have an inkling where Vietnam, the country's number one topic of conversation, even was. Dane had been acting more and more strangely lately, a result, my grandfather was certain, of too many bad acid trips. And Jessie, though mentally challenged and barely thirteen years old, was bringing new guys home regularly. But if there was one thing Papa Dick was sure of, it was that society was to blame for his children's troubles.

My grandfather's early golden view of California was fading fast. After three years there, he had begun to notice the hypocrisy of supposedly enlightened folks who professed their hatred of The Man by evening and then returned to their cog-grinding, hamster-in-the-wheel jobs by day. For all their talk about striking out against corporations and government, in the end these people still paid their taxes, kept their money in banks, and bought their burgers at

McDonald's. There were some exceptions—the commune-dwellers, for example, folks who started off with the best intentions but inevitably ended up using their emancipation as an excuse for one long, drug-fueled sex-fest. The antiwar crowd was more sincere in their convictions, but though the impending threat of the draft hung over his own son's head, it was freedom my grandfather craved, not retreat from the powers of authority he so loathed.

The idea that had been brewing in his mind since his teens was pulling at him stronger than ever now. He had heard talk about a movement up north in Canada, a land known for its harsh climate and gentle handling of disillusioned Americans. But a new country was only the start of my grandfather's plan. He knew how to hunt, how to survive in the wild, and he had some exciting ideas about shelter. What his kids needed was fresh mountain air and dirt between their toes. If he could just get them away from the city and into nature, back to the basics of food, water, clothing and shelter, they might still stand a chance. And so, he thought, might his marriage.

Papa Dick stood up and walked back into his house, filled with renewed conviction. He would wait until his wife's lover left, then he would tell her that the time had come for them to pursue a life far more meaningful than the clichéd hippie existence they had allowed themselves to slip into. He was almost certain she would agree. In fact, there was only one person in the family my grandfather was worried about convincing, and that was his sixteen-year-old daughter Michelle. Because only days ago, she had come to her parents with some happy news: she was madly in love, ready for marriage and two months pregnant.

THE FIRST TIME MY father set eyes on my mother, she was running toward him with her hair flying and bare breasts bouncing.

Like an X-rated ad for Breck Shampoo, she stopped in front of him, tossed her waves aside and gave him a coy smile. Greg blinked back at her, more intrigued by her complete lack of modesty than he was by her appearance. He was one of my grandfather's climbing students, and had just emerged from his VW bus to have dinner with my family. An aspiring artist and Catholic boy brought up within a hedged suburban community, he hadn't yet lived large, but had plans to: a little climbing and surfing, a few years of university, a summer in Europe funded by the sale of his vehicle, and some fun with the women he had no trouble attracting. Greg was tall, brainy and handsome, a man who others considered to hold great promise. He was twenty-two years old and Michelle was fifteen. He grinned back at her, carefully holding his eyes above chest level, and it never even crossed his mind to become involved with such a young girl.

There was, however, one small complication: it was the sixties.

The Person family was like none my father had ever met before. They got high together, shared the bathroom for showers and bowel movements, and didn't even bother closing their bedroom doors for intimate encounters. Fascinated by my grandfather's unique outlook on life and inspired by his unfailing confidence, Greg began spending more and more time at the Person home. He dug the music they listened to, the food they ate, the fact that they talked about sex right out in the open, and that the females, not the least bit self-conscious, didn't mind if he sketched nude drawings of them as they went about their day. Greg befriended everyone in the house, even Dane, but he was careful to avoid my perpetually topless mother.

Michelle, however, had her eye on a target and wouldn't be swayed. Although she was young, she had plenty of experience when it came to seduction, and in the end her persistence paid off.

She had a boyfriend, some short dude with bad teeth named Little Joe who appeared to be living in the backyard shed, but that didn't stop her from taking my father's hand at the beach one evening and leading him to a secluded sand dune. For Greg, one night would have been enough, but he also understood the complications of bedding the daughter of the man he had come to nearly idolize. My grandfather seemed to approve of the relationship, so Greg decided to go with it, at least until Michelle lost interest. But each day only seemed to crush my mother tighter against him, until he felt like he couldn't breathe. At night, she would trail her fingers over his body until he caught her hand in his own to stop it. Unabashed, she would leave the light on to stare at him as he slept, unable to believe her good luck. Here she was, not yet sweet sixteen, and she had already found herself a bona fide college man. My mother knew she wasn't the sharpest tool in the shed, and she had already seen her share of trouble and pain, some of which she had promised herself she would never tell another soul. But her love for Greg made her want to forget all the darkness, and dive headlong into the promise of everlasting devotion and protection.

WHEN MOM TOLD MY father she was pregnant, he asked her a few questions in disbelief ("Are you sure?" "Really sure?" "Totally positive?"), then left her house with the look of a trapped animal given the choice of chewing off his leg or waiting to die. A few days later, he came by and dropped off two hundred dollars in an envelope with the words *I'm sorry* scrawled across it, having sold his beloved VW bus to secure the cash. My mother, utterly devastated, spent an entire week bawling her eyes out and comforting herself with her mother's pot stash. Jeanne, at a loss to console her daughter, finally took a bus into the city to make the necessary arrangements.

A short meeting with a doctor, a couple of signatures, and she was able to go home and tell Michelle it would all be over soon. My mother took to her bed and vowed not to leave it until either the day of the abortion arrived or my father had a change of heart.

Against all probability, the house in Los Gatos had a telephone, though it was almost never used. But on an afternoon in May of 1969, less than a week before my mother was scheduled to abort me, the ringing of the telephone was the most beautiful sound she had ever heard. "I'm in Reno," Greg said to her over the line, his voice trembling with either excitement or fear. "Pack yourself a bag and get on a bus. We're getting married." Mom screamed and dropped the phone on the floor, she was that happy.

MY MOTHER WAS A wife for five months. And when Greg left her again, this time for good, Papa Dick decided it was time to make his move. He sold off most of his family's possessions, waved goodbye to his wannabe revolutionary friends and herded his wife and kids into the old VW bus. Mom once told me that her family left California on a Thursday and she didn't stop crying until the following Friday, nearly one week after they had set up digs in a tumbledown house in a town just over the Canadian border whose name she didn't even think to ask.

Chapter Three

If my mother hadn't nearly lost her mind, we probably would have made it into the wilderness a lot sooner. Our time in Hills, British Columbia, was never meant to be more than a stopover to accommodate my birth, but it became an eighteen-month delay stretched out like a frayed elastic by my mother's deteriorating state of mental health. And as my grandfather's patience wore thin and tensions among family members built, my mother came face to face with her darkest inner demon: the green-scaled serpent.

Just days after settling into our temporary home, a draughty old house negotiated by my grandfather in exchange for a side of bear meat, my mother took to pacing the worn floorboards with her hands at the small of her back. Still inconsolable over the loss of my father, she kept screaming at her mother, "What are we doing here?" Eventually, instead of answering, Jeanne just held her daughter's hands and told her to push. On the last morning of November, just as the sun was appearing over the distant mountains, I was born in a tiny hospital just down the road from Hills in a town called New Denver.

"A girl," the doctor said, holding me by the legs like a plucked chicken. "And Lord above, but she's a long and skinny one." He laid me across my mother's chest, and my eyes flew open and locked onto hers.

"She looks exactly like her father," she breathed to Grandma Jeanne, shaking her head sadly. "Cea. I'm going to call her Cea. That's the name Greg picked out for her. Before . . ." Her eyes filled with tears.

"Look out the window," Grandma Jeanne said, desperate to distract her daughter from her pain. "Look at that beautiful rising sun. Surely that's a wonderful sign." Just then, as if on cue, someone down the hall snapped on a radio and "Here Comes the Sun" filtered tinnily into the air. Mom lifted her face and smiled for the first time in weeks. "I love this song. That'll be her middle name. Sunrise."

Freshly named and scrubbed, I went home that evening. Mom placed me in a cardboard box in front of the fireplace. She looked down at me sleeping peacefully, then went to her bedroom and returned with something in her hands. "Suzie Doll," she said softly, tucking her childhood doll in beside me. "Who would have thought you'd be replaced by the real thing so soon?"

MY MOTHER TOLD ME that when I let out my first wail, shortly after my homecoming and just minutes after she herself had finally fallen asleep, it took hours to reach its end. "She's colicky," my grandmother declared as I continued to scream my way into day five, but that was just the beginning of it. I shrieked day and night, practically without pause, until even the neighbors inquired. My overwhelmed mother took to gazing straight ahead as if paralyzed while I cried, or walking in aimless circles with my head flopped sideways onto her hand. When I arched my back and wailed instead of feeding, she would lay me down on her mattress and leave the room to smoke a joint.

One evening, Papa Dick found my mother standing at an

open window with a pitiful look of defeat in her eyes and her arms wrapped limply around my writhing body. He scooped me up, led his daughter over to her bed, and then brought me outside while he chopped wood for the fireplace. Things hadn't been easy for his family since their move to Canada. Jan had already run away once, hitchhiking back to California to reunite with her biker lover, only to return home when she found him passed out with another woman's lips wrapped around his flaccid penis. Just recently, the family had had supper with folks at a local commune, a visit that resulted in a dose of the clap for Jan and a case of hep B for the rest of the family. Dane's increasingly erratic behavior—he left the house late at night and ranted on about aliens posing as government officials—was becoming more and more worrisome. And now Michelle's sanity seemed to be slipping. As much as my grandfather was itching to be on his way, he knew his dream would have to wait a little longer. There was no way he could afford to have two of his kids losing their marbles out in the bush.

As it turned out, Papa Dick was right to be cautious. My mother's day of reckoning came when I was about six months old. It happened when she was sitting in the bedroom she shared with her sisters, staring at herself in the mirror while she smoked a joint. The house was empty, and I was screaming. Mom had been trying to soothe me for hours, rotating like an automaton through a futile routine of lullaby, walk and swaddle. I hadn't nursed since morning, too wound up to latch on to her breast, so she finally gave up and just placed me in her lap. She knew it would only be a matter of time before I hyperventilated enough to pass out, which happened on the really bad days.

As my shrieks filled the room, Mom took a deep pull on her joint and plucked a photograph from the corner of the mirror. It was a picture of my father, taken during the time they had been together. He was wearing a fringed suede vest and playing the guitar. My mother let out a loud sob and collapsed in a heap beside me. How could he have done this to her? She hadn't even wanted a baby, but he had married her and given her hope, and then left her when she was too far along to do anything about it. And now her parents were going to move her to the wilderness, of all places, where quite possibly she would never meet another man as long as she lived.

Suddenly it all seemed too much to bear. My mother put me down on the floor and lay beside me with a brand-new idea in her head. Although the thought was a scary one, it was also strangely comforting: a permanent way out. She pondered her options. There were no pills in the house, no vehicle to sit in and asphyxiate herself, and no high buildings or bridges nearby. Her father's hunting rifles were in the basement, but she was pretty sure she wouldn't be able to reach the trigger if she aimed it at herself. Her only viable option seemed to be a rope. She considered this for a while, but all she could think of was a photo she'd once seen in *National Geographic* of a woman's face after she'd hung herself. Despite my mother's misery, ugly and bloated was not the way she wished to exit the world.

Still laid out on the floor, Mom finished up her joint and lit another. Her mind entered a sort of hazy state of emptiness. She stopped thinking about ways to kill herself, about my father, and even about me. She just smoked and lay there, staring up at the ceiling. After a while, she noticed an annoying sound in her ear that wouldn't go away, like the buzzing of a mosquito. At first she thought it was leaves rustling outside her window, but then she realized it was actually a voice, and that it was speaking to her. Yes—it was telling her to look in the mirror. She sat up and did so, and right there, coming out the top of her head, was a serpent.

My mother, more curious than afraid, stared at the reptile. It was small and shiny, with perfectly formed green scales, and it rose directly up from her hair like a curl of smoke. And as she gazed at it, she knew exactly why it had come. It had come for her mind.

As my mother listened, the serpent spoke to her. Her sanity had been crumbling for some time, the snake said, but it had now reached the end of the line. All that was left for her to do was to make a choice. She needed to decide if she wanted to enter into a world where everything would be easier, but where her days would be ruled by confinement rather than freedom.

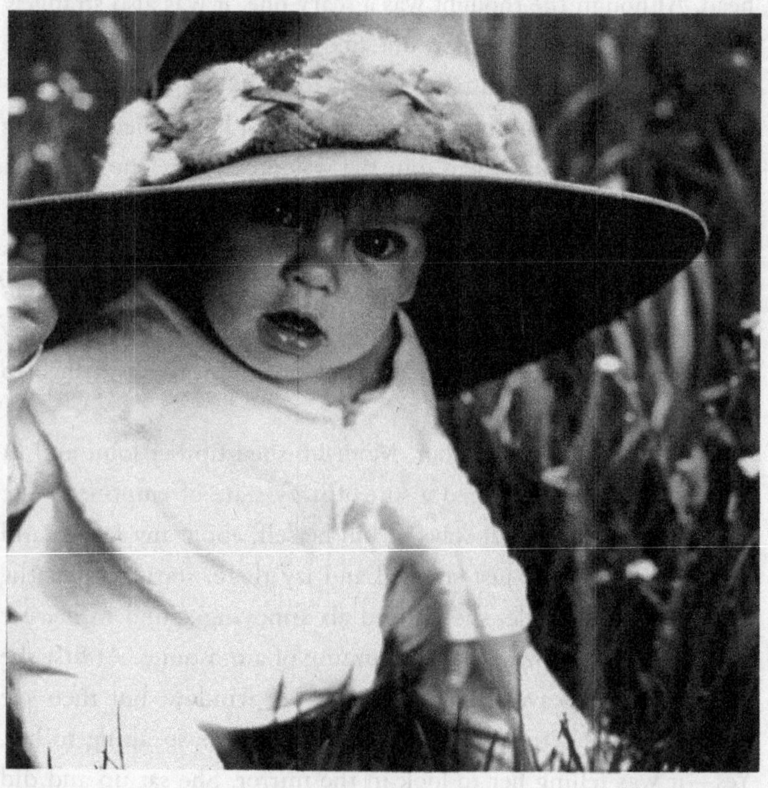

Me as a baby, wearing Papa Dick's hat.

Freedom. It was this word that jarred my mother from her trance. She knew it was something she wouldn't be able to live without, and she silently said as much to the serpent. It nodded, satisfied, and flicked its tongue at her one last time. *Now*, it said to her, *pick up your baby.* Mom shook her head to clear it, and her ears slowly tuned in to the sound of my cries. When she looked back at the mirror, the snake was gone.

After that, things changed. Mom put my father's picture away in a box, and swore off drugs for a good month or so. She was grateful for her narrow escape, but she also understood that her decision had come with a price: no more denial. No matter how unprepared she might be for motherhood, her fate was now tied to mine until the very end of her days.

Chapter Four

The journey from southern British Columbia to northern Alberta is a long but picturesque one, with each bend in the road revealing yet another view straight out of a Canadian tourism brochure. Wildflowers spring from green hillsides, dense forests give way to rippling bodies of water, and snow-topped mountain faces loom against bright blue skies. The scenery, however, was little more than a distraction from my family's anxious thoughts. It was May of 1971, eighteen months after my birth, and my grandfather was finally on the road to his dream. But for such a monumental day, the mood in the van was somber. My Aunt Jan had nearly convinced herself to get out at the next gas station and hitchhike, yet again, back to California. Grandma Jeanne alternated between worrying about the viability of their tipi—after all, she had made it herself and never tested it—and wondering if they would be able to survive a freezing northern winter at all. Aunt Jessie simply feared that they might all starve to death. And my mother couldn't help but think about her brother Dane, who had hit the dead end of mental soundness several months before and was noticeably absent that day. She could only hope that I, now sleeping straddled across her lap as the highway unwound behind us, would never learn why he was no longer with us.

But of everyone in the van, Papa Dick was probably the most tense. Usually immune to worries of a material nature, even he had to admit that the risk he was taking was huge. He had less than five hundred dollars left to his family's name, fewer worldly possessions than his vehicle could hold, and no backup plan. In fact, he wasn't even certain of our final destination. We were driving toward an expanse of the Rocky Mountains known as the Kootenay Plains, but where we would actually park and take the first footsteps into our new life remained to be seen. Papa Dick had heard rumor of a band of Cree Indians living along the river in the area, but he had also been warned that they could be unforgiving if they found white folk living on their land; there were reports of a small group of commune-dwellers who, not long before and after daring to trespass, had had their tents burned to the ground. Much better, my grandfather knew, would be to announce his plans to the Indians and obtain their blessing. Of course, we had to find them first.

Two days after we left Hills, Papa Dick pulled off the David Thompson Highway into a crop of evergreens and killed the ignition. Everyone sat in silence, recognizing the significance of the moment.

"Well," my grandfather said finally, setting the parking brake and peering up at the sun. "We still have a few hours of daylight left. Let's get going."

My family moved like a team of ants, gathering belongings and heaving canoes from the roof of the van. Everyone, that is, except my Aunt Jan, who moodily smoked a joint on the floor while I sat beside her, using her roach clip to pull threads from my shirt hem. Papa Dick fetched his axe and proceeded to hack off enough evergreen branches to conceal the vehicle from passing traffic, but still she sat in her darkened cave, sulkily blowing smoke into the air. My Aunt Jessie stood, staring into the van at her sister: the youngest and the oldest, the pleaser and the rebel. "Come on, Janny-wan, let's go," Jessie said in her slow and deliberate way, but Jan wouldn't be swayed. Tossing back her long golden locks, she shook her head and squared her shoulders.

Finally, my grandfather lifted me from the floor and gave Jan a sad shrug. "Lock up when you leave," he said to her quietly, and walked with Jessie to join the rest of his family on the riverbank.

Stepping close to the water, he surveyed the river in both directions. "Downstream," he declared. "Even tribesmen need to go to town sometimes. It's easier to paddle downstream with a boat full of supplies." And with that, he pushed his canoe into the flow of the river and waited for my grandmother to follow suit. She hesitated, peering up at the road in the direction of her oldest daughter, and then slid her boat into the swirling current. Just then Jan came running down the bank, joint in hand.

"Fuck it. Just fuck it all to hell," she said to her father, and he started to laugh. Pretty soon the rest of the family joined in, and one by one they placed arms around shoulders and waists, forming a loose circle. Whatever the future might hold for the Persons, they would face it together.

"YOU MAY STAY, BUT we will not look after you. Your survival is in your own hands." These words were spoken by the chief of the Stoney Indian tribe, a man by the name of Randall, whose powerful, stocky build seemed at war with the soft cascade of his waist-length braids. Papa Dick's instincts about the natives' location had been right, and we had found them just over an hour into our paddle. My grandfather, with his gift for convincing others to see things his way, hadn't taken long to win Randall over in our bid to stay on their land. Randall had even given us a brief tour of their camp. My family walked the pathways slowly, taking in the twenty or so tipis of canvas and rawhide, the cooking tent, the sweatlodge, and the corral of horses, all while forty faces stared at us curiously.

Finally, the chief led us back down to the river and pointed to a fallen log, positioned several feet over the water and bridging the two shores.

"There," Randall said. "Over that log and through that stand of birch trees, you will find a meadow where the land is flat. Pitch your tipi close to the trees to break the wind. This is not your first tipi, I assume?" He fixed his eyes on my grandfather, who smiled broadly and adjusted his hat.

"Of course not," he said.

Randall nodded and lifted a hand in farewell, his eyes lingering briefly on my mother. My grandparents stood facing the opposite shore, silently inspecting their new site. Nobody said the obvious: we may have found a home, but the real work was just about to begin.

ONE THING MY FAMILY hadn't anticipated was the rain. It came in a torrent shortly after we arrived, just when we were planning to fell trees to build our tipi frame. We took to our tents and remained there, trapped on our separate islands while we wrapped ourselves in sleeping bags and made our way through the dry food supplies. After three days, everything we owned was soaked, my mother was half-insane from listening to me scream in protest of my nylon prison and my grandparents' spirits were as sodden as their clothing. On day four, they decided that enough was enough. As the rain poured down, my family pitched a lean-to to build a fire under, took turns cooking over our Coleman camping stove, traipsed into the forest to fell trees and stripped and bound poles.

Within a week, the tipi frame was raised and readied for the shell. With her heart in her throat, my grandmother pulled the canvas from its bag and slowly unfolded it beneath the lean-to.

The rain had lightened that day, but the ground was still slick. Grandma Jeanne watched as her husband and daughters, slipping and sliding in the mud, attempted to wrap the shell around the poles. She couldn't even begin to count the number of hours she had spent on her treadle sewing machine, sewing strips of fabric together with nothing but a photo of a tipi from a newspaper clipping to guide her. If the seams didn't hold or the canvas didn't fit, her family had no backup winter shelter. Papa Dick tugged and stretched while her daughters pulled, but within a short time it became clear that my grandmother's worst fear had been realized. If we hadn't been so desperate for shelter, the scene would have been comical: our tipi ended a foot and a half short of the ground.

While her daughters sank to the ground in defeat, my grandmother circled the tipi. Giving up, she knew, was not an option. She scribbled some numbers down on paper, then instructed her husband and daughters to get her sewing machine. They pulled it out from beneath a tarp, carried it under the lean-to, and stripped the tipi shell off the frame. Then, thanking her lucky stars she had brought both her sewing machine and extra fabric along, Grandma Jeanne threaded the needle and attached a length of fabric to the bottom of the canvas. Mom said there was a moment when my grandmother was sitting at her machine, sewing furiously in the meadow while the rain poured down around her, when she just threw her head back and laughed until tears ran down her cheeks. Everyone else joined in. That was one thing about the Persons: if nothing else, they were good at seeing the humor in their predicaments.

BY LATE SUMMER, MY family was getting a handle on wilderness living. In many ways, it was everything my grandparents had envisioned: total privacy, a beautiful setting surrounded by mountains, clean water and air, and almost complete emancipation from the outside world. But in other ways, the work involved was much more grueling than even they had expected. Our diet consisted mostly of wild game, so my grandfather spent hours each day hunting bear, moose and grouse. And since he insisted on wasting no part of the animal, a successful big-game kill always meant weeks of work ahead. After the meat was cut, wrapped and stored in our tree platform, Grandma Jeanne would drain the blood to eat like soup, cut out the organs to eat, and boil the head and tongue to make a gelatinous mash known as headcheese. After that, almost every remaining part of the carcass was made into something useful: bones were carved into tools, antlers were made into hooks, and the hide was scraped with tanning knives and preserved with the mashed-up brain.

Every day there was water to haul, laundry to wash in the river, wild berries, mushrooms, onions and edible flowers to pick, and endless amounts of wood to collect and chop for the upcoming winter. Mice quickly overran our tipi, making baiting and cleaning traps a regular necessity. And despite our best efforts, occasional trips to town were unavoidable. These were all-day affairs, with Papa Dick leaving before sunrise to paddle back to the VW, removing its branch camouflage, driving four hours to town, and gathering what food and supplies we couldn't provide for ourselves. But even when he finally reached the grocery store, his task wasn't a simple one. With money so tight, instead of paying retail he would offer an employee a few bucks for their past-prime produce. And, if all else failed, he wasn't ashamed to head to the store's Dumpster.

The next day, Grandma Jeanne and her daughters would get out their paring knives and whittle every salvageable morsel of food out of the rot.

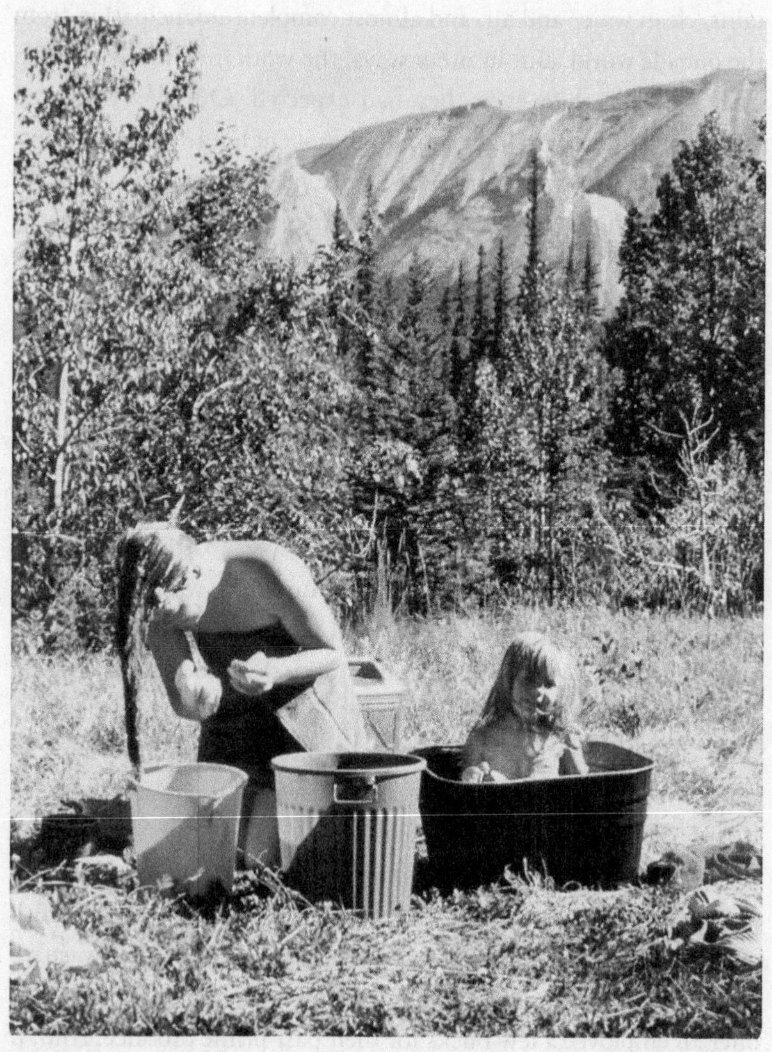

My mother and me, demonstrating the only way to keep clean on the Kootenay Plains.

To my grandmother, her work sometimes felt endless. Not only was there the cooking to do—she made bannock and yogurt, grew alfalfa sprouts, jarred berries, and stewed dried fruit—there was also the daily cleanup, which meant pots of water boiled over the open fire, several basins of dirty dishes, and the ongoing problem of where to put everything away. We were five adults and a toddler living in a twenty-foot circle, so to say quarters were cramped was an understatement. Besides my grandparents' bed (sleeping bags atop a bearskin pallet), the tipi contained several tree stumps for chairs, four plastic food coolers, my grandfather's book and rifle collections, our water barrel, a tape deck hooked up to a freestanding car battery that we used as a generator, some wooden shelving and two sets of antlers that acted as hooks mounted to the inside of the tipi frame. With no room for a table, food was prepared on the floor on chopping boards and we ate meals in our laps. My aunts, mother and I were sleeping in tents, but autumn was coming quickly and soon we would be forced to move into the tipi for warmth. Which brought us to a problem much more pressing than our need for more space: we desperately needed a woodstove, and with no money to buy one, even Papa Dick was beginning to worry.

TO MY GRANDFATHER, EMPTYING one's bowels was much more than the necessary evil it was to most folks. The way he saw it, almost every health problem could be traced to the intake and elimination of food, and he had even perfected a gut roll that he was fond of showing off. Starting at his diaphragm, his stomach muscles would clench and roll visibly downward to the base of his belly, releasing his colon in an impressive display. So it's no surprise that of all Papa Dick's creations, he was proudest of the shit pit. In lieu of an outhouse, this was our version of a toilet—quite simply, a ten-by-ten-foot hole dug in the ground with several boards over it to keep the flies out. Modern toilets were the cause of countless medical problems on account of the sitting position they forced their users to assume, my grandfather liked to say, but by contrast the shit pit allowed its customers to squat. It offered no privacy whatsoever, but by the time my family moved to the wilderness, such pretensions had long gone the way of refrigerators and running water. In fact the shit pit became a rather social place, and it was here that my Aunt Jan had her inspiration for our woodstove. My family was used to my aunt's unpredictability—on some days she would scream or toss cold water over the head of whoever had been stupid enough to piss her off, on others she was needy and apologetic, and at still other times she would cry nonstop. But on her good days, she could be very resourceful.

"I've got it!" she said to Grandma Jeanne, jumping up from the pit and zipping her cords. "The Indian camp! I saw something there we could use for a stove." And with that she ran off before my grandmother, loath to ask the natives any favors, could protest. "Don't worry," Jan yelled back, as if reading her mother's mind. "It'll be an even exchange!"

Two hours later, my aunt came back rolling a rusty old barrel, still dripping wet from being hauled through the river. Papa Dick looked at his daughter questioningly, and was just about to protest when she cut him short.

"It's better than nothing," she said peevishly, and my grandfather could only agree.

OUR NEW STOVE WAS christened The Guzzler on account of the amount of wood it burned. Using a metal saw, Papa Dick cut a hole in the barrel, creating a greedy belly that my entire family immediately became enslaved to. But by mid-October, we couldn't have survived without it. Winter came on with a fierce howl, sweeping a thick layer of white across our landscape and bringing a drop in temperature so extreme that, for several brief ugly moments, my grandparents looked at each other and seriously wondered if they had made a grave mistake. Not that turning back was an easy option at that point; the river had already frozen over, leaving the nine-mile trek back to the VW possible only by ski and snowshoe, which only my grandparents possessed.

By late November, Papa Dick was wondering if he'd chopped enough wood. He'd counted on two cords to see us through the winter, but with the stove burning constantly day and night, the woodpile was already looking picked over. We slept beneath layers of bearskins with heated rocks in our beds, but even then, we woke up with icy ears and snot frozen to the tips of our noses. It was the wind, though, that was the worst. Whenever it blew, it lifted the ill-fitting canvas off the poles just enough to let in a freezing billow of air. This caused some of the seams to rip, so after stormy nights my grandmother could be found inside the tipi with her needle and thread, furiously stitching it back together.

In April of 1972, my family felt confident; they had successfully made it through their first year in the wilderness living under canvas. Our food supplies were extremely low and our cash can empty but for a pitiful rattle, but we were all healthy and had the bounty of spring to look forward to: game, grouse, fish from the river and wild edible plants. But this far north, spring was a long-winded promise that rarely got fulfilled until late June, and as can so often happen, nature had one last surprise in store for us.

It started on a day like many others, cold but not forbidding as the season slowly shifted into warmer gear. Our handmade tipi was battered from the long winter but still hanging in there like a determined hero. The wind began to howl as we were settling down to sleep, prompting Grandma Jeanne to heat some extra rocks in the stove for our beds. Papa Dick inspected the weakened seams of the canvas with a neutral expression, then went outside to double check the stakes that held the shell to the ground. With nothing to do but wait, we all went to bed and lay awake, listening to the impossibly loud beating of the tipi flaps. Eventually, we all must have fallen asleep.

I remember one moment from this story, and that is being awakened by the sounds of a loud splintering and a horrifying ripping, and then a spruce tree crashing inside our tipi. It had fallen just shy of Grandma Jeanne's head, clawing a hole in the canvas from the apex of the tipi poles right down to the ground. The loose canvas thrashed in the wind. Snowflakes stung at our faces. Jan was yelling, Jessie was crying and Mom was crushing me to her chest. My grandparents grabbed at the canvas, trying to pull it back over the naked part of the frame. The wind yanked mercilessly at the fabric, finding the weakest seams and tearing right through them. Within minutes the shell was in tatters, floating away into the darkness like an enormous ghost. Snow settled on our beds, floor and table, sparing only a circular area around the still-warm woodstove.

The next thing we knew, Randall was beside us, holding a kerosene lantern and shouting at us to follow him. Mom yelled at me to find my boots, but they were crushed beneath the fallen tree. She finally hoisted me on her back, and we all traipsed through the swirling snow over the log bridge to the Indian camp. Randall led us into the cooking tent, where a warm fire was burning. We all gathered around the stove. Randall looked us over and then gave a low, rare laugh.

"My good friends," he said, "you must do something about that tipi of yours."

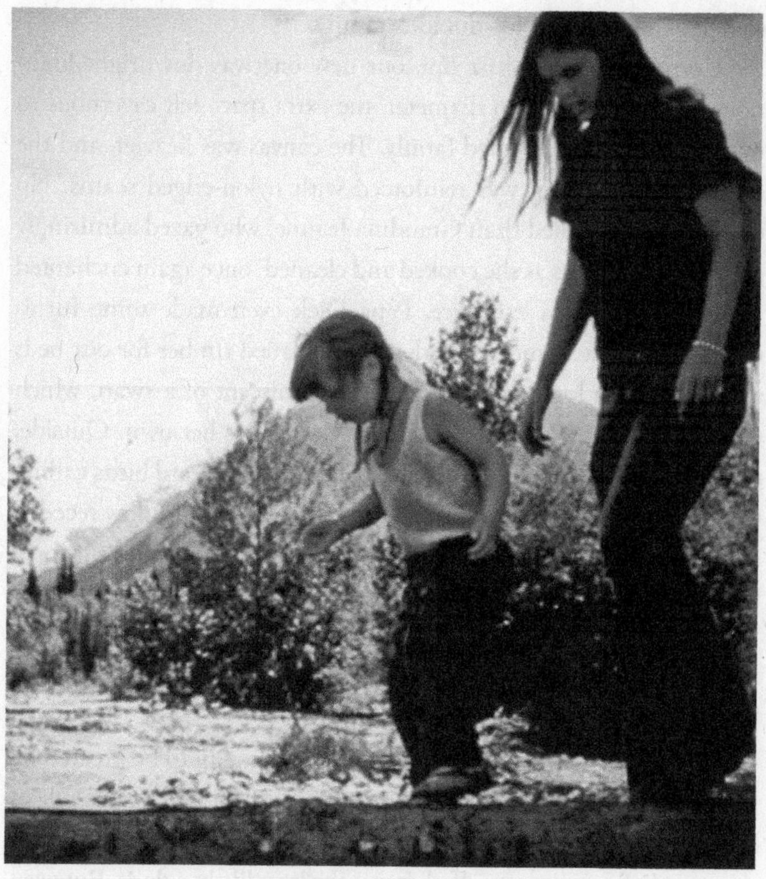

My mother and me navigating the log bridge from our camp to the Indian camp on a warmer day.

THOUGH MY GRANDFATHER WAS loath to admit it, the Indians saved our butts. They made a deal with Papa Dick: they would give us one of their tipis, but they wanted to be paid for it—with cold hard cash, not some bear or moose that they could very well hunt for themselves. My grandfather agreed, of course, and asked if he could have until summer to repay them. He would think of a way somehow, he assured his dubious family.

Compared to our first tipi, our new one was downright luxurious. Four feet wider in diameter, the extra space felt cavernous to my previously overcrowded family. The canvas was heavier, and the commercial stitching was reinforced with nylon-edged seams. No one was more thrilled than Grandma Jeanne, who gazed admiringly at her surroundings as she cooked and cleaned, once again enchanted with her wilderness existence. Papa Dick even made some furniture for our new home: a wooden table, planed timber for our beds and a chair—a log whose shape was reminiscent of a swan, which Grandma Jeanne went gaga over and claimed as her own. Outside, the ice on the river finally began to melt away. We heard birds calling to each other in the mornings, and the snow in our meadow receded to patches on the brown, winter-worn grass. Despite our still-sorry food situation, everyone was filled with renewed optimism.

And then the bear came.

ONE MORNING, MY FAMILY walked outside the tipi to be greeted by a chewed plastic cooler, a mess of ripped wax paper and a huge pile of bear poop. Of all the people who might forget to put our food back in the tree platform, my grandfather was the least likely culprit. But even he wasn't perfect. Wiping tears from her eyes, Grandma Jeanne assembled everything we had left while her husband and daughters gathered around: a few dried mushrooms, some nuts, a little pemmican, basic baking supplies. For the first time that year, our situation was dire.

"It's okay," Papa Dick assured us, lifting his hunting rifle down from its antler rack. "I'll go hunting." And he did, but returned later that afternoon empty-handed.

"We could ask the Indians . . ." Mom ventured, but Papa Dick shook his head.

"They just gave us a tipi. We can't go to them again. Anyway," he said, pulling out a large zip-lock bag from beneath his bed, "I have these. An excellent source of protein. I collected them last summer, exactly for an emergency like this."

My family gazed at the bag in horror.

That evening there was stew for dinner. Ravenous, I ate mine without hesitation, but the women dawdled over their bowls. "Just eat it," Papa Dick kept saying. "It's delicious. You won't know unless you try." He finished his bowl and started another, but still no one followed suit. "Oh, for cripe's sake," he said finally, setting his spoon down. "What's wrong with you people?"

The next day, my grandfather shouldered his rifle and vowed not to return until he had meat to bring home. The women settled in to wait, knowing this could mean anywhere from a few hours to a week or more. But despite their grumbling tummies, not one of them would touch Papa Dick's stew. They happily gave it all to me, and I, just as gladly, cleaned my bowl night after night.

With little to do while we waited, my mother and aunts busied themselves with trapping mice and skinning their hides to make polishing rags. And my Aunt Jan, always the funny one in the family, thought it would be hilarious to teach me to say the name of my favorite new food.

"Bug stew," I said obediently, smacking my lips. "Yummy-yum. Bug stew."

BY LATE SPRING, MY mother had had about enough of being single to last her a lifetime. The problem, of course, was that the pickings around our camp were rather slim. Other than Randall, there was no one she was interested in, and Randall was already attached to a woman in his own camp. But one evening, Jessie knocked over a kerosene lamp and caught our tipi on fire, and everything changed.

Our floor was made from packed dirt overlain with fir boughs. The boughs had to be changed every few weeks, or the dried brown needles would crumble and cling to everything we owned. "Changing the floor" was a job that no one enjoyed much, so as a result, it hadn't been done since we'd moved into our new tipi. Jessie was washing dishes when she knocked a lantern sideways with her elbow. Within seconds the flames spread across the floor, the dried needles perfect as kindling, sending a trail of fire toward the tipi shell before anyone even had time to react. Grandma Jeanne grabbed the water pail and doused the flames, then sat on the floor and cried. It wasn't the three-foot hole in the canvas that had moved her to tears; her swan chair was ruined, and she had loved that chair more than any piece of furniture she could remember owning.

That night, we slept in the Indians' cooking tent. I went to bed with my mother beside me, and woke up alone. She bounded in as I was eating my breakfast, sweeping me into a giant hug. I stuck close to her all day, as if sensing a change in her. And indeed there was. She had spent the night with the Indian chief, and she had already told her sisters that she was madly in love.

WHEN MOM FELL FOR a man, she did so like someone jumping from a cliff without first checking the terrain below. No matter what the consequences, it was the giddy feeling of attracting a man's attention that she lived for. I remember almost nothing about Mom's affair with Randall, except looking at him and hating him because he had stolen my mother from me. She began spending her nights at the Indian camp, leaving my care to the rest of my family. I would chase her across the meadow and try to cross the log bridge after her, sobbing inconsolably until one of my aunts came to lead me home.

But by the time the last of the snow had melted, Randall and my mother were finished. Crocuses sprouted in our meadow and the river began to flow freely, but Mom hardly noticed. She stayed in the tipi day and night, nursing her heartache. I would lay beside her, stroking her arm while she cried and wanting nothing more than for her to come back to me. When she didn't, I finally left her and went back to my play.

I don't remember falling into the river, but I do recall the feel of the current as it pulled me downstream. I flailed for something to grasp, but the rocks and branches in my path all slipped away. I must have screamed, because I can still see my Aunt Jan's face as she appeared at the shore beside me, her eyes wild with terror. She lunged into the water and made a grab for my ankle. Dragging me onto the rocky shore, she turned me on my side and let me cough until my lungs cleared. Then she scooped me up and brought me to my mother.

"There!" Jan yelled at her, dropping me unceremoniously onto the bed. "Are you satisfied? Your daughter just damn near drowned. Now will you please pull your head out of Randall's sorry ass and start being a mother again?"

Mom looked back at her sister with wide eyes, then ran to my side and crushed my soaked body into hers, sobbing.

Over the mountains, the sun was high. Summer had arrived, and we had survived our first year in the wilderness.

Chapter Five

How great my sorrow
And light my joy
That such a one as she should even be
A child of nature, love, goodness
Belonging and shared
To many, by many
Tomorrow is an endless trail
And would that on it
We should meet someday—
Then will be our time

Wow. Isn't that lovely?" Mom asked me, wiping away a tear. "It's all about you."

I kept my eyes on the ground, focused on the wall of pebbles I was building around a yellow caterpillar. She'd been reading a letter, and it wasn't the first time she had tried to interest me in the topic of my father, but I wasn't biting. Anyway, I already knew everything about him: his name was Greg, he lived in California and he sent Mom a hundred dollars each month to help support me.

Mom refolded the letter and tucked it carefully back into the envelope. "Sometimes I wonder if . . ." Her voice trailed off as she gazed into the distance. "You know, sweetheart, your dad said he'd really dig a new picture of you, but I think we can do even better than that. Hey . . ." She placed her finger under my chin and tipped my face up to hers. "You're two and a half years old now, and it's about time you met your father. We're going to California, honey. What do you think about that?"

I continued stacking my rocks, nonplussed, but Mom wasn't concerned. Everything would change, she was certain, when father and daughter saw each other in the flesh. Although her heart was still bruised from Randall, deep down she knew she would go back to my father in a second if he asked.

Arrangements were made. Papa Dick agreed to drive us as far as the highway, and my mother sent Greg a note saying we would be arriving in Sunnyvale within a couple of weeks—it was hard to say exactly when, since we would be hitchhiking—along with a copy of my astrological chart. Sag sun, Sag ascendant, and Leo moon. His daughter was a triple ball of fire, Mom enthused, and she just knew he was going to love me. He wrote back saying he would take some time off his new teaching job to see us, but his bachelor apartment was too small for guests so he had arranged for us to stay with his parents. He also said he was certain he'd love me on sight.

TEN DAYS AFTER MY mother and I left our tipi camp, I sat at my new grandparents' dining table staring at an untouched glass of milk. I had never seen milk before, and although I was impressed by its pure whiteness, the smell of it was making me feel a little sick. Across the table, my new grandparents grinned at me gamely. My grandfather had a ring of gray hair around his head, and my grandmother kept asking me if I wanted to learn how to play cards. I slid off my chair and climbed into my mother's lap, refusing to talk.

I had no idea what to make of these people, but their house was a different matter. When I was finally set free to explore, I tore through the rooms, picking up and dropping everything in sight. When I discovered the bathroom, I flushed the toilet so many times that Mom finally had to come in and drag me away from it, causing me to throw myself on the floor in a screaming fit. To calm me down, my grandparents led me into the backyard and showed me their aboveground swimming pool. After an hour of splashing me playfully while I floated, my grandmother smiled broadly when I let her lift me from the water. "Glamma," I said to her, shaking my wet hair over my face. "Glamma and Gampa have a nice pool."

IF I WARMED TO my grandparents rather quickly, the same cannot be said of how I reacted to my father. The day after my mother and I arrived, I was sitting on my grandparents' back step with a bottle of Dr Pepper in my hand. My grandparents seemed to be an endless source of new things to drink, and this was the most interesting so far. My mother, craving a toke, watched me from across the yard while she contemplated taking a walk to the park to get a fix. From inside the house, a door opened and shut. I took a sip from the bottle, and my mouth flooded with my first heavenly taste of refined sugar.

"Cea," a man's voice said softly above me. "Hi. I'm Greg. I'm your father."

Mom smiled at me encouragingly, but instead of looking up, I picked up my bottle again and drained it.

My father waited until I was finished, then sat down beside me on the stoop.

"I . . . I've waited so long to meet you. Can I just look at you?" I turned to him briefly, and he broke into a smile. "You're beautiful. Just like your pictures."

He touched me lightly on the shoulder. I didn't pull away, so he tried to put his arm around me. I jumped up.

"No!" I yelled, running into the house.

This was not how my father had planned our meeting. But then he had an idea. Dropping down on all fours, he followed behind me and began to chant. "Oh, little gir-r-l-l! I'm going to get you! I'm going to g-e-e-e-t you!"

That did it. I turned on him, holding my hand like a stop sign in front of his face. "No, no, *no*!" I said furiously. "Now *stop* it, asshole!"

Mom said that until our trip to California, she hadn't ever realized what a potty-mouth I had. After this memorable moment, my father stood up and brushed his knees off, saying to no one in particular that perhaps he'd try again later. But things didn't improve much. The following day I ignored him except for the one time I ran past him shrieking "Quick, get my boots, I gotta shit!" at the top of my lungs. I was so used to living in a tipi that despite my fascination with my grandparents' bathroom, I really didn't understand its purpose. Everyone had a laugh, but my grandparents worried at my behavior. They had already witnessed me tearing around their yard yelling "Fuckin' ant! Get this fuckin' ant off me!" after I found one crawling on my leg, and calling out "Mom, come wipe my twat!" while squatting beside their pool to take a pee. If this was how I acted in the city, they could only wonder at what my life must be like in the wilderness.

On our last evening in Sunnyvale, my grandparents waited

until I had gone to bed, and then sat down to have a chat with my mother. Mom said later that she didn't remember much of what was said, but she would never forget their last few sentences. "It must be terribly difficult for you," my grandmother said. "Being out in the bush like that, no running water and such. Anyway, we've talked about it, and Greg . . . well, we all know he's just not ready to take on a responsibility like this right now, but . . . we'd like to take Cea. To raise her. She'd have a good life, better than . . . I mean, you're just . . . so young. Have you thought about school for her?"

Mom shook her head, trying to absorb their words. "No," she said finally. "No."

My grandparents exchanged glances and waited, unsure if she was referring to their offer or their question about schooling, but my mother said nothing further. Finally, she wiped her eyes and wordlessly rose from her seat.

Just before we left the next morning, my father tried to pick me up one last time while my mother snapped a photo. In the picture, I'm arching away from him and crying while he looks at me with a soldiering smile. Mom said that when she looked at that photo, she finally knew it was over between them.

As for me, I'm not sure if this meeting really counts. Mom said that when she mentioned it to me a few months later back at the tipi camp, I had no idea what she was talking about.

This is the photo my mom took of my dad, Greg, and me at the end of that first ill-fated visit.

Chapter Six

"This," said my grandfather in a loud voice, waving a piece of paper in the air as he paced in front of the fire, "is the ultimate irony. Can all of you see what I have here?"

His audience gazed at the object in his hand. "A check. It looks like a check," someone said, and Papa Dick nodded.

"Indeed. A tax-return check, from the U.S. government."

"Hey, wait a minute," a man heckled from a fireside log. "You mean *you* paid taxes?"

Papa Dick smiled broadly, not missing a beat. "Sure I did, once upon a time. Like all good Americans, I watched more than a third of my paycheck get stuffed into some corrupt government official's pocket. That's when I decided I needed to quit forestry, stop paying The Man. So I start my climbing instructor business, and what do they do? Continue to rob me blind. So finally I say, *hey, man, this is bullshit,* and decide to switch things up a bit—"

"Switch things up how?" the heckler interjected, but Papa Dick just grinned and shook a finger at him.

"Find your own way, man, find your way. There's more than one way to skin a politician." Then my grandfather stood up straight, pausing for effect. "So there you have it, folks. The U.S. government, an institution I once fled from, will now *fund* my antigovernment lifestyle." Everyone laughed and clapped, but even then he wasn't finished. He adjusted his cowboy hat and held the piece of paper over the fire, not quite close enough for the flames to touch it. "The number on this check isn't small," he went on. "In fact, it would probably support my family for a couple of years. That's right—a couple of *years.* So the question is, what's more important? Sticking with your principles, or"—he snatched his hand back and stuffed the check in his shirt pocket—"sticking it to the government? I'll take choice number two, anytime I can!" His audience broke into cheers, and Papa Dick finally bowed and took a seat by the fire.

It was our second summer in the Kootenay Plains, and much had changed for my family. Our camp now included three tipis, each with its own woodstove, a summer lean-to kitchen, and a generous sprinkling of nylon tents, all of them occupied. My grandfather had achieved his dream, but even more important to him, he was now spreading his philosophy to others. It had all begun with a few letters to friends. He had started writing them during our first winter, telling of our lifestyle and inviting visitation. My grandfather's mission was not to recruit cohabitants for our camp as one would for a commune, but to teach others our way of life and then send them out to create their own. With a little education and inspiration, Papa Dick determined, anyone could—and *should*—live as we did.

It seemed that his friends agreed with him. A trickle of them had arrived after my mother and I returned from California, but it was nothing compared to the flood that would descend on us a year later. They came from everywhere—deserters and draft dodgers we had met during our time in Hills, free-love-and-marijuana-saturated folks from Minnesota, Missouri and Chicago in search of a more concrete movement than the loose promise of change that had yet to fully materialize in America. And my grandfather was a practical man. The visitors ate his food, smoked his home-grown weed and benefited from his knowledge, so he began to request a small fee. Before long, his unstructured daily teachings had become more formalized. He would round up his charges in the mornings and teach them how to fish and gut trout, how to skin and cook a porcupine, how to build a lean-to with a fire under it in the pouring rain, and how to fit enough survival items into a small knapsack to keep them thriving for a month. After a nightly game dinner provided by Grandma Jeanne, there would be parties around the outdoor fire pit complete with rock 'n' roll music and wild strawberry punch, occasionally spiked with LSD by one of the visitors. No one seemed to mind parting ways with their cash for such an experience.

By the middle of that second summer, our camp was overflowing with long-haired strangers, all in various degrees of undress as they clenched joints between their smiling lips. My grandfather encouraged nudity, casting dark glances at those fully clothed, but he did not insist upon it. Most often it was the women who shed their clothing first, lounging topless against their bell-bottomed men while inhaling pot smoke from their lovers' mouths. Boisterous laughter and deep discussions infused our camp, but most of the visitors knew better than to talk about war or politics within earshot of my grandfather. Such topics returned the speaker's energy to the woes of society, Papa Dick cautioned, which defeated the whole purpose of escaping it. "Talk the life you want to live," he would say, "and block the one you don't." The visitors nodded and murmured "Right on, man," as my grandfather spoke, beholden to his courageous choices. And it was during this time that the legendary government check came, acting as the perfect punctuation mark to my grandfather's successful new venture and high place among his pupils.

It happened one evening after a trip to town, when he came home waving a brown envelope.

"Look at this!" Papa Dick said while my family gathered around. "We can thank our old friend Wanda in Los Gatos for forwarding this to us." He held the envelope out in front of him and kissed it. All the women laughed. "A check from Uncle Sam! Just wait till I tell the visitors about it."

From my mother's arms, I looked at Papa Dick questioningly. "Uncle Sam?" I repeated. "Isn't he in the metal hospital?"

Everyone fell silent.

"*Mental*," Jessie said finally. "No, honey. That's your Uncle Dane."

"Oh," I said. When no one offered anything further, I finally went off to play. I didn't know much about my Uncle Dane, other than that he was in a place for people with head problems. Mom called it "the loony bin" when no one else was around, and to me it sounded fascinating. I wondered why everyone seemed more interested in talking about a dumb old piece of paper than they did my crazy uncle. One time, I asked Mom if I would ever get to meet him, but she just looked away and told me I already had.

OF THIS SECOND SUMMER, nearly all my memories are beautiful. I remember a feeling of lightness and freedom that seemed to expand around my heart as I ran across our meadow. I remember the taste of grouse meat, the sound of Fleetwood Mac and the Beatles on the tape deck, the feel of my stick horses between my legs as I galloped them through pink fireweed and orange tiger lilies, and the childish, outlined pictures in my *Illustrated Treasury of Children's Literature*, which I called the Big Blue Book. I remember riding high and bareback on Apache, the Indians' favorite horse, with Randall leading her. And I remember other children floating through our camp, brought along by their visiting parents.

I found the kids from the city intriguing. They had pale skin, covered themselves in swimsuits instead of going nude, and wore clothing made from slippery, shiny fabrics. They refused to eat our food and asked their parents for things I had never heard of, like Cheezies and Twinkies and Cap'n Crunch cereal. They talked about the Road Runner and Bugs Bunny, which they watched at home on a thing called a television. They brought toys with them, dump

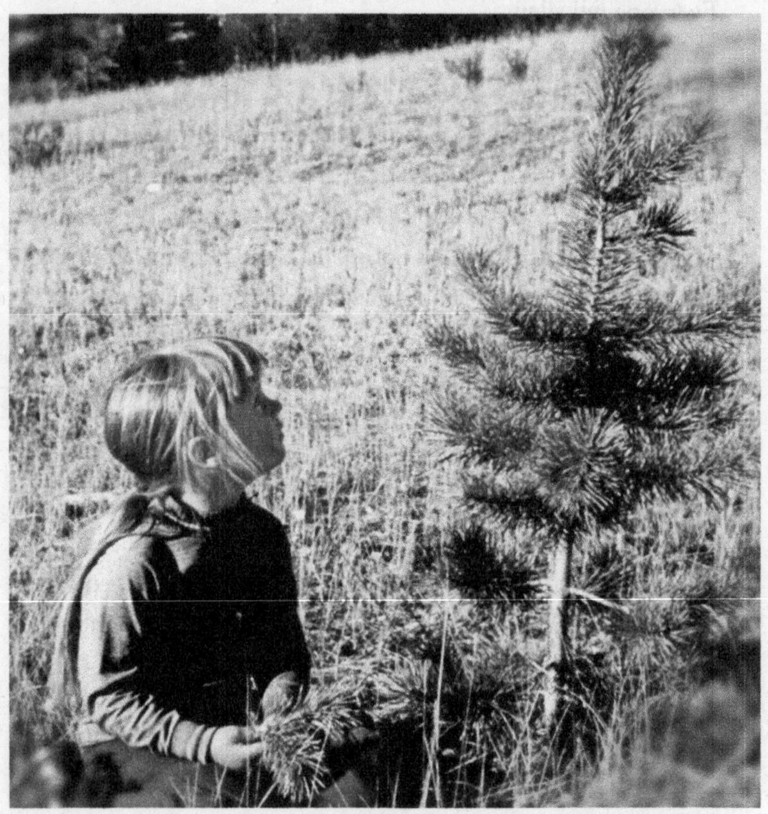

Taken on the Kootenay Plains, this was always Papa Dick's favorite photo of me because I look truly at home in nature.

trucks and little plastic men holding machine guns and Lite-Brites made useless by our lack of electricity. But I had never wanted anything the town kids had until one of the visitor's daughters showed me the most beautiful thing I had ever seen. It was still in its box, visible only through a plastic window. I almost hyperventilated with excitement when I saw it, but the girl cruelly held it out of my reach. When I asked if I could play with it, she shook her head and swiftly stuffed it back under her sleeping bag. "Mine!" she said firmly, but it wasn't enough to put an end to my desire.

The next morning, I snuck into the girl's tent and removed the doll from its box. Stroking her silky golden hair with the palm of my hand, I gazed down at her in adoration. Barbie was wearing a pink dress, a silver tiara and tiny shoes with pointy heels. I hid her under my shirt and ran to my tipi. Later that day, the girl discovered her missing treasure and knew exactly where to look for it. But her relief at finding her doll soon turned to shrieks. I crouched on my bed as she cried, wondering why on earth she was so upset. In my mind, I had done her a favor; since Barbie had no twat under her dress, I had drawn one on with a felt pen.

Just as commercialism was entering my life in the shape of a Barbie doll, the visitors' enchantment with our lifestyle was coming to an end. By early that fall, almost all of them had returned to their lives in the city. And the one family who stayed behind to create their own wilderness existence would meet an unfortunate fate. While crossing a river to save his pot crop from a storm, the father got his shoelace tangled in a fallen tree and was dragged underwater, leaving his wife widowed and his two young children fatherless. Years later, when Mom tried to tell me that pot was harmless, I would repeat this story back to her.

Chapter Seven

My family was always good at celebrating my birthday. Grandma Jeanne would make my favorite meal, fried bear meat with wild mushrooms, and there would be either a wheat germ or carob cake for dessert. There weren't any candles or presents, but I didn't know there were supposed to be. The first birthday I clearly remember is my fourth. I spent it sitting on a bearskin outside the Indians' sweatlodge, licking maple-syrup frosting off a piece of cake. It was late November, so the air was well below freezing, but since it was a special occasion I had insisted on wearing a buckskin dress sewn for me by one of the native women. My teeth were chattering, and snow crunched under my rear end as I shifted on the ground. I could have gone to the cooking tent to warm up, of course, but on that night I wanted to be close to my family. And they were inside the sweatlodge, smoking from a pipe and listening to the Indians tell stories.

I watched as the door to the lodge flew open and a row of naked brown and white bodies streamed outside. Hooting and hollering, they threw themselves in the snow and started rolling around. Mom's voice was high and breathy, the way it always got when she smoked joints. I set my cake down, pulled the bearskin around my shoulders and walked over to her. She was lying beside Randall, screaming playfully as he rubbed snow on her nipples.

Mom had spent her summer nights in some of the visitors' tents, but a little while ago she and Randall had rekindled their affair.

"Mommy," I said loudly.

"Cea! My beautiful girl! Come here, sweetheart."

I smiled and fell into her arms. Her skin was freezing against my cheek, but I didn't mind. I liked it when Mom smoked joints, because it seemed like she couldn't give me enough hugs and kisses, and she loved to tell everyone how beautiful I was.

"I'm cold," I said.

"Why don't you come into the sweatlodge with us? It's nice and warm."

"No. I don't want to."

"Okay. But I'm going to go back in for a little while, all right?" She nudged Randall's arm. "Look at her, Randall. Isn't she just the most gorgeous thing you've ever seen?"

Randall nodded and gave me a little smile. He didn't talk much. I tried not to stare at his wiener, which was dangling on his thigh as he lay on his side. Mom reached out and stroked my hair.

"We're going to have to fight the men off of her someday. You know, darling, I was thirteen the first time I had sex—"

"—and smoked pot," I finished with her, and she giggled. For some reason, Mom really liked to tell me that story.

"Yeah," she continued. "And you're so gorgeous, it'll probably happen really young for you too. But . . ."—she circled her arm around me—"I'll be right here with you. You can always tell me anything, okay?"

"Yeah. Okay." I nodded, then looked up at the dark sky and pointed. "Mommy, look!"

She followed my eyes and laughed delightedly. "The Sagittarius archer! Oh, honey, isn't it wonderful? Consider that your birthday present."

I nodded happily, and together we gazed up at the starry sky. Mom always said Sagittarius was the most *resilient* of all signs, and she had even read to me what the word meant from the dictionary. *Resilient.* My mother sure did love that word.

I SAT ON MY bed, coughing and hacking as Mom patted me uselessly on the back. I doubled over, unable to stop, and finally spit a wad of blood and saliva into the basin. When the coughing finally settled, I flopped back onto my bearskin like an abandoned marionette.

"Open your mouth," Mom said, unscrewing the lid from a small brown bottle, and I obeyed. One, two, three drops of Rescue Remedy landed under my tongue. Mom loved Rescue Remedy, because it was made from flowers and she said it cured everything from head colds to bad moods. I closed my mouth as Mom turned to my grandparents.

"It's been weeks now," she said to them quietly, shaking her head. "The juniper berry steam isn't working. Neither is the raw garlic. She . . . she can barely leave the bed. And she's so pale . . ."

Papa Dick nodded. "I'll go get Randall," he said. "I guess we should have done this a while ago."

He stood to leave, but I rolled over and reached for his hand. I was rarely ill, but when I was it was usually my grandfather I wanted.

"I'll go," Grandma Jeanne said, and ducked out of the tipi.

Papa Dick sat on the tree stump stool beside my bed while Mom stroked my face. Her palm felt cool against my warm cheek.

"Now," Papa Dick said, patting my hand, "I can think of one thing that might make you feel a little better."

I turned on my side to face him. "What?"

"Maybe . . . a childhood story?"

I smiled. I had probably heard all of his stories by then, but I could have listened to them a hundred times.

"Okay, let's see," he began, adjusting his hat. "Hmm. Did I ever tell you the one about the snake?"

"No," I said with a grin. It was my favorite.

"Oh dear, how could I have forgotten to tell you that one? Well, now. It all started when your Papa was just eight years old. You know how I sometimes killed rabbits and squirrels with my slingshot, right? Well, it wasn't just for fun. This was during the Depression, you see, and my family needed the food. My mother had six mouths to feed, so she wasn't picky—grouse, squirrel, whatever I could bring home was always welcome. Anyway, we had this one neighbor, old Mrs. Lagestrom, and she was about as grumpy as they came. She used to scowl at me when I came home with my kills, and call my family mean names because we had to eat such poor food. But the thing was, she wasn't any better off than us, and we all used to wonder how she didn't starve to death herself. My mother used to say she was full of foolish pride, but at the time I didn't really understand what that meant.

"So anyway, this one day I was on my way to the woods with my slingshot when Mrs. Lagestrom comes banging out of her house, going on about what a horrible kid I was, so I decided it was time to get back at her. When I got to the forest, instead of looking for a rabbit or a grouse—"

"—or a porcupine?" I added.

"Right," Papa Dick said. "Or a porcupine, I decided to look for a snake. I knew where they liked to hang out, and it didn't take me long to find a nice long green garter. I grabbed my snake, took it back to Mrs. Lagestrom's house and rang the doorbell. And when she opened up, I pulled out my jackknife and right there in front of her cut the snake in half. So now I've got half a snake in each hand and they're both still wriggling, because that's what happens with snakes when you do that, and Mrs. Lagestrom is screaming her head off—"

I laughed. It was so funny that I just couldn't help it, but then I started to cough again. Mom ran to my side, and her and Papa Dick waited until I could breathe.

"So," Papa Dick continued, carefully wiping the spit from my chin. "My mother hears the racket and comes running over, and finds this scene in front of her. Let me tell you, did I catch hell. She said it didn't matter how awful Mrs. Lagestrom was, I should never have done such a thing, and also it was really mean to the snake, which I hadn't even thought of.

"Well. We were having grouse for supper that night, and as my punishment, my mother made me take my portion over to Mrs. Lagestrom, tell her it was chicken and offer it to her. Well, boy oh boy, my mother was some cook, and that grouse smelled so good that I was just about faint with hunger by the time I passed it over to Mrs. Lagestrom. I was just hoping she wouldn't take it, but she did, right before she slammed the door in my face. Well—"

"The next day . . ." I cut in, for I knew the story by heart.

"Right. The next day, would you believe that Mrs. Lagestrom came over to our house to return our plate, and didn't she just go on about how good that chicken was. Well, that's when Mom admitted it was actually grouse, but suddenly Mrs. Lagestrom didn't seem to mind so much anymore. So after that, I would bring her a grouse every now and then, and we all became much better friends."

I grinned weakly as Papa Dick stroked my hair from my face. His shirt smelled like wood smoke. Just then the door flap opened, letting in a cold gust of air, and Randall came into the tipi. I barely recognized him. He had traded his usual jeans and flannel shirt for a buckskin robe decorated with eagle feathers, and his hair fell in loose waves over his shoulders. He also seemed larger somehow, and more in control. He pointed to the stove.

"More wood," he said, even though the room already seemed too hot.

Mom did as he asked and returned to my side as a fresh coughing fit squeezed my lungs. She helped me into a sitting position, and I spat blood and lay back again, catching my breath. I opened my eyes and Randall was above me, staring into my face. His eyes looked as big as planets. I tried to block them out by closing my own, but his irises grew bigger in my mind like a zooming telescope. I felt his hair brushing over my cheek, then his hand on my forehead. After a few minutes, the tipi filled with the smell of sweetgrass. Suddenly, I was so incredibly tired that even though I wanted to open my eyelids, they felt as heavy as if there were rocks on them. And then Randall was making a sound, a sort of chant that I couldn't understand. I began to sweat. My entire body felt bruised, as if I had taken a tumble down a hillside.

And then, far above me, I heard Randall asking the evil spirits to leave me. I began to shake, and I realized the tipi had gone ice cold.

Randall stopped then, and everything fell silent. That's when I heard it, like the call of a chickadee, right next to my ear. I turned to look, but nothing was there.

"The bird," I said. "Where—?" But then I needed to throw up.

"Basin," Randall barked, and Mom shoved it under my chin.

I heaved until my stomach clenched and then fell backward.

Mom said I slept for thirteen hours straight, and that she had to keep prodding me through the night to be sure I was alive.

Two days later, I was well enough to leave my bed. I was still weak, but Mom said a bit of color had crept back into my cheeks. I sat on the floor and made a bird out of feathers and wood.

"Look, Mommy," I said, holding up my creation, "it's the bird who came to save me."

Mom grinned and kissed the top of my head. "It's beautiful, sweetheart. I heard it too."

"Where was it? I tried to see it."

"I know, so did I. Randall . . . he said it was the spirit. The good spirit, the one that helped heal you."

Later that day, my mother walked me across the log bridge to the Indian camp. I left the bird at the door of Randall's tipi and hid behind a tree while Mom chatted with one of the Indian women. After a few minutes, Randall came outside with a bridle in his hand. He paused when he saw the bird, and then picked it up and tucked it into his shirt pocket with a smile.

THE ONLY THING I loved more than my birthday was Christmas, and I remember my fourth one well. Since Mom and I didn't have a stand for our tree, Papa Dick strung it from the tipi poles so it dangled a few feet above our woodstove. My mother and I decorated it with long strings of popcorn that Papa Dick brought from town and little animals that we made from walnuts and mouse fur. On Christmas morning, I awoke to a stocking brimming with oranges, paper, crayons and a vial of colored beads. Squealing with excitement, I made roach clips for everyone in my family, and then Mom and I went over to my grandparents' tipi so I could present them.

We could hear my aunts yelling at each other long before we saw them. Mom lifted my grandparents' door flap just in time for us to see Jan hurl a small cardboard box at Jessie's head.

"Fine. Just *take* them!" Jan said furiously, her blond hair a tangled mess.

Jessie, who was cowering on the tipi floor, picked up the box and started stuffing tampons back into it. "You don't need to get so *mad*, Janny-wan," she said sulkily, but Jan wasn't done.

She walked over to the water barrel, picked it up, carried it over to Jessie and dumped it over her head. Jessie ran out of the tipi, screaming and crying.

Later, Mom told me that Jan had been using sphagnum moss for her periods for months, and when Papa Dick finally bought her some tampons for Christmas, Jessie had tried to steal them. Out here in the wilderness, with modern conveniences so rare, Mom said it just wasn't a good idea to mess with certain gifts.

IN MAY OF 1974, our fourth spring in the tipis, my grandfather made a sudden announcement. Our camp had been compromised, he said, and it was time to move on.

"Com . . . promized?" I asked, but he wouldn't explain. Even Mom didn't run for the dictionary the way she usually did when I asked about a new word.

But several days later, when my Aunt Jessie and I were at the river fetching water for the weekly baths, I learned the truth.

"So, kiddo," she said, lowering her yoke to the ground and passing me a bucket. "Do you know why we have to split camp?"

"Yeah," I said, dipping my bucket into the flow of water. "We got *com-promized*."

Jessie nodded. I loved my Aunt Jessie, but sometimes she was hard to look at. Mom said she hadn't brushed her teeth since we'd moved to the wilderness, and that was when I was just a little baby.

I switched my gaze to her eyes, which were green and looked like Mom's. "Yep. The cops finally found us."

"The cops?"

"Yeah. Found our pot plants, said we'd better scram or they'd throw us all in jail. It's illegal, you know."

I stared back at her. I didn't even know what "illegal" meant, but I had seen plenty of bears and cougars during our years in the wilderness, and this was the first time I could remember feeling real fear. I wondered where we might be going next, and hoped upon hope that it wouldn't be to town, a place that loomed huge and mysterious in my mind. I'd never been there, aside from the time I couldn't remember visiting my dad, but Papa Dick said it had big stores filled with food that would give you every disease under the sun, lots of concrete and calamity, and some sort of jam made out of traffic.

There was much to do over the next week as my family prepared for our departure. Belongings were loaded into the canoes and paddled to the VW, our few bags of trash were taken into town, the shit pit was filled in and the food platform was torn down from the tree. The last to go were the tipis themselves. My grandparents stripped the canvas shells from the poles, leaving them standing like wooden skeletons. When the poles were finally untied and lowered, we all took a moment to gaze at the three worn circles left on the ground.

"Don't cry, Mommy," I said, taking her hand as she wiped her tears. Then everyone was crying, even Papa Dick. I stood close to my mother, my arm around her waist, and waited for her to stop.

Three years to the month after we first set foot in our campsite, we were ready to leave it. All the Indians came down to the river to say goodbye. My grandfather stepped toward Randall and took his hand, and they stayed like that for a long time. Then Randall hugged my mother and lifted her into one of the canoes. The rest of us piled in, and Randall pushed us off from the shore.

At that moment I finally understood what was happening. As water droplets flew from Papa Dick's paddle, I fell into my mother's lap and wept for the home I was leaving behind. My mother shushed me and stroked my hair, but Papa Dick didn't turn around. I peered over the edge of the canoe toward shore and saw forty faces shrinking into the distance. Randall, standing on the riverbank with his long black braids shiny against his suede jacket, lifted a hand. I lifted my own hand and held it there until he disappeared from my view, then I collapsed into my mother and cried some more.

Chapter Eight

As much as Papa Dick believed in steering clear of political topics, even he couldn't resist sometimes poking fun at the government. He liked to say it was so messed up that often one hand had no idea what the other was doing, or "while one hand's in the corporate cookie jar, the other's wiping the devil's ass." This was demonstrated by our move from the Kootenay Plains. Apparently, someone in the government's native affairs department had gotten wind of my family's lifestyle and decided that Dick Person was the man to teach an experimental new program: Native Culture Re-Instigation. In other words, in an effort to reduce alcoholism and violence among the native population, my grandfather, a white man, was being paid to teach Indians how to be Indians. Adding to the absurdity was that the Royal Canadian Mounted Police had just driven us from our camp for a bit of pot, and this double dose of irony made the opportunity irresistible to my grandfather.

Our new home was the Stoney Reservation, located on the golden plains of southern Alberta. It consisted of about fifty run-down cabins and trailers; the problem was that we were required to live in one of them. And even though Papa Dick assured us we would only live there for a few months and then sneak back to the bush, for the first time I could remember, Grandma Jeanne seemed mad at my grandfather. She scowled at the Indian who handed over our key, then she unlocked the door and pushed it open so hard that it hit the wall. We all stepped inside.

The place was a shambles. Floorboards were rotted through in several places, and the blankets on the single room's two beds were soiled and riddled with mouse-chewed holes. The building's lone window was broken out and covered with plastic, framed by a nicotine-yellowed curtain. The electric stove was crusted with what looked like years of careless cooking. Cockroaches scuttled across the floor, even though such insects were almost unheard of in this part of the world.

Wordlessly, Grandma Jeanne fetched her cleaning supplies from our van, and the Person women got to work. They stripped, washed, scrubbed and wiped, and by that evening our home was livable. I slept on the floor beside Mom, staring at a wall that looked like it was crusted with boogers.

While Papa Dick got to work trying to win over his new pupils, I spent my days exploring the reserve. But try as I might, it was impossible for me to relate these natives to the ones we had just left behind.

"Papa Dick," I asked him one day, finally, "why are the Indians so different here?"

"You hear that?" he responded, pointing at a nearby cabin window, and I leaned toward the sound coming from within. "Television," he said scornfully. "It rots the mind. Not to mention white sugar. Have you seen what they eat here?"

I shook my head and kept quiet, thinking guiltily of the Mars bar I had devoured that morning. I had found it half eaten on the ground, but I knew where it had come from. There were lots of children at the reserve, and one of their favorite activities was raiding the supply cabin. They didn't play with me, but I didn't much care because I didn't want to play with them, either. They ran together as a pack, their hair flying out long behind them and their noses in a permanent state of runniness. I would stand on a bed inside our cabin, pushing the plastic aside so I could stare out the window at them. They pulled each other's hair and tried riding the dogs like horses. Another thing that was strange about the Indian kids were their parents. With the summer visitors, I had always known which kid belonged to which grownup, but here I never saw any adults around the kids, and when I did, they just seemed to ignore each other. It made me extra-glad to have Mom. I knew I could usually find her in our cabin, smoking a joint with my aunts or Grandma Jeanne. And whenever she saw me, her arms would always open up for a great big hug.

PAPA DICK'S GOVERNMENT JOB with the natives didn't last long. After several months of trying to interest them in hunting, canoeing and tipi-raising, he wrote the band off as hopeless. They drank all night and slept all day, my grandfather complained, and spent the remainder of the time so hungover they couldn't tell a tipi pole from their asshole. He didn't even tell the Indians we were leaving. We just woke up one morning and Papa Dick announced that it was time to go. Then we piled into the VW and headed thirty miles west, until Papa Dick found a spot he liked well enough to pitch our tipi and call home.

Chapter Nine

By the time I was five, I understood why my Uncle Dane hadn't made it into the wilderness with us. Not only was he in the loony bin, he also had a disease. I had even learned to pronounce it: *skit-so-fren-ee-a*. Mom said it meant you were crazy, but that it wasn't really your fault because you couldn't help all the weird thoughts that came into your head. "Like what kind of weird thoughts?" I wanted to know, but it seemed like nobody in my family wanted to talk about my uncle. In fact, the only time he really entered our lives at all was when my grandparents received his quarterly psychiatric reports from the mental hospital.

I could always tell when Papa Dick was reading one, because instead of reading out bursts of news the way he would from a friend's letter, he would skim it silently. Sometimes Grandma Jeanne would dab at her eyes. After Papa Dick finished reading, he would place the letter in a tin box along with some money I knew he was saving to buy Dane a new set of false teeth. Mom told me Dane had stolen a hammer from the hospital storage closet and smashed his old set to pieces. So that summer, when a man with a toothless grin showed up at our new tipi camp, I knew exactly who he was.

One evening shortly after my uncle arrived, the whole family gathered in my grandparents' tipi for supper. I couldn't stop staring at Dane's mouth, which sunk into his face like a little cave. It seemed funny to me that even though he was the one with no teeth, he was also the only one doing any talking. As he gummed his fried rabbit and dandelion-green salad, he told us his good news: he was cured. The doctors had released him, and he was doing so well he was even planning to go off his meds.

"What are meds?" I asked, but no one answered.

Papa Dick removed his hat and smoothed his hair with his hand before clearing his throat.

"How did you find us?" he asked.

Dane grinned and leaned back on my grandparents' bed, lacing his hands behind his head. "I knew you were close to Morley. I hitchhiked there, then asked around town. Phil Mesker down at the post office gave me a ride out to the dirt road. After that it was easy—I just followed the trail."

Papa Dick nodded. Close to a creek, our new camp was a three-mile hike through the forest from the nearest dirt road. And although we had only been there a few months, our route through the trees had already worn into a telltale trail. "Well," he said, "what say we go and pitch you a tent for the night."

Dane sat bolt upright, nearly smacking his head on the overhead antler rack. I jumped. "For the night?" Dane shouted. "What are you talking about, old man?" He thumped his chest. "I'm here to stay. Just look at me—I'm *cured*!"

"I heard you," my grandfather said quietly. "Let's just take it one day at a time."

Dane stood up and stormed out of the tipi. Papa Dick followed, and the women glanced at each other. Then Grandma Jeanne started filling the basin to wash the dishes, and nobody said a thing.

"LOOK," DANE SAID, HOLDING out a stick to me. "It's a beetle. I made it for you."

I took the carving and turned it over in my hands, wondering what my uncle was talking about. Even though I had seen him whittling away at it all day, this piece of wood looked like exactly what it was, a stick of wood and nothing more. I set it down on the ground beside Suzie Doll.

Ever since my uncle had arrived, it had been hard for me to get away from him. In the beginning, he had spent most of his time away from our camp, going for walks in the forest and bathing in the creek as part of a healing routine my grandfather had put him on. "He needs to get back to what's important," Papa Dick explained to me. "Earth, sun, fresh air and water . . . he's out of touch with nature. That's what happens when you live among concrete and pollution. It rots your mind."

But it didn't take long for Dane to start spending more time at home. One day, I walked by his tent and noticed something new at his doorway: a folded piece of cardboard with letters on it. I knelt down, sounding out the words the way Papa Dick was teaching me: *Dane lives here*, it said in bright red marker. And after my uncle put that assertion down on paper, things began to change. He would find me wherever I was playing, then sit close to me and tell me a story. At first I wasn't really interested, but then he started being nice to Suzie Doll. He would pick her up and hold her like a real baby when he talked, so after a while I started to pay attention. The truth was that he had some pretty good stories. My favorite was the one about the time a friend of his at the hospital put a spider in his mouth, then opened it up to scare the shit out of a nurse.

"Grandma Jeanne told me you knew me when I was little," I said to him one day, holding Suzie Doll by the hands and somersaulting her over and over. "But I can't remember. What did I look like then?"

Dane smiled. He was whittling, the wood curling off the blade of his knife as he spoke. "I knew a baby," he replied, "but she didn't look like you." He turned his stick around and started working on the other end. "You're pretty."

"I am?" I brought my fingers up to my cheeks, pressing at the bones under my skin. If I'd ever seen my reflection before, I couldn't remember what I looked like. Besides, I didn't really understand what "pretty" meant, except that Barbie was for sure. I decided that the next time I went to my grandparents' tipi, I would try to see myself in one of Grandma Jeanne's pie plates.

AFTER A MONTH OF having my uncle around, I was secretly hoping he might go crazy again so he would have to go back to the loony bin. With each passing day, he was acting weirder and weirder. One day, he told me he had no bones in his body and that the U.S. government wanted to capture and study him because of it. Then he made me walk around camp with him, looking behind bushes for hidden FBI agents. Sometimes he'd punch his fist into the palm of his other hand with a loud *whack* for no reason. He was also looking pretty scary. He had taken a pair of scissors to his hair, cutting it so close to the scalp that he'd left several bloody cuts that he hadn't even bothered to clean. But none of this seemed to concern Grandma Jeanne. She smiled whenever Dane was around, and once she even had an argument about him with Papa Dick right in front of me. Their son had changed, she said to my grandfather, and it was time for him to let bygones be bygones. But Papa Dick wasn't having it. He said he would allow Dane to stay for her sake, but after he had gone down the hill he just couldn't be trusted again.

I looked up from my sewing project. "What hill did Uncle Dane go down?"

Papa Dick blinked back at me, confused, and then gave me a little smile. "Not gone *down the hill*, sweetheart. *Went down in Hills.* It means what happened there."

"Oh. So what happened?"

"Nothing," he said, turning away. "Nothing you need to worry about."

I went back to my sewing, wondering why everyone seemed so mad that my uncle was here.

"Mommy," I said to her one day. "Yes or no. Are you glad Uncle Dane is here or not?"

"Am I . . . ? Oh." She finished crumbling pot into her joint and licked the edge of her rolling paper. We were in our tipi, and had just finished eating dinner.

I glanced over her shoulder at the dark-haired man sitting on a stump chair. He had arrived at our camp a few weeks ago as a visitor, but he'd spent almost every night since in Mom's bed. Our tipi walls were now stacked high with his collection of canned goods, broken household appliances and worn-out cowboy boots, but Mom didn't seem to mind.

"I, uh . . . it's complicated, sweetie," she said, lighting the joint and inhaling deeply. "What I really want is for him to get well."

"But . . . he told us he was all better."

"Yes, I know, but . . ." She exhaled and passed the joint over her shoulder to the dark-haired man. "Just do me a favor, okay? Don't spend too much time with him."

I knew Mom and my Uncle Dane didn't like each other. I never saw them talk, and when Mom saw Dane coming she would turn around and walk in the other direction.

"How come?"

Suddenly, the man leaned forward over Mom's shoulder and as she turned to him, he blew smoke into her mouth. She inhaled and smiled up at him.

"Mommy, how come?" I repeated, but by that time they were kissing with their tongues sticking out, so I stood up and went outside to play.

A FEW DAYS AFTER Mom told me to stay away from my Uncle Dane, I was making mud pies in the dirt when I sensed someone behind me. I turned and saw Dane, scratching at his balls as he stood naked in the morning sun.

"Hey. Do you know where your mother is?" he asked me.

"I don't know. In her tipi, I guess." I continued stirring pine needles into my pie, wishing he would leave.

"No. I mean your *real* mother. Do you know where she is?"

I stopped and looked up at him. "What do you mean? She's in the tipi," I replied, waving my hand in her general direction.

Dane stared at me for a moment, then slowly kneeled down in front of me.

"Okay," he said, looking into my eyes. "It's time I told you something."

"About Mom?" I said, my voice sounding far away. I could hear my heart thumping in my ears. "What about her?"

"Okay, here it is." He placed his hands on my shoulders. "Your real mother died."

The hair on my forearms stood up. *"What?"*

"That's right." He nodded. "She poured gasoline all over herself and set herself on fire. I was there when it happened. I tried to stop her, but . . ." His voice trailed off and he shook his head. "She was beautiful. Blue eyes, curly black hair, a real fox. Debbie was her name.

Crazy Debbie. That woman who calls herself your mother . . ." He gestured toward our tipi scornfully. "She's nothing but a cheap impostor."

Dane was still talking, but my ears were ringing too loudly to hear his words and I couldn't seem to swallow. I stood up on legs of rubber and walked away, my mind racing. It couldn't be, I thought. Hadn't Mom always said Dane was crazy? But nothing could soothe my fear. Adrenaline zinged through my body and my eyes welled over. Who could I possibly ask? Aunt Jessie, my usual source of honesty, had recently gone off to live in a yurt with her new boyfriend. Stumbling blindly through my tears, I rounded the side of my grandparents' tipi and saw a blurry figure sitting on the sawhorse. It was my Aunt Jan, coughing loudly as she rolled herself a joint. I stopped in front of her, sobbing.

"Hey, kiddo," she said lightly. "What's with the leaky faucets?"

"Dane," I replied shakily, pointing in his direction. "He said—"

"Dane? Don't listen to him. He's full of lies."

I wiped at my eyes. "But—but he said that Mom isn't—"

"Let me guess. He said your mom isn't really your mom, and that your real mother's name is Debbie. Right?"

"Yes." Relief swept through me, immediately stopping my tears. "But . . . but how did you know?"

"Ah . . ." Jan waved her joint dismissively at me. "He's been going on about that one for years."

"What do you mean?"

She plucked a stray pot leaf from her tongue and examined it on the tip of her finger. Then she flicked it into the air and jabbed her joint at me. "Do you know why Dane didn't move to the wilderness with us?" she asked me.

"Yes. He had to go to the metal hospital instead."

Here's a happier memory of my Aunt Jan; we're snowshoeing near Morley.

"*Mental.* Yes. But do you know why?"

I shook my head.

"Okay. Well, it was because of this story he'd made up about your mother. That's what started it, anyway. But mostly it's because of you."

"Me?"

"Yup."

"But how could I make him go crazy?"

"You didn't. But you made him prove to us all just how crazy he was. Your uncle is a very sick man, kiddo. I'm telling you,

you need to stay away from him." Jan exhaled a slow stream of smoke into the air. Then she turned toward me, her pale blue eyes boring into mine. "I think it's about time I told you a little story."

IT HAPPENED JUST AFTER my first birthday, my aunt told me, when we were living at the house in Hills. My grandparents and Aunt Jessie were out one evening, and Mom and Jan were giving me a bath in the kitchen sink. All was fine until Dane came into the room. He stood there, just staring at Mom, and then pointed a finger at her.

"You!" he barked. "What are you still doing here?"

Mom ignored him, lifting me from the sink and wrapping me in a towel. Dane had been acting pretty strangely for a while now, but lately he seemed to be focusing more and more on Mom, going on about fake mothers and orphaned babies.

"What is it?" she asked him finally, holding me to her chest.

"That baby," Dane said, reaching for me. "She belongs with her real mother. Give her to me."

Mom glanced nervously at Jan and tried to push past Dane, but he grabbed her arm. Mom twisted away from him, and she and Jan bolted down the hall to their bedroom and shut the door. Since there was no lock on it, Jan grabbed a chair and shoved it under the doorknob. Dane hammered his fists against the other side, cursing and yelling, while I screamed in Mom's arms. Jan ran to the window and looked down, but she already knew it was too high. Mom was just about to shove me into the closet when the chair slipped to the floor with a clatter. Dane stormed into the room, yanked me out of Mom's arms and took off down the stairs to the cellar. Mom and Jan chased him to the laundry room, but he slammed the door in their faces and slid the dead bolt.

Through the wall, they could hear me wailing. Mom covered her ears with her hands and slid to the floor, where she curled into a ball. After a few minutes, I went quiet.

Not too much later, my grandparents came home. When Papa Dick learned what had happened, he removed the hinges from the laundry room door and threw it aside. The room was dark inside. Jan pulled the cord on the bare bulb, and they saw Dane in a corner, rocking with his head in his hands. The laundry sink faucet was turned on, running water onto the floor. Mom, Jan and Papa Dick crossed the room and found me lying in the sink, unconscious. Mom scooped me up and held me, sobbing uncontrollably, while Papa Dick went upstairs and stuffed some clothes into a bag. Then he led his only son to the VW bus, placed him in the back seat and, as the story goes, didn't stop driving until he got to the nearest mental hospital, almost five hundred miles away.

AFTER HEARING THIS STORY from my aunt, I wished I could take it out of my head again. It hung around in my mind like a bad dream that I couldn't wake up from. Now I knew what Papa Dick meant about *what went down in Hills*.

A short time later, I was walking by Dane's tent when I noticed that his cardboard sign looked different. I knelt down in front of it and sounded out the words: *Dane's—I'm watching you SO GO THE FUCK AWAY!*

I jumped up and ran. The next morning, my grandfather came home from his hunting trip. He took one look at Dane, packed his belongings into his knapsack and led him down the trail for the long drive back to the loony bin. I clutched Suzie Doll to my chest as I watched Dane disappear into the trees. All I could think was how glad I was that she was safe in my arms, and that if my Uncle Dane ever came back to visit us again, I would never ever let him hold her again.

Part Two

Cracks

Chapter Ten

While my Uncle Dane had been busy scaring the crap out of me with lies about my mother, love had blossomed at home.

"I've finally found my mountain man," Mom told me happily, sweeping me into a giant hug. "And you know what the best part is, sweetheart?"

"What?" I asked into her hair.

"He's an Aries. That means he's the most sexually compatible with my sign, Pisces. Isn't that wonderful?"

I nodded, happy that she was happy. Her eyes looked as shiny as our creek did when the sun hit it just right.

Mom's new love was Karl, of course, the man who had moved into our tipi some weeks before. With his perfectly straight white teeth and long, wavy hair, even I could see he was handsome. He wore a thin gold chain around his neck, baby blue bell-bottom cords that matched his eyes, and he liked to stretch his long legs out by the fire while he read a book called *I'm OK, You're OK.* Sometimes he would chat with Papa Dick about the world's most boring stuff, like food preservatives and the crisis of modern progression. But mostly Karl liked to talk about himself. It was grief that had brought him to the wilderness, he told us. As a teen, both of his parents had passed away within months of each other and left him orphaned; to escape foster care, he ran away to the bush and built himself a small cabin. It was a story my mother never tired of hearing. She would massage his shoulders as he spoke, nodding sadly and rubbing her bare breasts against his back. Sometimes Karl would pull her into his lap and fiddle with one of her nipples while he talked, and Mom would stick her tongue into his ear. I thought that was pretty gross, because there was probably wax in there.

But there was another side to Mom's new relationship. It seemed that when she and Karl weren't screwing, they were arguing. They fought about everything: Karl was messy, Mom was lazy, Karl was an asshole, Mom smoked too much pot, Karl should get himself some sensitivity and Mom should get herself a brain. One subject that came up often was where we lived. Karl grouched that he had never intended to stay at our camp longer than a few weeks, and that he had a pot crop back at his cabin that needed tending. Mom reminded him that she had a child to raise and needed her parents' help doing so. Karl countered that it sounded to him like Mom was picking her parents over him, so maybe he should just be off on his jolly way. Karl won.

"PAPA DICK," I CRIED, leaning out the open window of Karl's green pickup truck. "Don't let us go! Please! I want to stay here with you. *Pleeeeeaaaase* . . ."

I clung to my grandfather, pleading and crying. Beside me, my mother was in tears of her own, heaving great sobs as she reached for Grandma Jeanne's hands through the window. Papa Dick held me for a moment, and then gently eased his shirt out of my clenched fists.

"Peanut," he said to me, shaking his head, "there's no reason for such tears. Don't you remember what Papa's always taught you?"

"N-no," I replied, wiping furiously at my eyes.

"That nothing is real except the moment you're in. The past and the future are just illusions. Much like a dream—interesting, but useless. People who live in the past are living in a place of fear, and you're not a fearful girl. You're a brave girl. Okay?"

I sniffled and nodded. "But . . . but when will I see you and Grandma Jeanne again?"

"I don't know. Someday, probably. But until then, you need to live as if your grandmother and I never even existed. All right?"

I tried to smile through my tears.

"Good girl." He leaned in the window to hug me, and my arms went around his waist.

My fingers touched something cold on his belt loop, and I realized it was the roach clip I had made him the Christmas before. I unclipped it and hid it in my hand. In the driver's seat, Karl tipped his hat back and lit a cigarette.

"Come on," he grumbled, starting the engine. "Let's get this crybaby show on the road."

We pulled away in a crush of gravel and cloud of dust, Mom still crying beside me. I leaned against her arm and closed my eyes. *He doesn't exist, he doesn't exist,* I thought to myself over and over again, but it was no use; I knew very well Papa Dick was right where we had left him, in fact he was probably walking back through the forest to our camp by now. I twisted my head around to look out the back window, but it was already too late. Smooth blacktop unwound behind us, dotted on each side by green and white signs. I opened my hand and gazed down at my treasure, breathing in deeply to stop a fresh flood of tears.

"Mommy, where are we going?" I asked.

"Karl's place. He lives in a house," she replied quietly, and I felt a stab of excitement in spite of myself.

After a little while, I fell asleep with my head slumped against my mother's heaving shoulder.

I SAT UP AND rubbed at my cheek, cold from being pressed against the window. It was almost dark outside. We had left the highway, and were now on a dirt road with a shaggy strip of grass growing down the middle. Elton John sang "Daniel" on the tape deck.

"Mommy," I whispered, rubbing my eyes. "When will we be there?"

She didn't answer, so I glanced to my left. She was lying across the seat with her rear end pressed up against my thigh. Karl's pants were down, and Mom's head was bobbing up and down in his lap. I turned away. The road was getting bumpier, but Karl wasn't driving any slower. I snuck another peek at him. He was pumping his crotch up and down under Mom's face, gripping the steering wheel hard enough to make his knuckles turn white. He reached around my mother's back, threw the truck into low gear and steered toward the trees. Ahead of us, I could just make out a faint set of tire tracks. Mom's head was bobbing faster beside me. I squeezed my eyes shut.

"Don't stop," I heard Karl say breathlessly. "Don't stop."

Branches scraped across our windshield. I opened my eyes again and saw that we were climbing a slope. There were red flags tied to branches here and there, and I wanted to ask what they were for, but I didn't dare. The engine strained as we climbed over a fallen log, making the beam of the headlights bounce up and down. I heard Karl moan, my mother gag, and a few seconds later she sat up and wiped her mouth. The truck burst through the forest into a small clearing.

"Now how's that for timing?" Karl cackled to Mom, stomping down on the parking brake. "We're home."

SO THIS IS A house, I thought when I awoke the next morning.

There were no windows, so I could only tell it was morning by the crack of light framing the caribou-hide door. I sat up in my bed, scratching at my legs. They had felt itchy all night long. I lifted up the army blanket I was lying on. My bed was made of hay bales, just like Mom and Karl's across from me. At the center of the room was a woodstove, and beside it a table with two graying tree stumps for stools. Other than that, it was difficult to see any furniture for all the clutter. Shelves built from orange crates held books, curling magazines, tape rolls and tins of food. I could tell that the floor was made of packed dirt, but only because it looked as though Mom had cleared a path through Karl's junk from the door to the bed.

I pulled on my clothes, grabbed Suzie Doll and slipped out the door. Bright sunlight hit me square in the face, making me squint. I stood back and stared at the outside of the cabin. It was made from logs, plywood sheets and orange crates, all hammered together to form four walls. The roof was covered in tinfoil. I walked around the building and started down the trail back to the truck. Along the way I found an outhouse, a woodpile, a heap of empty tin cans and a small greenhouse filled with marijuana plants. I hugged Suzie Doll to my chest. Ever since my Aunt Jessie had told me that pot plants were illegal, my belly always jumped at the sight of them. At least Mom had told me that we didn't need to worry this time; Karl had lived in his cabin for almost six years, and nobody had found his secret garden yet.

"MOMMY, WHY WOULD A chair have a hole in it where your ass is supposed to go?"

"Hmm? What was that, honey?" Lifting her basin from the table, Mom crossed the room and pitched the dirty water outside.

"A chair," I repeated, swinging Suzie Doll around by the arm. "I found one in the bushes behind the cabin, but it had a big hole in it. I sat down and my ass fell right in."

"Oh," Mom said, giving me a little smile. "That sounds like a toilet. I think Karl tried to install one, but the pipes kept backing up with mud."

"Oh." I sat down and returned to drawing my picture, glad I had made Mom smile. She hadn't been laughing as much since we arrived at Karl's cabin, and she said it was because Karl was a slob and she missed my grandparents. We weren't even allowed to go visit them, because Karl said trips in the truck were for emergencies only. As it turned out, the red flags I had seen on the way here were put there by Karl to throw the cops off his trail. Anyone who followed them would be led on a wild-goose chase, so he couldn't afford to let the tire trail to his cabin become too worn in.

I had trouble sleeping. I would lie in my straw bed at night, holding Papa Dick's roach clip and trying to convince myself that my grandparents had never existed. I even created a new life story for myself: I was born in California, but my father died right afterward, so Mom put me in a canoe and paddled until she got to the Kootenay Plains. We lived in a tipi, just the two of us, until Randall saved me when I tried to die. After that my Uncle Dane found us, so Mom and I got back into our canoe and paddled down the river to Karl's cabin. But one day, my mother and I would get into our canoe again and move to that concrete jungle Papa Dick always talked about and wear fancy dresses, just like Barbie.

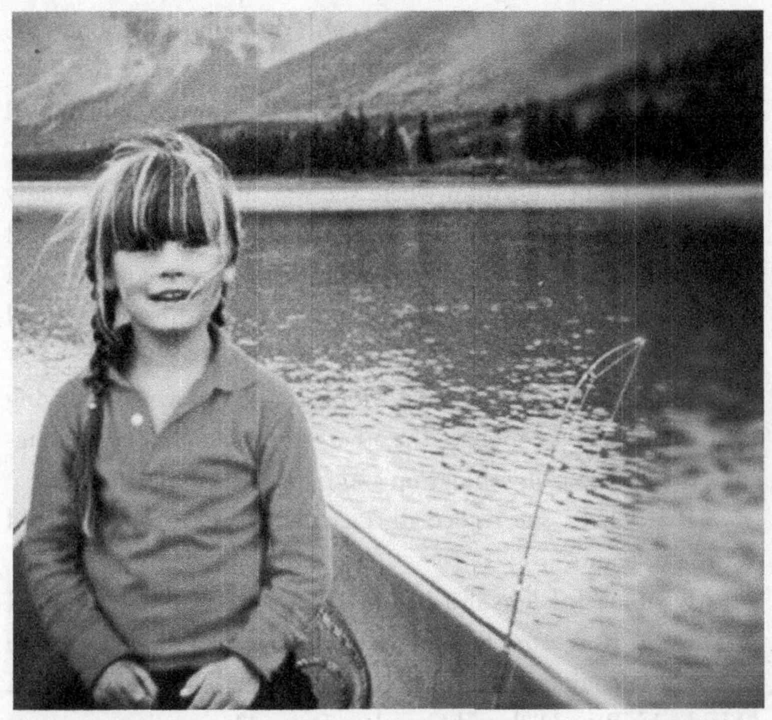

I spent a lot of time in canoes during my wilderness years, as they were often our primary form of transportation.

Sometimes, if I focused hard enough on my story just before I fell asleep, I could actually make myself believe it. But when I woke up the next morning, my first thought would always be that my grandparents were right where we had left them, going on about their lives without me. I wondered if they ever talked about me, or if they just tried to pretend that I didn't exist too.

ONE DAY, I WAS sitting on the floor drawing a picture of Barbie from memory when I heard running footsteps outside. They came closer and closer, and then Karl burst in through the caribou-hide door.

"The heat's on our asses!" he shouted at Mom. "Goddamn it! Get our shit together!"

Mom jumped up from where she was sitting, looking wildly around the room. She had been butchering a rabbit Karl had brought home that morning, and her hands were covered with blood. She rushed over to the basin and started washing them. Karl grabbed a duffel bag from a shelf and ran outside again.

"What's going on?" I asked Mom, who by now was hurrying from one side of the room to the other trying to collect our belongings. She kept picking things up and putting them down again.

"The police," she replied distractedly. "I guess they've found Karl's pot plants."

My stomach felt as if it had been punched. I swallowed hard and strained my ears. Faintly, I could make out the low rumble of a vehicle engine getting closer. Then I had an exciting thought. "Maybe it's Papa Dick and Grandma Jeanne!"

"It can't be. You know nobody knows where Karl lives, not even them. Come on now, get your boots and coat on." She tossed them to me and I did as she asked, then slid off my bed and stood uncertainly. Mom glanced over at me. "Get your things together. Suzie Doll, your books . . ." She reached up to a high shelf to grab her backpack.

"Mommy, are we going to the slammer?"

"What?"

"The *slammer.* Where they put people who do bad things like grow pot plants."

"Who told you that?"

"Aunt Jessie. That time when the cops came to our tipi."

Mom shook her head as she stuffed a sleeping bag into a nylon sack. "Don't worry about it. You're only five, that's way too young to go to jail."

"But what about you?"

She shook her head again. "Just don't worry about it. Now come on, we have to get going."

Outside I could hear the engine coming closer, joined by the rumble of Karl's truck starting up. Mom shouldered her pack, took my hand and pulled me out the door. I broke away from her and dashed back inside to grab Suzie Doll and my Big Blue Book.

Through the trees, Karl was shouting at us from the truck. "Let's *go,* goddamn it!"

"Quickly," Mom said to me, pushing me ahead of her on the trail.

I glanced at Karl's greenhouse as we hurried by it. All the pot plants had been picked, leaving only a patch of bare stems. Karl was in the cab, motioning for us to hurry. Mom threw her pack into the back of the pickup and we piled in beside him. Behind us, I could hear a low drone.

"Hang on," Karl said, popping the parking brake.

Mom pulled me close while he hit the gas. We lurched forward across the clearing, heading for the trees. Karl veered to the right and slid between two evergreens, tires squealing against the trunks. He crunched through a frozen creek, came up the other side and drove on, looking for an opening.

"Shit," he said, stomping on the brake. He turned to look out the rear window, and I did the same. From where we were parked, I couldn't see the clearing. "We'll wait them out," Karl said, sitting back in his seat and crossing his arms.

"Wait who out?" I asked. "What, Mommy?"

"Shh . . . the cops. Don't worry about it, Karl knows what he's doing." She pulled me close and cupped her hand around my head.

"What? What are we doing? Are you going to jail now?"

Nobody answered.

After a few minutes, Karl jumped wordlessly out of the cab and walked back toward the clearing. Panic clutched me. Was he leaving us? The cops were less than a mile away, we didn't know the way from Karl's cabin to the road, and Mom didn't even know how to drive.

"Where's he going? *Mommy.* Where's he going?"

"It's okay . . . shh . . ."

I twisted around in my seat and watched the trees until I saw Karl jogging back toward us. He got behind the steering wheel and slammed the door. "All clear. Cruiser's still there, but it's empty. We're gonna go for it."

"Go for it?" Mom said uncertainly. "What do you mean?"

"Use your brain, woman! There's only one way back to the road!"

"Then let's wait until they leave. They can't see us where we are."

"Don't be stupid. As soon as they find out we're gone, they'll search the area. Then we'll be fucked. It's now or never. Unless you want to walk your way out of here, that is."

Mom pursed her lips. Then she stuck her hand into the crack of the seat, fished out the seat belt and snapped it around me.

"What about you?" I asked.

"I'll be fine." She reached into her purse and took out her bottle of Rescue Remedy. Three drops for me, five for her. "Okay," she said to Karl. "Let's go."

Karl put the truck in reverse and was about to hit the gas when he stopped. "Oh, fuck it," he said, hitting his head with the heel of his hand. "*Fuck it.* I forgot. Reverse is busted."

"Busted?" Mom asked. "What do you mean?"

"I mean the reverse gear's broken. I meant to get it fixed last time I was . . . Come on, get behind the wheel."

"But I can't—"

"I know you can't drive, okay? Just get behind the goddamn wheel! I'm going to push us out of here. Hurry up!"

Mom took his seat and Karl started pushing the front of the truck. "Crank the wheel left! Left! Around the tree! *Around* it!" he yelled at Mom, his face turning red.

Mom steered and Karl pushed until the truck slid into the creek bed. Then he got behind the wheel again, put the gear in drive and jammed his foot down on the gas.

"Hang on," he said, and we shot out of the trees and into the clearing.

I saw the police car right away, parked at the head of the trail to Karl's cabin. Red and blue lights pulsed in silent circles on the vehicle's roof. I felt like throwing up. Karl shot past it, engine roaring, and headed for his track through the woods. I turned in my seat and saw two men running toward the car.

"Mommy!" I squealed. "The cops!"

I faced forward in time to see Karl throw his head back and laugh. His eyes shone with excitement, as if he were riding a toboggan down a hill instead of escaping from the cops. "Ha!" he cackled. "They'll never catch us!"

Mom pulled me hard against her ribs. The truck rocked crazily from side to side as Karl gunned it down the slope. Mom's head slammed into the roof, so she braced herself against it with her hands. Finally, after what felt like forever, we burst through the trees onto the dirt road. From far behind us, I could hear the distant wail of a siren.

"You see that?" Karl shouted, pumping his fist in the air. "I'm unstoppable! Un-fuckin'-stoppable!" He hit the gas hard, spraying a cloud of slush and gravel into the freezing December air.

While Mom stayed silent, Karl wound through back roads

until we got to a long driveway with a farmhouse at the end of it. "Best get rid of this shit," he said as he hit the brakes, flung open the door and hopped out. Whistling a little tune, he swung the duffel bag out of the back and jogged up the front steps of the house. A man wearing a plaid shirt answered the door, clapped Karl on the back and took the bag from him. Then he handed Karl a small wooden box and shook his hand. Karl walked back to us, locked the box into the bolted-down storage trunk in the truck bed, and swung himself into the cab.

"We're all set," he said. "I'll switch the license plate at the next rest stop, and we'll be on our way with the cops none the wiser." He settled back into his seat and started rolling a joint.

Mom looked at him nervously. "Okay. But where—where are we going to go now? I mean, we can't go back to the cabin, right?"

"Of course not," Karl said, inhaling deeply. "But we've got plenty of other options."

Mom brightened. "Right, like my parents. Nobody would find us there."

My heart leapt hopefully, then sank when Karl made a face. "You're twenty-one years old," he said to her. "Don't you think it's time to stop running back to Mommy and Daddy?"

Mom opened her mouth, but then closed it again. Karl dropped an arm around her shoulders and softened his voice. "Anyway, babe, it's time to move on to greener pastures. I'm done with Alberta and these goddamn deep-freeze winters."

Mom took a drag on the joint and talked through held breath, making her voice sound low and rough. "What did you have in mind?"

"Let's head for the water. British Columbia. I know—"

"B.C.?" It was Mom's turn to make a face. "I haven't been there since Cea was a baby. The place doesn't exactly hold good memories for me."

"Aw, come on, it'll be different this time. You got me now, don't you?" He grinned sweetly at her, and after a moment Mom smiled back.

"Listen, I know this great little place called Scotch Creek. I passed through it a few years ago, and I just know you'd love it. It's a summer beach town, lots of open-minded folks just like us. Who knows—maybe we can even find ourselves a cottage to call home."

"A cottage? What's that?" I asked.

"It's like a house, but smaller," Mom explained. "Kind of like . . . a big doll's house."

My heart leapt, and I bounced excitedly in my seat. "Say yes, Mom, please say yes!"

Mom turned to Karl and blinked up at him happily. "You mean it?" she asked.

"Of course."

"Far out, babe, far out." Mom giggled and gave me a stoned hug. "You see?" she said to me, squeezing my shoulder. "It all worked out for the best."

Karl took one last pull on the joint, extinguished it in his mouth and slipped a Steely Dan tape into the dash. "One thing, though," he added, starting the engine. "First off when we get to Scotch Creek, I need to take care of a little business."

Mom's smile faded. "What kind of business?"

"You'll see. Your man's got an enterprising spirit, babe, and a plan to go with it. You'll see."

Mom pursed her lips again, and I dropped my head against her shoulder. Just before I drifted off, I heard Karl laughingly ask her if the pot smoke had finally gotten to me.

Chapter Eleven

I started awake to the sound of breaking glass and looked around wildly, trying to remember where I was. The clock on the dashboard glowed yellow numbers. I didn't know how to tell time, but I could tell by the darkness that it was late. *Scotch Creek*, I thought, glancing around for Karl's promised lake, but we appeared to be parked in a gravel driveway. At the end of it, I could just make out a small house. I looked for Mom's face in the blackness beside me.

"Mommy, what was that noise?"

"Nothing," she said, staring straight ahead. "It's okay."

I followed her gaze, and for the first time noticed Karl. He was standing on the front step of the cottage, holding a penlight with one hand and sticking the other through a broken window.

"What's he doing?" I asked, my hand on the door handle. I opened it and started to slide out, but Mom caught me around the waist and pulled it shut again.

"Shh . . . just stay here with me, okay?"

"But—"

"No, it's all right. Come here." She lifted me into her lap.

Other than the sound of her beating heart the night was silent, but I could feel teardrops dripping onto my forehead.

"Mommy, why are you crying?"

She didn't answer. After a while, I picked up Suzie Doll from my seat and started tipping her slowly back and forth, watching her eyes open and close by the light of the clock. More than half an hour passed. I knew because my mother kept announcing the minutes to me as they ticked by. I laid Suzie Doll down again and covered her with my sweater.

"Mommy," I whispered. "What's an enterprising spirit?"

"Shh . . ."

I heard the grinding of shoes against gravel and looked up. Karl was walking toward us with the penlight in his mouth and two cardboard boxes stacked in his arms. He lifted the boxes into the back of the truck, slid into the driver's seat and lit a joint. Then he propped a foot up on the dash and shone his light on it.

"Look at that," he said to Mom, tapping his matchbook against a scuffed cowboy boot. "Just the right size and everything." Then he slapped her knee playfully and started the engine, and we were on our way.

WHEN KARL TOLD US we were going to Scotch Creek, I had pictured water flowing around yellow rocks made of butterscotch, so I was disappointed when all I saw were houses spaced miles apart between sweeping power lines. Karl hadn't lied about there being a lake, but so far I'd only glimpsed it through the trees as I sat in the driveways of some of the cottages. Since our arrival, Karl had gone on to hit one almost every day. At first, Mom tried to reason with him. Why did he have to steal, she asked him, when he had all that money from his pot plants?

"First of all," Karl said, with a tip of his head toward me as he drove, "we don't use that word. I'm 'stocking up.' And here's a little piece of reality for you, woman: that money ain't gonna last forever.

I got you and the kid to take care of now, and it doesn't look to me like you're planning to get off your ass anytime soon to support us. Huh?"

Mom looked away peevishly.

"Yeah, that's what I thought. You want your piece of paradise on the lake, just show me a little patience. Besides"—Karl's tone softened as he stroked her thigh—"we're in this together, right? We're a family now—you, me, and Small Fry here. For better or worse."

Mom smiled and leaned into him. "Yeah. A family," she said, and that was the last time I heard her bring it up.

BEFORE LONG, WE FELL into a routine. Each evening we would park off a remote forest road, eat granola or bread and dried salmon for supper in the cab, brush our teeth in a cup of water, sleep in the back of the truck under piles of down and wool, have breakfast, then spend the day driving around looking for Karl's targets.

Sometimes, on really cold mornings, we got to go to a restaurant to warm up. Mom called the place a "greasy spoon," but the utensils looked perfectly clean to me, and it was my favorite place on earth. As soon as we arrived, Mom would shoo me into the bathroom and have me hold my hands under hot running water to stop the chill. Then she'd wipe my face with a cloth, give my hair a quick comb and get me to brush my teeth. I liked to linger, flushing the toilet and turning the taps on and off, but Mom would usually rush me back to the table to order.

Karl was always at his nicest during these visits, smiling widely and chatting with everyone. While Mom and I wolfed down scrambled eggs and toast smeared with jam from little packets, he would casually ask about this neighbor or that cottage, saying he was looking at properties for sale. Then he would give a friendly wave and we would climb back into the truck, while I secretly hoped for another cold night so we could come back the next morning.

One time when we were there, I was eating pancakes when I felt the waitress's eyes on me. I looked up, and she was holding out a piece of paper from her order pad.

"Can you tell me what this says, sweetie-pie?"

I glanced at Mom, and then I looked back at the piece of paper. "I . . . ice . . . ice cream," I said.

"Very good. I knew you'd be able to read."

"Yeah. Papa Dick taught me," I said proudly.

"Is that right? What a smart girl. What grade are you in, one? Two?"

I had no idea what she was talking about. I flicked my eyes to Mom uncertainly.

"Oh," Mom said quickly, "she's a lot younger than she looks. It's the height. Um, she's actually in kindergarten, but we're taking a little break right now. To travel around." She ducked her head. "I mean, it's not like kindergarten is mandatory or anything . . ."

"Of course not," the waitress said kindly, and winked at me before walking away.

After I was finished eating, she brought me a bowl of strawberry ice cream with a bright red cherry on top. Then she told Karl it was on the house, which made about as much sense to me as talk of Grade One and kindergarten and taking a break.

A FEW TIMES, MOM got mad at Karl because it was so hard for her to keep everything clean, including herself. The greasy spoon was fine for brushing our teeth or washing our hands, but our bodies began to smell and sometimes our dirty laundry and dishes would pile up until we were completely out of clean ones. Karl finally came up with an idea, but he warned us we would only be able to do it once: we would visit the local hotel.

I didn't know what a hotel was, but when Mom explained it was a place where people slept and bathed and that some of them even had swimming pools, I got super excited.

"Hold your horses," Karl said as he pulled up to a building with a flashing neon sign in front of it. "We ain't sleeping here, princess."

My heart fell, but I slid out of the truck and took Mom's hand. She swung a duffel bag over her shoulder and fell in step behind Karl. It was a Tuesday afternoon, and the parking lot was mostly empty. As we passed the glass entrance doors, I could see a lady in a yellow dress standing behind a long counter.

"Don't look at her," Karl muttered as we walked by. "Just keep your eyes straight ahead." He picked up the pace and turned the corner, leading Mom and me to the back of the building. "Look," he said, pointing, and my heart jumped.

There was a huge window in front of me, and through it I could see a blue swimming pool. Beside it, a woman in a swimsuit was sitting in a chair, reading a magazine while two children played in the water. I could hear laughter through the glass as they splashed.

"Let's go. Keep an eye out," Karl said, pulling out his lock pick and approaching the back door. Mom glanced around nervously while he fiddled and rattled. Finally, he swung the door open. "Your spa awaits, madame," he said to Mom. "Compliments of Mr. Slim Jim."

Mom giggled quietly, then led me down the hall and into the changing room. "Good, it's empty," she said. "Let's hurry up, okay?"

I nodded distractedly as I looked around. I had never seen a room like this one before. There were two shower stalls, a toilet, a sink and a line of wall hooks, white towels hanging from two of them. The floor was wet and dotted here and there with clumps of hair.

"Here you go," Mom said, opening her bag and taking a swimsuit out for me.

I took it and held it in front of me, rubbing the slippery fabric between my fingers. It reminded me of the clothes the summer visitor kids used to wear at the tipis.

"What about you?" I asked.

"I'm going to stay here. I'll take a shower and wash some clothes in the sink. You go have some fun."

"But . . ."

"Go on, you'll love it." She kissed me on the forehead and turned away, already emptying our laundry into the sink.

"But I can't swim!"

"Honey, just stay in the shallow end. You'll be fine. Anyway . . ." She filled the sink with water and grabbed the bar of soap, rubbing it to work up a lather. "There are other people out there. You'll be fine," she repeated.

I stood watching her for a moment to be sure she was serious, then pulled the swimsuit on and opened the door to the pool deck. The smell of chlorine filled my nostrils. The lady with the magazine glanced up and gave me a quick smile, and her kids paused in their play for a moment before turning away again. I sat down shyly at the edge of the pool and dipped my feet in.

"Wendy," said the woman to her daughter, "why don't see if that little girl wants to play with you?"

The girl swam up to me and spun in circles. She had red hair and freckles that started at her forehead and ended at her shoulders. "Hi. I'm six and a quarter. Watch this, I can do a handstand!" She plunged into the water and stuck her legs in the air.

"Did you see that?" she asked me breathlessly when she came back up.

I nodded, wishing I knew how to swim. I stood and started making my way to the shallow end with Wendy chattering at my feet. They were from a place called Vancouver, they were on holiday but it wasn't like a real holiday because they actually had to go to her godmother's funeral because she had gotten too old and died, her brother was ten and liked to do skateboarding, her favorite Archie character was Betty because she was way nicer than Veronica, and where were my mom and dad?

"Oh," I said, stopping in my tracks, "my mom will be out in a minute. She just takes a while to change, that's all."

"Yeah, mine too. Where do you live?"

It was the worst question she could have asked me. I could feel my face turning red. "Um . . . wha— Pardon me?"

"Live. Are you from Vancouver too?"

"No, I, uh . . . well . . ." I looked down at her. She was holding on to the side of the pool, smiling up at me expectantly. I glanced around and then knelt down beside her. "I, um . . . I sort of live in the wilderness. I mean, not really right now, but . . . usually."

Her eyes lit up. "Wow. That is sooooo cool! You mean like Laura Ingalls in *Little House on the Prairie*?"

"Yeah, kind of . . . I mean, who is she, exactly?"

"Laura Ingalls? She lives with her ma and pa way out in the country, and they make all their own food and stuff. She has to walk really far to get to school. Now, let's play water tag. You're it!"

She poked me in the leg and ran away, and I chased after her. Her brother joined in, and before long we were laughing and splashing each other like we'd been friends forever. Too soon, Mom poked her head through the door and called for me.

"Mom!" I said breathlessly as she toweled me off. "I made a friend! Her name is Wendy! We played tag and it was so much fun!

And—and I even told her about living in the wilderness, and she thought it was super cool!"

"That's wonderful," Mom said absently, leading me over to the hand dryer. She pushed my head in front of it and hit the big silver button. Hot air blasted out at my hair.

"Can't we stay? Please can't we stay?" I begged over the roar.

"We can't, darling," Mom said. "Karl is waiting for us."

"But . . ." I stepped away from the dryer and looked at her pleadingly. She was putting the last of our laundry, clean but still wet, into her duffel bag. She stacked our tin dishes on top of the clothes and pulled the drawstring shut.

"Come on, honey," Mom said. "We need to get going before people start asking questions. You'll have other friends, I promise."

I crossed my arms and bit my lip as my eyes welled with tears. Before I could stop it, my hand swung out and hit her squarely in the chest. *"No fair!"*

"Cea!" she said, catching my wrist in her hand. "Listen to me. You can't have everything you want in life. You have a mother who loves you, and that's more than a lot of kids in the world have. Be grateful for that."

It wasn't the first time my mother had said these words to me, and they never failed to fill me with a strange, crawling feeling of guilt. I sank to the floor, completely deflated. As I cried, I tried to block out the sight, burned behind my closed eyes, of my mother's hurt and shocked face. Because what she didn't understand was that for forty short minutes, I had felt almost normal.

STOCKING UP WAS LIKE a business, Karl liked to say to us. You started off small and got bigger, and you always kept in mind that time was money, which meant you never left empty-handed. With each passing day, Karl was getting bolder. In the beginning, he had seemed happy enough with his finds of toilet paper rolls, crackers, and canned pork and beans, but now he was going for bigger prizes. Among the items under his tarp were a ten-speed bike with flat tires, a pair of fishing rods and a huge canvas tent that he had had Mom help carry out of someone's garage. As for never leaving empty-handed, Karl had that covered too. Some of his odder treasures were a blender jug with no base, a moth-eaten business suit, a metal barrel filled with some sort of liquid and a set of hair rollers. The back of the truck was so full now that Karl was storing stuff in the cab. Cans of soup rolled around at my feet, army blankets scratched at my ankles and a pile of musty *Rolling Stone* magazines sat on the seat between Mom and me. When my mother complained that we no longer had anywhere to sleep, Karl got out the tent and pitched it by the side of the road, and there we spent our nights for the next week.

One rainy evening, we were driving down a back road when I saw in the distance an old farmhouse with peeling yellow paint.

"Why are all those windows covered up?" I asked Mom, pointing.

"It's abandoned. That means nobody lives there."

"Why did the people leave?"

"I don't know, sweetheart."

"Well, what do you think?"

"I'm not sure. Maybe . . . maybe they died. Or they couldn't pay for it anymore."

"Pay who?"

"The bank."

"Oh." I thought for a moment, wondering why anyone would leave their home instead of just giving their money away. If it had been up to me, I'd have given that bank place anything to keep that house. "So then can we sleep there tonight? Please?"

Mom glanced at Karl, who shrugged, and when we reached the driveway, he pulled in. He drove around to the back of the house, where we found a sagging barn and, beside it, a rusted tractor with tires so flat and dusty that it was hard to tell where they ended and the ground started.

"Yep. This was a farm, all right," Karl said, sliding from the cab.

Mom and I waited in the truck while he pried the plywood from the back door with a crowbar, then we ran inside with our heads lowered against the pouring rain.

It was hard to imagine anyone had ever lived here. In the kitchen, the cabinet doors hung off their hinges at crazy angles. The roof was full of holes, letting the rain pour down here and there in noisy streams. In the living room, the floorboards were so rotted through that when I knelt down, I could see right into the dirt cellar. A chandelier hung at the center of the room, stripped of its crystals. Every corner was draped in spiderwebs. But there was also a pretty ceiling made from stamped tin, and a dark wood banister as smooth as the inside of my forearm.

Karl went to look for forgotten goodies while Mom searched the main floor for the driest room. Finally she settled on the bathroom, and went to work making a bed for me in the claw-foot tub.

"There," she said, tucking my sleeping bag around me. "Isn't that nice and cozy?"

"Yeah," I said, fingering Papa Dick's roach clip in my pocket. I let Mom bend down to kiss me, and put my arms around her neck before she could pull away. "Mommy?"

"Yes?"

"Why couldn't we live here?"

She smiled down at me. "Oh . . . it would just be a lot of work to fix up, that's all."

"I wouldn't mind. I could help! And we could even get that tractor going again, and plant our own garden . . ." I looked up at her hopefully.

"Sweetheart . . ." She gazed at the wall above me. "It's just . . . even though nobody lives here, someone still owns the property—that means the land this house is on—and if they found out we lived here, we'd have to pay them money."

"But Karl has all that money from his pot plants."

"Yeah, I know, it's just . . . we're better off looking for a free place to live, that's all. That's why we love the wilderness so much. Nobody even knows we're there. It's like our own secret little world, right?"

"Yeah, I guess so. Are we ever going back?"

"To the wilderness? Eventually, probably."

"No, I mean . . ." I hesitated, and then blurted it out. "I mean are we ever going back to live with Papa Dick and Grandma Jeanne again? And what . . . what about Aunt Jessie and Aunt Jan? Will we ever see them again?"

"Oh, I . . ." Mom looked at me sadly. "I don't know, sweetheart. Jessie and Jan . . . they're hard to keep track of. I don't even know if they're with Mom and Dad anymore. And right now . . . well, we're just taking it one day at a time, that's all."

I dropped my chin to my chest, but then I had an exciting thought. "Mommy, you know that cottage Karl talked about before? The one he said we could live in on the lake?"

Mom nodded, softly stroking my hair from my face.

"How about it? Do you think we might? That would be so neat?"

"Yeah, sweetie, it would. I hope so. We'll just have to see what happens. Okay?"

She placed Suzie Doll in my arms, then lay down on the floor beside me in her sleeping bag. I dozed off to the sound of rain pattering on the roof, happy to be snug and safe, and dreamed of living in a floating cottage that was just big enough for Mom and me, and no one else.

I WAS LEARNING THAT although Karl liked to play the tough guy, inside he really wasn't. The truth was that I liked him. Our relationship never crossed into the territory of stepfather and step-daughter—he didn't hold my hand when we walked, kiss me good-night, or teach me how to throw a ball—but it never occurred to me that he should. I didn't imagine that Karl would be with us forever, and I didn't imagine that he wouldn't. Karl just was. But if I was ever unsure of his feelings for me, there was one thing that happened in Scotch Creek that changed that.

A few days after the night in the abandoned farmhouse, my mother and I were snoozing in the truck waiting for Karl to complete a stocking-up session. Suddenly he rapped on the window, scaring the crap out of both of us. Mom scrambled across the seat and rolled down the window.

"What is it?" she asked in a panicky voice.

"Hey, loosen up, will ya? I thought we'd sleep here tonight, that's all."

"Here? You mean in this cottage?"

"Sure. Why not?" Karl was already reaching under the tarp to pull out our sleeping bags.

"Oh, well . . ." She glanced at me, and I smiled back at her.

Maybe it was the farmhouse that gave Karl the idea, I thought, and maybe he would like it here at this cottage so much that we would stay. I looked at it again with different eyes. With its brown siding and flat roof, it wasn't one of the prettier houses, but I thought it would do just fine. I helped Mom gather our stuff, and we went inside.

As soon as we entered the door, my hope dissipated. It wasn't that the house wasn't fine; it was that I could feel this wasn't nobody's home like the farmhouse. It was someone else's.

I didn't sleep well that night. Mom put me in the kid's bedroom, which had bunk beds and Winnie the Pooh curtains, but I tossed and turned as the clock ticked. I closed my eyes again and again, trying to calm my beating heart, but I couldn't stop thinking about doors flinging open and lights flipping on and owners dragging me outside and slamming the door in my face. Finally, I left my bed and went to find Mom, who was camped out in the bigger room with Karl. I fell asleep next to her, but when I woke up the next morning, I was back in the bunk bed. I blinked against the bright sunlight, glad the night was over.

Then I rolled over and saw it: there, sitting on the bedside table, was a pink satin music box. I sat up on my elbow and stared. How had I not noticed it before? Besides Barbie, it was the most beautiful thing I had ever seen. I opened the lid, and a tiny ballerina popped up and started spinning to tinkling music. More than once, Karl had offered me left-behind toys from the cottages, and I always shook my head no. But that was before I saw this. I snatched the box up and ran into the kitchen, where Mom and Karl were sitting at the table eating cereal out of blue bowls.

"Mommy, look!" I held the box out for her to see.

"Wow," she said slowly, taking it from me. "I . . . I think we should probably leave that here. It looks like someone's treasure."

"No!" I said angrily, snatching it back. Mom looked at me in shock. "If they really cared about it, they wouldn't have left it here." I turned to Karl. "Right, Karl? They wouldn't have."

Karl finished drinking the milk from his bowl and dropped it onto the table with a clatter. "It's all yours," he said. "Pink. Your favorite color, right?"

"Karl—" Mom started.

"Just cool it." He took the box from me, opened it and lifted a slip of paper out from under the tray. "See?" he said, holding the receipt up for Mom to see. "Bought and paid for. It's a present, from me to Small Fry." He winked at me, and I looked back at him in shock.

A present? From Karl? It was the first brand-new thing I had ever owned. I gave him a hug, then skipped outside and played with my new toy until Mom swept me up an hour later and placed me in the truck to go steal some more.

AFTER OUR FIRST SLEEPOVER in a cottage, we started staying in them more often. Karl never let us stay longer than one night for fear of someone catching on to us, but even though it was risky we all preferred the cottages to sleeping in the tent. One of the best things about them was the hot water. Most of the cottages left it on for the winter, so we were able do a load of laundry in the washing machine or take a bath. Mom would sit at the edge of the tub to shampoo my hair while I washed Suzie Doll, and then lift her up to drain the water from her body.

With each passing night, my worry of being caught was fading. Now and then, I would wake up early to search for treasures while Mom and Karl slept in. I never took anything, but I liked to turn things over in my hands, wondering about the kids who had left them behind and looking for clues about who they were. There were books with names in them—*This book belongs to Cathy M.*—and frames around photos of smiling, gap-toothed children wearing shorts or swimsuits. I always put them back exactly where I found them, using the bare spots in the dust as a guide.

Even when Karl just wanted to finish up a job and move on, I was getting braver. Mom still waited in the truck, her eyes glued to the road while she smoked Karl's Player's Light cigarettes, but I began leaving the cab to run around in the yards. Whenever I made a big show of jumping off a swing or hanging from a tree branch, Mom would give me a smile. Sometimes I'd get too loud, shouting, "Watch me, watch me, Mommy!" and she'd glance down the road and then bolt out of the truck, shushing me with a finger to her lips, but mostly I remembered to be quiet. Sometimes I thought about the kids from the photographs, the ones who got to spend their summers there without hiding, but I never felt jealous of them. Mom liked to remind me that I was a Sagittarius, which meant I was destined for great adventures. I was willing to bet the kids who lived in Scotch Creek didn't get to do half the stuff I got to do.

IN THE YEARS SINCE, I've wondered how long we would have gone on like this if we hadn't been caught. Probably not long, considering there was barely a square inch left in the truck to store anything. It was mid-March, nearly three months since Karl had begun his stealing spree, and he was starting to make some noise about moving on. One morning, we went to the greasy spoon for breakfast and everyone was talking about some recent break-ins. My stomach dropped in fear. Karl sipped his coffee slowly, clucking his tongue and shaking his head as the waitress filled him in. Apparently a friend of hers had been dismayed to arrive at his cottage to find not only his bottle cap collection missing, but also the contents of his sock drawer.

"Can you imagine?" the waitress said into the air, holding her coffeepot at a dangerous angle. "I mean, who would take *socks*, for land's sake?"

Back in the truck, Mom and Karl got into a huge fight. It was time for Karl to stop, Mom said, but Karl told her that business was business and he still needed some power tools. Just a couple more houses, he swore to it. Mom held her ground for a few minutes, but in the end she gave up with a cross of her arms and turn of her cheek.

"All I can say," she said, lifting her chin, "is that the next house you hit better have enough power tools in it to fill a frigging store!"

Karl nodded distractedly, his mind already on the job ahead.

Twenty minutes later, we pulled up to a cabin with a play area in the backyard. I jumped out of the truck and went to explore. And as I was digging a moat in the sandbox with a plastic shovel, I heard the voice.

I stopped, leaning toward the sound. The voice belonged to an unfamiliar man. I could hear Mom talking too, then a brief silence before he responded. My heart thumped. I tiptoed to the end of the wall and peeked around the corner. Mom was leaning out the window of the truck, talking to a man in a red baseball cap. Karl was nowhere to be seen. I walked to the truck and slipped in through the driver's side door beside Mom.

"Well, hey there, youngster," the man said, tipping his hat to me. "I was just talking to your mama about this fine cottage you folks are renting."

I nodded silently. The man's eyes swept the floor, taking in the soup cans, half-burned candles and a picture frame holding a photo of the wrong family. Then he peered over Mom's shoulder at the back of the truck.

"Looks like you folks've got quite the load here."

"Yes, well . . ." Mom glanced at the front door of the cottage for the hundredth time. Luckily, Karl had used his lock pick to break into this one rather than a rock through the window. "We were actually just on our way to the dump. Spring cleaning, you know?" She smiled weakly.

Just then, I heard a door slam and looked up. Karl was walking toward us, smoking a cigarette and carrying a large black plastic bag. He spotted the man and smiled at him, and then pitched the bag into the garbage bin. I stared at it, wondering if Karl had just thrown away his power tools.

"Well, hello there! Lovely day, isn't it?" Karl said to the man, hurrying over and shaking his hand. "Sorry about that, just doing a little cleanup. Matthew is my name, Matthew Stokes. You new to the area?"

The man shook his head and scratched it through his baseball cap with a thumb. "Nope, been here almost ten years. Hadn't realized the Andersons were renting their cottage out this season. They friends of yours?"

Karl smiled again. "Just acquaintances. Look, I hate to be rude, but we really have to run. The wife—" He waved his hand at Mom. "Late for an appointment."

"Yes," Mom said quickly. "Before we go to the dump, that is."

"Mm. Well . . ."

The man looked like he wasn't really finished talking, but Karl was already climbing into the truck, closing the door and starting the engine. He pushed the gearshift into drive, waved once more and pulled down the driveway toward the road. I turned to look out the back window. The man was standing with his arms folded, watching us pull away with a mad sort of look on his face. I lifted my hand to wave goodbye, but he didn't even wave back.

THAT ASSHOLE IN THE red baseball cap's timing had been perfect, Karl declared as he drove, as he was getting bored of Scotch

Creek and its one-streetlight-and-a-barbershop mentality anyway.

"Besides, didn't I tell you?" he said to Mom with a grin. "All that stocking up has paid off. I've barely had to touch my cash supply. Which means . . ." He paused while Mom and I looked at him expectantly. He waited for the lighter to pop out of the dashboard, then he lit the end of his cigarette and exhaled. "I got a line on a cottage for rent. That's right," he continued while Mom and I clapped our hands excitedly, "just sixty or so miles down the road. We're gonna put us down some roots!"

I bounced up and down while Mom laughed and hugged me. We were on our way to greener pastures, Karl said, and greener pastures deserved a party. Mom slid Steve Miller into the tape deck and rolled a joint while Karl popped the cap on a bottle of stolen beer. We all sang along to "Jet Airliner" and boogied in our seats. A while later, Karl pulled off the highway and started down a road lined with maple trees, their shadows dancing on the pavement in the late-afternoon sun. We came to a dirt lane, and he touched the brakes.

"Here, I know a shortcut," Karl said, turning in.

I swallowed hard and moved closer to Mom. We were on a logging road with potholes that looked big enough to swallow me, but Karl was picking up speed. With one hand on the steering wheel, he used his other hand to open his fourth bottle of beer. It sloshed onto his lap, so he drained it and threw the bottle on the floor.

"Here we go. Hold on!" he said, and hit the gas even harder.

Mom yelled at him to stop, but Karl was too busy drumming his fingers on the steering wheel and bopping his head to the music to pay her much attention.

"Karl!" she shouted, louder this time. "Slow *down*, please!"

"Hey, cool it, woman!" Karl yelled back, cranking the music up. "You wanna get there before midnight, don't you?"

Mom huddled beside me, wrapping her arms around my body. I grabbed the bottom of my seat to try to stop bouncing. Karl cackled and took a pull on the joint, and as I turned to look at him, something caught the corner of my eye. It was an orange flash, and it was coming from behind us. I turned.

The back of the truck was on fire. Flames jumped at the rear window under a cloud of black smoke.

"*Mommy!*" I screamed. "*Fire!*"

"What the *fuck*?" Karl slammed on the brakes and the truck lurched to a stop.

Mom pushed my door open and shoved me outside. I fell to the ground and she landed on top of me, jamming my face into the dirt. A wave of heat washed over my body. I lifted my head and looked for Karl. He was already out of the cab, hopping into the back of the truck and trying to throw a blanket over a large object. Whatever it was, it was burning like a small sun as Karl tried to get it under control. He finally pushed it over the side of the truck and it hit the ground rolling, flames moving slowly around it like orange liquid. Liquid. It was the barrel, I realized, the one Karl had stolen. He grabbed a shovel from the back and started throwing dirt over it, then stomped around on the ground to put out the last of the blaze, cursing all the while. Finally he tossed the shovel down, lit a cigarette with shaking hands and blew a long stream of smoke from his nostrils.

"God *damn* it!" he yelled, kicking the truck with his stolen cowboy boot.

THE FIRST THING KARL looked for was his cash. The storage trunk was burned partly through, so he reached inside it and pulled out the small wood box. The top was black, and the money sat inside it in an ashy little pile.

"*Fuck it!*" Karl shrieked, throwing the box against a tree trunk. He walked away from us with his hands folded over his head, paced back and forth a few times, then came back to the truck. What was left of the tarp had melted into almost everything, making a huge mess. Karl pawed through his loot like a dog digging for a bone, tossing out anything that was ruined. When he was done, it was nearly dark outside and piles of junk were spread in every direction around the truck. Karl raked his hair back, jumped into the cab and slapped his hand on the dash for us to join him.

"Well, you can forget your fucking cottage now," he said to Mom angrily as we piled in beside him. "You see? If we hadn't been on our way to your goddamn palace on the lake, this never would have happened."

"Fuck you," Mom replied, and it was the first time I had ever heard her pair these two words together. "You're the one who stole the barrel of gasoline. You should be thanking Cea—she saved our lives."

Karl glanced at her sideways, then placed his hand lightly on her thigh. "Anyway," he said, his tone softer now, "not to worry. Your man has a plan B up his sleeve."

Mom scooted away from him, still mad, and put an arm around my shoulder. I slumped against her, willing myself not to cry. No cottage on the lake, not to mention that my face was pounding painfully from being slammed against the ground. Mom looked my wounds over and cleaned them with some spit on a paper napkin. I dug in my pocket for Papa Dick's roach clip, relieved to find it still there, and then closed my eyes, grateful that Mom hadn't asked what plan B might be. As long as we were driving, I thought, there was always the possibility that we might never stop.

Flames shot from my ankles like jets. I was weightless, flying over a clear green lake with Barbie in my hand. Far below, I could see my cottage. It looked like a delicious birthday cake, pink with white trim. I steered my jets and zoomed down to it, and then—

It was the screeching sound that woke me up. I flew forward over the dashboard and bounced back hard on the seat, my face slamming sideways against the window. Our headlights spun in an arc across tall grass, picking out the gaping hole in the barbed wire fence we had just crashed through. The truck lurched to the left, landed back on its tires and shuddered to a stop.

Nobody spoke. A ticking sound rose from the engine, breaking the silence. We were in a farmer's wheat field. In the distance, a golden square of light glowed yellow. One square became two, and then three. People jogged toward us, their flashlight beams bouncing up and down as they ran. We stared into the darkness.

"Well," Mom said finally. "Fuck a duck. Talk about your bitch of a day."

Karl started to laugh. A moment later Mom joined in, and then so did I. Before long we were all cracking up so hard, doubled over in our seats with tears streaming from our eyes, that the farmers had to tap on Karl's window to get his attention.

"You folks okay?" the man asked us, his face confused, but we couldn't even stop laughing long enough to answer him.

That night, the farmers let us pitch a tent in their field. They called a tow truck for us the next morning, and the three of us rode into town and waited for Karl's truck to be repaired. He even had them fix the reverse gear while they were at it, so when we left the next morning, our ride was as good as new.

Chapter Twelve

Karl said that after all he and Mom had been through, they deserved a break. "What say we do a little camping trip, babe?"

"Camping trip?" Mom echoed. "Isn't that kind of like going to Mexico when you live in Hawaii?"

Karl shrugged. "Maybe, but at least we can hang by ourselves for a while. Let's take off, just the two of us. I know a place we can drop Cea off for a few days."

I suddenly felt ill. Drop me off for a few days? I moved closer to Mom's side. "Please, Mommy. I don't want to."

"Oh, sweetie . . ." She glanced over at Karl. "It'll be fine," she said to me decisively. "It's just a few days. You'll probably have fun!"

My caregiver for the week turned out to be a lady friend of Karl's who lived in a tipi with her four-year-old son. "Don't worry, he ain't mine," Karl added when Mom looked at him sideways. Karl's friend wore a paisley scarf around her head and heavy gold earrings that stretched her earlobe holes into long, thin lines. Her son, Mica, had crusted snot under his nose and hair so matted that it looked like it would take a full day to brush out. His long fingernails had crescents of dirt beneath them. And even though he didn't have shoes, his feet were filthy enough to make it look like he was wearing a pair.

After the adults had a toke, Mom started rounding her stuff up to leave. I clung to her and cried for all I was worth, but it seemed there would be no changing her mind.

"Five days," she said to me as she unwound my arms from around her leg. Reaching into her knapsack, she withdrew her bottle of Rescue Remedy and opened my mouth with her hand. Drip, drip, drip went the cold drops beneath my tongue. "Six days at the most. I'll see you soon, my love." And then Karl hurried her out. There was a gap between the bottom of the canvas tipi shell and the ground, and I saw her moccasins walking past as she left. I fell on the floor and bawled.

"Hey, cool it, kid," the lady friend said to me. "Us mamas need a break sometimes, you know? It's tough work raisin' you little ones." She handed her son and me each a baby bottle filled with milk. "Why don't you guys go feed Rainbow or something?"

"Wainbow! Wainbow!" Mica yelled, tearing out the tipi door, and I finally dragged my feet out behind him.

Rainbow turned out to be their goat. She was tied to a tree with a leather strap, and she was as grungy as Mica. While she sucked greedily at the bottle Mica held out to her, he told me her story.

"She lost her mama. Some dummy hunter thought she was a deer. So now I gotta feed her and stuff."

"Oh," I said, wishing he would wipe the snot from under his nose. Mica couldn't seem to say the letter *r*, so he said *hunt-tuh* and *dee-uh*. The bottle drained into Rainbow's mouth until it was empty, but instead of removing it, Mica shoved it in even farther.

"Watch this," he said. "She makes a funny sound." Rainbow took a few gulps of air and began to hiccup.

Mica squealed with laughter, but I didn't really think it was very funny. He finally pulled the bottle out, and I replaced it with my own.

Mica picked up a stick and started whacking it on a tree trunk. "How come your mama leaved you he-uh? She gonna come back?"

"Yeah, of course," I replied confidently, but the lump in my throat was back. I tried to swallow it down again, but when I couldn't, I yanked the bottle out of Rainbow's mouth, ran for the tipi and buried myself inside my sleeping bag, not even peeking out an hour later when the mom said it was time to come on out and eat some borscht.

Other than feeding Rainbow, there wasn't much to do at Karl's lady friend's tipi. I wasn't used to being entertained, of course, but Mica's mother paid us almost no attention at all. She usually made us dinner, but Mica and I scrounged up our own breakfast and lunch from whatever we could find in the tipi. She never tucked us in at night, and once when Mica burned his knee on the woodstove and started to cry, she didn't even move from her place in bed. One night, she grabbed a wooden spoon and smacked him on the bum for no reason that I could see. Mica seemed to cry for hours afterwards, and I could feel the weight of his sadness filling the small space of the tipi. After that, I vowed not to leave my sleeping bag until Mom got back. I ate my meals in bed and just stared at that gap in the tipi wall between the ground and the canvas, waiting for her feet to come walking back to me.

And one afternoon, about a week after she'd left me, they finally did. I jumped up from the floor and ran outside, joyously slamming my body into her legs in the biggest hug ever. As far as I was concerned, I had the best mother in the whole wide world.

REJUVENATED AFTER HIS CAMPING trip with Mom, Karl was good and ready to tackle our problems. As he often liked to tell

Mom, he was a man with a plan, and if ever we were in a situation that needed a plan, it was now. Karl ticked the facts off on his fingers as he drove the highway eastward.

One: except for the sixty-five dollars he had left in his wallet, we were flat broke, which led to two: we had to rebuild our cash supply. This brought us to three: we needed to set up house somewhere private enough to grow a marijuana crop, and finally, four: Mom was dead wrong if she thought we were homeless now, because we had that canvas tent Karl had found during one of his stocking-up sessions. Guessing from the weight of it, he thought it was around the same size as a tipi, and lucky for us he had put it on the bottom of the truck bed, where it had been saved from the worst of the fire.

"Right on," said Mom agreeably, well into her first joint of the day. "Far out, babe." She blew me a smoke ring, and I poked through the middle of it with my finger.

Karl grasped the steering wheel as he nailed down the final point of his plan. "I got the perfect spot in mind to re-grow our wealth—no pun intended," he said, elbowing Mom in the ribs. "Lake Minnewanka, Alberta."

"Alberta? I thought you were done with—"

"Forget that," Karl said, waving a hand at her. "B.C. wasn't all it was cracked up to be." He rubbed Mom's thigh. "Listen, babe, I know the past few months haven't been easy on you, okay? What you need is a support system. Some friends you can rely on."

"You mean like a commune?" Mom asked, passing the joint to Karl. "Not really my cup of tea. All they ever gave me was a bad case of hep B."

"Not a commune, no. Just some friends. I've got some—Larry and Susanne—who live out in Minnewanka in a tipi. At least they did last I heard from them, which was about a year ago. They were city folk before moving to the bush. They even have a kid, a little girl around Small Fry's age."

"That would be nice for you, wouldn't it, sweetheart?" Mom said to me. "You'd have a friend."

My heart leapt. "You mean Wendy will be there?"

"No, honey. Another little girl."

"Oh. What's her name?"

"Kathy . . . er, no . . . Kelly," Karl said.

I turned away and gazed out the window, trying to imagine her. A girl who lived in the wilderness, just like me. I wondered if she would have any stick horses, and if she liked to pick the pitch off tree trunks like I did to chew like gum. Kelly. A real friend. I wasn't sure why, but suddenly my tummy felt funny, like if someone had put a plate of fried bear meat in front of me, I wouldn't have been able to eat even a single bite.

"KEEP YOUR EYES PEELED for a Winnebago," Karl said to us six hours later as he turned off the main road onto a dirt lane. "Should be somewhere in the trees." I watched the side of the road as we bumped along, wanting to be the first to spot the prize. After a while we rolled over a cattle guard and came to a metal gate, which Karl hopped out to inspect. "Lock's already been broken," he said as he swung back into the cab. "Looks like we're on the right track."

Ten minutes later, we pulled up beside a purple camper van with a huge pot leaf painted on the side. Karl and Mom jumped out of the truck. I slid out slowly, and then stood close as Mom went through our belongings.

"Mommy, are there cops around here?"

"Of course not, sweetheart," she said distractedly, holding up a piece of orange fabric that was burned half away. "Will you look at that? Damn it. This was my favorite dish towel. And look at this—" she continued to Karl, pulling her backpack out. "Burned to a crisp. How are we supposed to carry our stuff to camp?"

Karl came over and took it from her, then tossed it aside and dug around for his own pack, which was just as damaged. "Shit," he said, throwing it to the ground. He placed his hands on the edge of the truck bed and leaned forward, head down. After a minute he popped it up again. "I've got it," he said. "You've got yourself one smart man here, babe."

Karl pulled the canvas tent out, unfolded it on the ground and tied a rope at each end to form a hammock. Then he threw all our stuff onto it, grabbed an end, told Mom to do the same and started dragging the tent through the woods. It looked like it would be a fun ride, so I asked if I could get on too, but Karl barked that I'd be better off making myself useful by picking things up as they fell off. So I scrambled along behind, Suzie Doll under one arm, tossing pots and tin plates and underwear back onto the canvas as it snaked through the trees to our new home.

Larry and Susanne must have heard us coming, because they were both standing in front of their tipi when we got there. When Larry saw Karl, he let out a whoop.

"Madman!" he said, thumping Karl on the back. "What the hell are you doing here?"

"Just passing through, Larry. Although, we may stay awhile."

"Goddamn, it's good to see you. What's it been—like, three years?" He turned his eyes to Mom. "And who do we have here?"

"This is Michelle, my woman. And her daughter Cea. Where's your kid?"

"Out playing with bears somewhere, you know how it goes." He looked down at our canvas tent, overflowing with camping equipment, and shook his head. "What the hell kind of contraption is that, Madman? Glad to see you haven't changed. Come on inside, let's roll ourselves up a j."

AS IT TURNED OUT, the j was just the start of it. An occasion like this deserved a real celebration, Larry announced, and he brought out a little plastic bag filled with something wrinkly and brown. Karl laughed and twisted his arm behind his back as if it were Larry doing it.

"What's that?" I asked Karl.

"Mushrooms," he said. "A special kind."

He held the bag under my nose so I could take a sniff. They smelled horrible. I went back to my Big Blue Book, tracing my fingers over the Brownie Yearbook story. It was my favorite because it was all about my birth month, November, and I could almost read the whole thing by myself. I finished my page and glanced up at Karl's friends. With their matching long hair, colorful woven ponchos and tie-dyed bell-bottoms, Larry and Susanne looked more like twins than husband and wife. Larry ate another mushroom, then held the bag out to Mom and Susanne.

"Ugh, I hate those things," Mom said, taking a hot butter knife off the stove and dropping a chunk of hash onto it. "Never brought me anything but trouble."

"What kind of trouble?" I piped up, looking away from my book.

She hesitated, and then held the knife under her mouth to inhale a curl of smoke. "Never mind," she said, her voice strained as she spoke with held breath.

I sprawled out on my stomach and rested my chin in my hand. "Mommy, when will Kelly be here?"

"I don't know, sweetie. Soon."

I went back to my book, but the adults were talking too loud for me to focus. Not only that, but Larry had a battery-powered boom box that was blasting Led Zeppelin's "Dazed and Confused."

"I'm tired," I said to Mom. "Can I go to bed now?"

"In a little while," she replied. "Karl still has to put the tent up. Why don't you draw a picture or something?"

Her voice sounded too breathy. Her eyes looked funny. But that was nothing compared to Karl and Larry, who were now in the middle of the tipi wrestling like a couple of gorillas. Susanne kept laughing and telling them to watch out for the hot stove.

"What's Karl doing?" I asked Mom. "Why is he acting so weird? And why is that other guy—?"

"*Cea!* Please! I just need a little grownup time right now," Mom said sharply, and I jumped back. She leaned toward me and placed her hands on my shoulders. "Look, honey, I'm sorry. I didn't mean to yell. But I just can't be your mom all the time, okay? I try my best, I really do, but I can't. Now why don't you go and play outside." She shoved a flashlight at me and turned away.

I wiped my eyes and stared at her back, wanting nothing in the world except for her to turn toward me. When several minutes passed and she didn't, I finally lifted the door flap and slipped out into the near-darkness. The air felt cold. I walked over to our canvas tent, still spread out on the ground beneath our mess of belongings, and bounced the flashlight's beam around until I found one of Mom's sweaters. It smelled like her as I pulled it over my head. Through blurry eyes, I went to work, taking everything off the canvas and placing it in a heap under a tree. The tipi glowed yellow in the dark. I heard stoned laughter, and then the sound of breaking glass. I untied the ropes from the tent and tugged and pulled until it was flat. Then I found the poles, took them out of their nylon bag and snapped them together, and stood beside the tent and started to cry again. I knew perfectly well I wouldn't be able to put it up by myself.

I went back to the heap and found my sleeping bag, which smelled like smoke but was undamaged, and unrolled it on the ground. *I can't be your mom all the time,* she had said to me. Did that mean she didn't want to be my mother at all anymore? I didn't even know my dad, and my grandparents were pretending I had never existed. I went to sleep with tears soaking through the neck of Mom's sweater, wondering what would happen to me if she ever decided to give me away.

The smell of hash woke me up. I turned my head, and Mom was curled behind me with her arms around my waist. "I'm sorry," she said as she cried into my hair. "I'm so sorry. I'm here now."

I hugged her back and glanced around. Karl and Larry, both of them sober and quiet in the light of sunrise, were busy building the tent around us. I closed my eyes again, and when I woke up a few hours later, the tent was built. Mom was still at my side, fast asleep. And a strange girl was dangling a hacked-up earthworm in front of my face.

"I chopped it up with my very own knife," she announced, flicking a switchblade out of her pocket to show me. I blinked back at her. She leaned forward and stared at me, almost hissing into my face. "But you can't use it even if you say pretty please."

KELLY AND I COULD not have been more opposite. She was dark where I was blond, short where I was tall, chubby where I was thin, and fearless where I was shy. At least, that's what I thought at first.

Next to Kelly, I felt about as exciting as a bowl of cold cream of wheat. She was eight, three years older than me, and she took every chance to show me how tough and/or daring she was. During our first weeks together, she ran barefoot through a swarm of red ants, threw herself from a tree branch twenty feet off the ground, mixed spit into her parents' tub of yogurt, and showed me a blister on her arm the size of a banana that she got from falling against the woodstove. She wore a too-small T-shirt with an iron-on rainbow nearly every single day, and she always had something in her mouth; if it wasn't food, it was one of her fake joints. She liked to dry clover, roll it into one of her dad's Zig-Zag papers, and then smoke it while pretending it was a reefer—something that always gave her parents a good laugh. And she did like to chew gum, as it turned out, but not the kind you could make from tree sap. Her gum was pink and rubbery and sweet smelling, and she blew it into huge bubbles that popped onto her face in a sticky mess.

Kelly and her family had been in Lake Minnewanka for a year and a half, but they still lived much like city folk. Their reason for coming to the bush was never completely clear to me, but Larry did spend a lot of time writing letters to the government (with no return address), which he would drive to the town post office once a week with his family in tow. Since they weren't big on bathing and cleaning in the lake, they would also hit the Y for showers and laundry while they were at it. Not much of a hunter, Larry kept a large store of wheat puffs, Kraft dinner and canned pork 'n' beans in the tipi to feed his family.

Maybe it was because of this constant pull between two worlds that Kelly hadn't taken well to the wilderness. I would walk along the shore with her, pretending to be interested as she went on and on about how much she missed things "back home," a place where she was able to watch TV, lie on her waterbed and neck with her ten-year-old boyfriend.

Me around the time we lived in Lake Minnewanka.

"I've even Frenched, you know," she said to me, digging in her pocket for her father's roach clip. "It's really gross. But cool."

"Wow," I said flatly, thinking of the many times I'd seen Karl and Mom's tongues touching. I couldn't imagine anything grosser, except maybe real sex.

Kelly struck a match and lit up one of her joints, blowing smoke through her nose like a bulldog. "Your parents are pretty dumb to be growing pot, you know," she said.

"They're not my parents," I told her for the fiftieth time. "Karl isn't my dad."

"Whatever. You know what'll happen to you if the cops find out?"

"Of course," I said lightly, picking at a line of tree sap. "We'll go to the slammer."

"Not true. Your parents will, but *you'll* go to the orphanage."

"Orphanage? What's that?"

"A place for kids with bad parents. Or parents who don't want their kids anymore."

I swallowed hard. Well, now I had it, my answer to where I would go if Mom ever gave me away. But Kelly, I knew, was not someone to show fear in front of. Casually, I rolled my tree pitch into a ball and popped it into my mouth.

"Oh yeah? Well, Karl isn't scared of the cops. We already got busted once, but we escaped. The cops chased us down but we were faster. So there."

I turned away, but not before I caught the look of shock on Kelly's face. After that, I became a bit more interesting to her.

LARRY AND SUSANNE SEEMED to do almost everything in the nude—cooking, eating, wood chopping, even hiking. Susanne had a body like a Buddha, skinny legs with a huge belly and boobs. As for Larry, he had a funny-looking wiener. Unlike Karl's and Papa Dick's, Larry's looked like it was inside out. Sometimes, when he sat by the fire, it would inch out of its skin like a fat purple slug. I couldn't help but stare, even though he caught me looking once and shook his finger at me like I was a naughty girl.

One night, I was sleeping soundly when I heard a scream. I sat up in bed, my heart racing. "Mommy!" I called out into the darkness. "What was that?"

She didn't answer, so, clutching Suzie Doll by one arm, I got up and felt my way across the tent. Mom's bed was empty. Tears sprang to my eyes. From outside I heard another shriek, this one even louder than before. I crept to the door and peeked out.

Larry and Susanne's tipi glowed orange in the night. That's where the screaming was coming from, I realized. I tiptoed down the path and quietly lifted their door flap.

Susanne was lying naked on her bed, turned away from me as she moaned. Mom was sitting beside her, rubbing her lower back while Larry paced the floor with his arms wrapped around his head. Karl sat on the tipi's only chair as if none of this was happening, reading a *Rolling Stone* magazine with a picture of John Denver on the cover. I looked for Kelly, but she was nowhere to be seen.

"Cea," Mom said calmly, waving me inside. "Come on in. Susanne's baby is almost here."

My jaw dropped. "Baby?"

"Yes. Didn't you know she was pregnant?"

I shook my head. Not only had I not known, but also I was pretty sure I had never seen a baby before. In fact, I hadn't even seen a picture of one; Mom had told me that Papa Dick took lots of pictures of me after I was born, but most of them were burned in the fire in our second tipi. And then I remembered Suzie Doll. I held her up in front of Mom's face.

"Mommy, will the baby look like this?"

She smiled. "A little."

I crept closer and looked at Susanne's sweaty face. "Why was she screaming?"

"She's in labor. It can be really painful."

Larry stopped pacing and bent over his wife. "Here, babe, this'll help take the edge off," he said, holding a joint to her lips. Susanne tried to inhale, but her breath caught in her throat and she started to cough. She squeezed her eyes shut and finally let out another long scream.

I clapped my hands over my ears and backed away. "Mommy—"

"Shh, it's okay. This is how it's supposed to happen. This is how it was when I had you."

She smiled at me, and I relaxed a little. But the screaming didn't stop. In fact, it only seemed to be getting worse, turning Susanne's face into a mask of pain as she panted and puffed. Sweaty strings of dark hair clung to her bare shoulders.

Finally, after what seemed like hours, Susanne turned onto her back and started rocking side to side. "I think . . ." she said breathlessly, "I think it might be time . . ." She lay back on her elbows and pushed her hips in the air.

"Okay," Mom said, grabbing a basin. "Your water hasn't broken yet, so let me take a look."

Susanne opened her legs wider, and I peeked over Mom's shoulder. What I saw there looked nothing like a baby. A big balloon was bulging out of Susanne's crotch.

"Mommy, what's—?"

Just then, the balloon broke with a *pop*. Water gushed everywhere as Mom jammed the basin under Susanne's butt. Most of it sloshed onto the bed and some even hit me in the face. I crouched down on the floor, and a soaking wet towel landed on top of my head. I clawed it off just in time to see another one flying toward me.

"Cea! Help me clean up. Take that towel and start mopping."

I watched, frozen, as Susanne let out a scream that made the old ones sound like whispers. I dropped the towel and slammed my hands to my ears.

Larry ran to Susanne's side and knelt beside her, his face pale. "You can do it, babe, I know you can. Just—"

"I can't I can't I can't! It hurts too much!"

"You can!" He held the joint out again. "Here, have a toke—"

She batted his hand away, sending the joint flying across the bed. Mom reached over and handed it back to Larry. Then she pointed at Susanne's shoulder.

"She doesn't need drugs right now, she just needs you."

It was the first time I had seen my mother look so in control.

Larry nodded and took his place, and from the other side of the tipi, Karl glanced up from his magazine and smiled.

"Do you feel ready to push now?" she asked Susanne. "Okay. Take my hands. Try to pull me toward you. My mother taught me this."

I watched as Susanne did as she was told. Her eyes squeezed shut, her face turned red and her hair fell forward as she grunted. She looked like she was taking a giant poop. I looked down at her crotch again, but all I could see was lots of black pubic hair and some whitish stuff leaking out in a thin trickle.

"Mommy," I whispered when Susanne grew quiet again. She was lying on her back, breathing hard as she moaned. "Where's the baby?"

"It's coming. It might take a while. Why don't you go find Kelly?"

"Where is she?"

"I'm not sure. She can't be far, though."

I hesitated, torn between my urge to watch things unfold and my urge to escape. Finally, I turned away and left the tipi. The sky had brightened to a dark blue canvas painted with darker clouds. Over to the east, I could see the first rays of morning sun.

I found Kelly down at the lake. She was sitting against a tree trunk with one of her fake joints. I could still hear Susanne from this distance, yelling and carrying on.

"Hi," I said, dropping down beside Kelly. "My mom says the baby's almost here. Don't you want to see it being born?"

"Nah." Kelly lit her joint and inhaled.

It was cold out here. I wrapped my arms around my legs and hugged them to my body.

"I think it's going to be a boy," I tried again, but Kelly stayed silent. I gazed out at the lake, silver in the moonlight, and wished she would say something. "What do you think it's going to look like?" I meant a baby in general, but such a thing was obviously nothing new to her.

"I don't know. My parents, I guess," she replied.

From the tipi, we heard a roar follow the screams. Kelly glanced toward it, but she didn't move. A moment later there was a sound that I'd never heard before. It was a high-pitched cry, but it sounded like it was coming from inside a tin can.

"The baby!" I shouted, jumping up. "It's here!"

Kelly ground her fake joint out under her heel and put her arms around her knees. I stood beside her a moment longer, hoping she would get up, but when she didn't I broke into a run back to the tipi. Even an hour later, when my mother and I returned home, Kelly still hadn't shown up.

I HAD BEEN RIGHT: the baby was a boy. Larry and Susanne named him Benjamin, and Benjamin really liked to cry—especially during the night. Since their tipi was easily within shouting distance, Mom gave me cotton pads to stuff in my ears when I went to sleep. Other than that, Benjamin was pretty boring. When he wasn't crying he mostly slept, except when he was stuck to one of Susanne's boobs, whose nipples had turned dark brown.

Mom liked to sit beside Susanne while she nursed the baby, stroking his soft head.

"Isn't he precious?" she said to me. "It reminds me so much of when you were little."

"Yeah." I touched his tiny fingers. "Will I have a baby someday?"

"If you want to, honey. I hope so. I would love to be a grandma."

"Yeah. I guess I'll have a little girl then. Boys are kind of noisy."

She smiled at me. "Wasn't it magical watching the birth?"

"Yeah, I guess," I answered, suddenly shy, and then I thought of something. I knew perfectly well how babies were made, and yet Mom never seemed to get pregnant.

"Mommy, why don't you get pregnant too?"

She smiled, stood up and led me out of the tipi. When we got to our tent, she brought me over to her bed and reached under her pillow, taking out a shallow plastic cup. "I use this," she said. "It's called a diaphragm."

I gazed at it from a safe distance.

"Here, I'll show you how it works." And with that Mom pulled down her pants, squatted over the bed and stuck it up her crotch. "You see? It rests against the cervix and keeps the sperm from getting in."

"Oh." I blinked and turned away, more than a little put off. I had been planning to ask her if I could use her diaphragm thingie as a dish to feed Suzie Doll, but I didn't really feel like it anymore.

IF KELLY WAS LOOKING for trouble before her baby brother was born, it was nothing compared to afterward. Which would have been fine, except that she also wanted someone to get into it with, and of course that someone was me.

She would seek me out each morning to bug me about setting the outhouse on fire, putting ants in the alfalfa sprout jar, or running away back to the city with her. Reminding her that we would be caught was pointless, as she would just shrug, blow a bubble until it popped on her face, and then continue on to her next badass idea. By the time we'd been in Lake Minnewanka for a couple of months, I'd had about as much of her as I could take.

One day, feeling worn down, I waited until her mother called her in for lunch and then took off into the woods by myself. I liked being alone in the forest. I had already hiked it in every direction from our camp, so I knew my way around really well. Besides, I had Karl's red flags to keep me on track. Karl liked to go into the woods to tie them onto tree branches, doing what he called "marking his territory." Every now and then, he would bring along his surveyor's tape to measure how much land he had and then write it all down in a little spiral notebook, which he told Mom he would use one day to prove something called "squatter's rights."

Today seemed like a good day for horse riding. I picked up a long branch from the ground, put it between my legs and started running through the trees. It felt good to be away from Kelly, who always laughed at me when I rode stick horses or talked to rocks like they were my friends. Twigs scratched at my bare legs, but I didn't care. I was pretending that Papa Dick was hiding in the bushes, admiring me as I rode. *Wow, Cea sure can control that wild beast*, he was thinking. I had long ago given up trying to pretend he and Grandma Jeanne never existed, but I wondered if I would ever see them again.

I heard a twig snap behind me and turned. I knew to hold perfectly still if I saw a bear, and to play dead if that didn't work. There didn't seem to be any animals around, but I decided to head back to camp just to be safe. I set off running, leaping over logs and crashing through bushes. After a minute, I saw a path up ahead and stopped. It petered out into the bushes behind me, but ahead it forked into two trails. They weren't real trails—the ground was just a little worn in places from Karl's footsteps. I knew he tied his flags about every half mile, and from where I stood, I couldn't see any. After thinking for a while, I chose the path on my left, but a few minutes later I noticed an unfamiliar clearing. I went back and tried the right fork, hoping to recognize something, but nothing jogged my memory. Come to think of it, I wasn't even sure I had taken a path at all that morning, especially in my hurry to get away from Kelly. Increasingly desperate, I looked for a tree trunk and found moss growing on one side. I knew that moss always grows on the north side of trees, but since I had no idea which direction the camp was, it did me little good. I sank to the ground and took a deep breath.

I was lost.

Stay put and someone will come, I said to myself in my head. It was one of Papa Dick's top five rules of the wilderness: *stay where you are if you get lost, know your edible plants, avoid a large animal's eyes, dress warmly in layers* and *never leave home without matches and a knife.*

I put my face in my hands and started to cry. I had left home wearing shorts and a T-shirt, and the early-afternoon sky was quickly turning cloudy. I had no matches, and I certainly didn't have a knife. And, having skipped lunch, I was starving. One of Papa Dick's phrases rung in my head: *Hypothermia can also happen in summertime.* He would have been furious with me.

I looked around, suddenly aware of every little sound. From far away, a woodpecker knocked at a tree. Birds called and squirrels chattered. I stood up and did a few jumping jacks. I was chilly but not really cold yet.

An hour later, I was wishing for a sweater. A few hours after that, all I could think of was food. By the time the sun started dropping in the sky, I would have given up my shorts for a glass of water. I held my breath for the twentieth time, listening for the sound of a stream, but there was nothing. My mouth felt like cotton. My tummy growled. Goose bumps crawled across my skin. I wished I had Papa Dick's roach clip with me.

Too soon, the sun's orange glow was almost gone. I had to pee. Briefly, I considered going in my pants to give me a moment's warmth, but then decided it wouldn't be worth the wet coldness afterward. I went beside a tree and returned to my spot, scraping a blanket of dried leaves and moss over my legs. I lay back and looked up at the treetops. Birds called their good-nights. The sun dipped behind the horizon, leaving the sky dusky blue.

"Papa Dick," I whispered. "Please let her come soon."

I closed my eyes and saw my grandfather's face under his cowboy hat. *Welcome this*, he said to me, *for life lessons come by experience and not by chatter.* Papa Dick always loved to say that to me, but I had never understood what it meant. Now I did. I opened my eyes, and when I closed them again the leaves overhead danced behind my lids in red and gray.

"CEA! *CEA!*"

It was my mother's voice. I sat up and looked around wildly, my teeth chattering. I had dreamed of Mom calling my name so many times that I wasn't even sure if it was real now.

"Mom! Over here!" I jumped up from the ground, rubbing my hands over my freezing arms.

I heard running footsteps, and then I saw a flashlight beam

bouncing through the trees. I felt Mom's arms around me before I even saw her.

"*Cea!* Thank god, thank god, thank god . . ."

She crushed me to her chest and covered my face with kisses. When she was finished, Karl walked over to me and grabbed my arm.

"What the hell were you thinking?" he said angrily. "Your mother was worried senseless. I'd like to just—"

"Leave her alone, Karl," Mom said, pulling me out of his grip. "Just leave her the fuck alone." She tugged her sweater off and pulled it over my head, then turned me away from Karl and started walking me home.

Back at the tent, Mom put me to bed with some rose hip tea and sat with me while I drank it. She had started to wonder where I was at around two o'clock, she said. She had done a quick look around camp, and then called on Karl and Larry to help. They had searched until they found me, almost ten hours later. Mom swore she'd never been so scared in her life, because the whole time they were looking she had been secretly afraid that I'd drowned in the lake.

"It was awful," she said, crumbling pot into a rolling paper. She licked the edge and reached for her matches. I plucked the joint from her fingers, and she looked at me in surprise.

"What are you—?"

"I just . . . do you think you could maybe not?"

"But why? It makes me happy. Don't you want a happy mama?"

"Yeah. I just . . . I don't know . . ." I shrugged, and she picked up the joint again.

"Someday you'll understand," she said, lighting up and inhaling.

Across the room, Karl was snoring.

"Mommy," I said quietly. "Why was Karl so mad at me?"

"Oh, honey, he was just worried, that's all." She shook her head. "Anyway, he's just upset because of his pot plants."

"His pot plants? What happened?"

"It was Kelly. She picked them all today and tried to hide them in her pillowcase. And they, uh . . . weren't ready yet. Karl was pretty furious."

I stared at her in shock. "She did?" I finally said. "Wow. Well . . . at least the cops can't find them now. Right?"

"Yeah, right." Mom cleared her throat again. "The thing is, honey . . . Karl is under a lot of pressure. He was counting on the money from those plants for us to live on. He wants to build us a cabin. But it looks like he'll have to replant them, and . . . well, we might be stuck here a while longer."

I nodded, thinking about the first shack we had lived in with Karl. If that was his idea of a cabin, I figured the stolen canvas tent wasn't half bad.

"That's okay," I said, taking Mom's hand. She smiled at me, and I could tell she was starting to get stoned. Her eyes shone in the candlelight. "Just as long as I'm with you."

She leaned down and hugged me for a long time, and when she pulled away, my neck was wet with her tears.

AFTER THE TIME I got lost in the forest, Mom decided she needed to come up with a plan to keep it from happening again. Her first idea was to give me a bell to wear. But when Karl pointed out that the bell would be useless if I strayed too far, she suggested that instead I take some of Karl's red flags with me to mark my way, sort of like Hansel and Gretel. Karl argued that after a few months, the trees would have so many flags in them that I wouldn't be able to tell one from another, and said that maybe I should carry a long ball of string tied to a branch outside the tent. The idea was that I would unwind it as I walked, leaving a line behind me to find my way home. After a test run, though, we decided to scrap this plan too, as the string got so tangled in the bushes that it was impossible for me to walk even as far as the lake without going back twenty times to pull it loose.

In the end, Mom decided that I should just tell her where I was going before I left each morning. This worked for a little while, but since Mom liked to sleep in, I got tired of waiting for her to get up so I could fill her in on my plans. I would sit by her bed with my fists under my chin, bored and restless as I watched her doze. Sometimes I would reach out and touch her bare shoulder or blow lightly on her face, hoping to wake her up, but she would just moan and turn away. Finally, I went out one morning without telling her, and when I got home she didn't say anything, so that was pretty much the end of that.

Chapter Thirteen

"Just take what you can't live without," Mom said, tossing me a small backpack. "Make sure you can manage the weight. I'll take care of your clothes."

I stopped coloring in mid-stroke and lifted my crayon from the page. "Why? Where are we going?"

"Somewhere. Anywhere. Let's just get going before Karl gets back." She was already stuffing tin plates and cups into the larger of the two packs she had just taken from Larry and Susanne, who were in town for the day.

"But what—?"

"Please, honey. No questions right now. Okay?"

I nodded and started putting my crayons away. It wasn't really surprising that it had come to this. Since arriving here several months ago, things had been relatively calm between Mom and Karl, but recently they had started fighting again. Last night had been the worst one yet. I awoke to Mom yelling at Karl that she was sick of worrying about the damn fuzz showing up and busting their asses, plus she was tired of Karl's limp-dick excuses because they hadn't gotten it on in a month and her twat was about to shrivel up and die. Karl shouted back at her that he had shit on his mind and could she maybe just show a bit of appreciation for what he was trying to do to support her and her damn kid. Eventually Karl stormed out, and by this morning he still hadn't come back.

Take what you can't live without. With her words echoing in my head, I collected up Suzie Doll, my Big Blue Book, my pink jewelry box, Papa Dick's roach clip, my crayons and some paper. Then I put my pack on and stood ready by the door. The book made it heavy, but there was no way I was leaving it behind.

"Okay," I said. "I'm ready."

Mom nodded and glanced over at me. I was wearing what I had put on that morning, my cutoff denim shorts and orange T-shirt with brown trim. She looked down at my bare feet and reached behind my bed for my snowmobile boots. "You need to change. Jeans, a sweater, and these boots."

"But it's summer!"

She held up a hand to stop my chatter, and I shut my mouth and changed my clothes. Then Mom wrote a quick note for Karl, put her own pack on and reached for my hand. She looked a little scary with Karl's .22 rifle slung over her shoulder. "Okay. Let's get a move on." We walked out the door and down to the lake without looking back.

When we got to the shore, Mom stopped to look in both directions. "We have to stick close to water. But not the lake," she added with a shake of her head. "There's a creek this way."

We started along the beach toward the Point, a finger of land I was never allowed to go beyond because of the thick trees and bushes just past it. We reached it and Mom took my hand, pulling me along the wall of growth until she saw a small break.

"If we can make it through here," she said, "I know there's a boulder patch on the other side, and from there we can go inland and find the creek. I've seen the waterfall from the lake while I was swimming." She pulled a hatchet from a loop on her pack and started hacking away. "Follow me," she said, crouching down and holding an arm in front of her eyes. "Put your hands over your face."

I did as she said and pushed into the bushes behind her, covering my face with one hand while I used the other to swat branches away. Mom moved slowly, stopping every now and then to hack at the growth, but branches still snapped back and twanged me in the head and arms. After about half an hour, I could see blue water sparkling through holes in the trees.

"We're almost there," Mom said. "Keep going."

"Then what? Where—?"

"*Please*, Cea. Just trust me. Okay?"

I nodded and pushed forward.

A short time later, we stepped out into patchy sunlight and a beach piled with gigantic boulders. I rubbed at my arms, trying to erase the red scratches with my hands.

"Let's go," Mom said, holding her arms out for balance as she climbed the rocks.

I watched, tin pots clanging against her backside, and then I followed. The weight on my back made it hard to stand up again when I leaned over. My heavy boots were awkward, but I was glad I had them on, because my feet slid on the rocks and more than once made me fall. Each time Mom would stop and wait for me, calling out to be sure I was okay before moving on.

"It's getting dark," she yelled out once. "Keep up the best you can, okay?"

"I'm trying."

A few minutes later, I scrambled over the last boulder into Mom's arms. She gave me a quick hug and pointed ahead of us.

"There," she said. "The waterfall. We just have to follow it along the creek until we get to a good camping spot."

"Why can't we just stay here?"

"It's too close to the lake. I don't want anyone to . . . I just want something a little more private, that's all. Like Papa Dick and Grandma Jeanne would choose."

I could hear the waterfall from where I stood. Mom took my hand, and together we walked over to the creek. It was a wide one, and about three feet deep.

"Perfect," Mom said, and pulled me forward into the woods.

I hesitated. "What if we get lost? Did you bring a compass?" I asked.

"No. Don't worry about it, though. We can't get lost as long as we follow the water. Let's go."

The creek gurgled as we walked. We made our way quietly, sometimes sloshing through the water when the bushes got thick. When it got too dark to see, Mom pulled a flashlight from her pack to light our way. Finally, she stopped and wiped her forehead with the back of her hand.

"This should do," she said, pointing to a small clearing.

We found a tree that was tall enough for Mom to stand up under, and then she pulled the cord on her backpack and laid the tent out under the branches. When she took the tent poles out of their sack and started fitting them together, I saw that her hands were shaking. She yanked on one of the rods a little too hard and snapped the elastic inside, and that's when she started to cry. I sat down beside her and tried to help, but she took the pole back from me and hammered it together with a rock. Sniffling and hiccuping, she threaded the poles through the tent loops, pulled it up straight, pounded the stakes into the ground, unrolled our sleeping bags and gathered some moss and branches to start a fire. After she got the fire going, she sat down and opened her arms for me. The flames cast an orange glow on her face. I went to her and curled against her chest.

"Shh," she said, even though she was the one crying. "It's all right. It's okay."

"I know," I said, the heat making me drowsy—and I did. No matter where my mother and I had ended up so far, it had always turned out to be okay. She would find something for us to eat, tuck me into my sleeping bag and maybe even read me a story.

Just before I fell asleep, I couldn't help but feel just a bit sad for Karl. He would be home by now, wondering where we were, and he might even be crying. The thought made me feel a little windless, as if a large animal had decided to settle on top of me for the night and I couldn't roll him off.

THE BEST THING ABOUT living in the wilderness with Mom was that I had her all to myself. The worst thing was that I knew we wouldn't be able to stay there forever. I could tell just by looking at our supplies—besides our tent, sleeping bags, hatchet, flashlight and rifle, we had some dry food, clothing, cooking equipment, candles and matches, a sewing kit, a small saw, a Swiss Army knife, some twine, four rolls of toilet paper, a bar of soap, a towel and a box of ammunition—that we didn't have what it took to stay long. But you would never know it from the way Mom and I went about our days. It was as if we had entered a time bubble when we set foot in our new camp. We never talked about the past, the future, Karl, my grandparents, or anything at all other than our daily routine.

We woke up early, fetched our water, ate granola for breakfast, bathed in the creek when the sun was hottest, collected firewood, washed our clothes and dishes, ate supper and went to sleep. Sometimes we would go for walks in the forest, always staying close to the creek so we wouldn't get lost. Mostly, though, we looked for food. Mom was trying to save what little she had brought, so we ate what-

This photo of Mom is exactly how I remember her in the seventies: windblown hair, youthful face, with the wilderness behind her.

ever we could find—mostly wild berries, dandelion greens, mushrooms and small game when Mom could get it. She picked rose hips and boiled them into tea to boost our immune system. Blackberries were everywhere, so I ate them until my stomach hurt. I was hungry nearly all the time, but I never complained. Mom was twice my size, but she seemed to be eating about half as much as I was.

The sun pushed the dusk slightly forward each evening, and the days turned into weeks. I spent my evenings using Mom's pocketknife to whittle twigs into stick people, finger-painting mud onto stones to make them look like animals, and drawing on every last inch of the little paper we had brought with us. When the paper ran out I began sewing the way Grandma Jeanne had taught me, covering my only sweater in embroidered thread flowers and stitching up holes in our socks. The only thing Mom had for fun, besides her pot stash, were two Conan the Barbarian comic books she had found in the front pocket of Larry and Susanne's backpack. "Look at this," she said when she discovered them, tossing them on the ground. "Even *Time* magazine would have been better than these." The next night, though, she picked up one of the comic books and leafed through it. Before long, she was reading into the dark. She allowed herself two pages each night, sometimes reading out loud to me and commenting on Conan's gentle but take-charge way with women. Conan, she said to me, was a real man, and she could only dream there might be someone like him in the real world.

Every night before I fell asleep, Mom would read me a bedtime story from my Big Blue Book. I chose a different one each time, saving the best for last. When I finally asked for it, Mom just dropped the book on the ground and let it fall open to the right page. She placed the open book in front of me and curled her body around mine, reading aloud over my shoulder.

"November's winds
are keen and cold
As Brownies know
who roam the world
And have no home
to which to run
When they have had

their night of fun
But cunning hands
are never slow
To build a fire
of ruddy glow."

I turned on my back and gazed up at the stars. Beside me, Mom closed the book softly.

"I'm sorry," she whispered. "I'm so sorry. I never meant for this to be your life."

I kept looking at the treetops, pretending she wasn't crying. "That's okay," then, "Mommy?"

"Yes, darling?"

"If I had a baby in my tummy and I read that story to her every single day, would she come out of my vagina knowing it?"

Mom laughed in spite of her tears. "No, sweetie. But I'm sure she'd love it all the same." I nodded, and she kissed the top of my head. "Cea? I want you to know something. If you ever get pregnant, like I did when I was really young, don't worry about it. I'll help you raise the baby. Okay?"

"Um, okay, but that would be kind of silly."

"Why?"

"Because. Isn't it better to have a baby when you're old? Like as old as Susanne?"

Mom laughed again. "Yeah, sweetie, I guess so. Does she seem old to you?"

"Yeah. Way older than you, anyway."

"Well, that's probably because I'm only twenty-two. Most mommies are a little older than me when they have their babies."

"Oh." I snuggled into her chest and closed my eyes happily. Mom just didn't understand. What I wanted was for it to be like this forever—just the two of us, living on our own and becoming friends with the wolves we heard howling at night. If we got to stay, I wouldn't even care if we never got to move to the big city and live like Barbie with pretty pink dresses in our closets and pointy high heels on our feet.

AFTER A MONTH IN the woods, it was getting pretty hard to deny reality. Although we were eating daily, both Mom and I had lost so much weight that we had to pull the cords from our backpacks to string through our belt loops. Game was hard to come by, our dried fruit and dried milk had run out, and we only had a handful of granola left. Our flour supply was low, but worse than that, what was left of it was full of bugs. I saw Mom picking weevils out of the bag one morning, but she still mixed the flour with water to make bannock and we both still ate it, pretending not to see the black flecks baked into it. Our clothing was too light to take us past fall, and our tent wasn't nearly sturdy enough for winter. Mom's rifle wasn't designed to take on big game, and we had already had one bear roam through our camp. Mom had tried to shoo it away with a holler and loud clanging of pots, but when that didn't work she had to fire a few warning shots of precious ammunition. Though we didn't talk about it, we both knew our time in the woods was nearing an end. Mom stopped reading her Conan comics at night and instead just lay with me by the dying light of the fire, stroking my hair until I fell asleep.

But of all the things that could have brought us back to Karl, the one that did was something neither Mom nor I could have imagined. I woke up one night with an itchy rear end, and when Mom lit a candle to inspect, I heard her breathe in sharply.

"Pinworms," she said grimly. "I've seen this before. One of the summer visitors' kids had it on the Kootenay Plains." She pulled my jeans on and wrapped her arms around me in the dark.

Neither of us could fall sleep again.

"Mommy," I said as we gazed out at the lightening sky. "What did you write to Karl in that note?"

"Oh . . . not much, sweetie. Just that we were leaving, and not to come looking for us. We'll see . . . we'll see if he's even still there."

"And if he's not?"

"We'll figure something out." She kissed the top of my head. "Don't you worry about it, okay?"

"Okay. Mommy?"

"Yeah?"

"Do you think we'll ever live somewhere else? Like not in a tent or a tipi or another person's cottage, but maybe, like, in a house or something?"

I waited for a minute, and when she didn't answer I turned to look at her. Her eyes were bright with tears.

"Maybe," she replied, and her voice was barely a whisper.

Chapter Fourteen

The first person to see us walking along the shore in the August sunlight was Susanne. She was doing laundry in the lake, wringing a T-shirt out with bright red hands. She dropped the shirt back in the water.

"What the hell? Where have you been? We've all been wondering . . . Karl is a wreck." She pointed in the direction of the camp. "See for yourself."

Mom nodded wordlessly and walked into the trees with me tagging after her. Susanne followed, spewing questions at Mom that she didn't answer. She reached our tent and lifted the door flap, and we both looked inside. It seemed empty at first, but then I noticed a lump with a spray of dark hair at the end of Mom and Karl's bed.

"He's been like that since you left," Susanne said to Mom. "Barely moved from his bed. I've been bringing him food, but he's hardly touched it."

Mom took off her backpack and walked over to him. I stayed where I was, waiting for the lump to move, but it remained still as a rock. Mom lifted the sleeping bag and climbed in beside him. A minute later, the lump moved toward her. I heard a sound like a crying child, a sound I didn't even know a man could make. I backed quietly out of the tent and sat on the sawhorse to wait.

THANKFULLY, KARL DIDN'T STAY down in the dumps long. In fact Mom's return seemed like a magic potion. The morning after we came back, I watched Karl roll out of bed, head outside to build a fire and return with a cup of coffee. He walked over to Mom, who was still sleeping, and whispered something in her ear. She sat up and smiled, then lay back naked against the pillows, and took the cup from Karl. I got out of bed and ran over to join her.

"Listen, babe," Karl said to Mom, rubbing her arm. "Things are going to be different now. I've made a decision. This pot-growing thing—it's losing its appeal, you know? Too damned unreliable. I think it's time for me to go straight."

"What are you saying?" Mom asked, reaching out to twirl his chest hair with her fingertip.

"A job, that's what I'm saying. Logging's booming out in B.C. The money's good, and the weather's a whole lot better than in this shithole place."

"B.C.? Again? Okay, but we . . ." She shook her head, then sipped from her cup and lowered it into her lap again. "Well. Where did you have in mind?"

"Celista. I got a line on a job there. It's right on Shuswap Lake, not too far from Scotch Creek in fact. I make us a little money, maybe we can even get that cottage we talked about. Hey, Small Fry?" He winked at me, and I bobbed my head up and down.

"Okay," Mom said with a slow smile. "Let's do it!"

Karl grinned and gave me a high five. I was so excited that I jumped up and took off through the woods as if we were leaving right that second.

"Hey, Small Fry, I think you're going to need these," Karl said, tossing me the truck keys, and that just made Mom crack up even harder.

I ran back to her and threw my arms around her waist. We were going to get our cottage!

AT FIRST MOM THOUGHT she could treat my pinworms with her medicinal plants, but after checking in her natural healing book, she decided I needed to see a doctor after all.

"We're going to town?" I asked when she told me.

"Yep! Come on, let's get your best clothes on."

I ran for the tent, feeling a little trembly. Scotch Creek was kind of a town, but today we were going to Calgary, which Mom said was a real city. I shuffled through the stack of clothing at the foot of my bed and finally decided on brown cords and my favorite pink T-shirt. It was a little small for me, but it was my favorite color.

As we hit the highway in the truck and drove west, Karl behind the wheel, I peppered Mom with questions about the city.

"Just wait and see," she kept saying, and an hour later I did.

In the distance across the plains, I could see a nest of buildings rising into the sky. I leaned closer to Mom as traffic got heavier. We hit the city limits and headed into town with cars zooming at us from every direction. As Karl zigzagged through them, I gazed at houses so close together that I wondered if they all shared one big backyard. After a while, Karl pulled up to a small building with a sign that said CLINIC over the door. Mom took my hand and led me inside, and within a few minutes we were sitting in a small room with gleaming silver instruments hanging on the wall. The door swung open, and an elderly man with a short gray beard came inside.

"So," he said to Mom, glancing at his clipboard. "Five and a half years old, no vaccinations, no medical history, and no family physician. Where have you been keeping this child, under a rock?"

Mom's eyes widened. I dug in my pocket, searching for Papa Dick's roach clip.

"She—she's very healthy," Mom replied finally. "Never been sick, really . . . except whooping cough, we nearly lost her then, but that was a long . . ." She cleared her throat. "Anyway, it looks like she has pinworms—"

The doctor waved a hand at her. "Yes, I can read her chart, thank you very much. Pinworms are an expected childhood ailment. What concerns me is your daughter's apparent lack of care. Why hasn't she seen a physician before?"

"Because, um . . ." Mom shifted in her seat. "I just haven't seen the need, I guess. And we live . . . kind of far away from the city."

The doctor scribbled something on a slip of paper, ripped it off and handed Mom the prescription. As he put his hand on the doorknob, he turned to give Mom one last look. "Children aren't meant to live like wild animals, you know."

My stomach lurched as the door clicked closed behind him. *Wild animal?* Was that what I was? I looked down at my clothes. A few hours ago I had been proud to put them on, but now I saw the torn knees, the smudges of grime from places I'd wiped my dirty hands and the moccasins coming apart at the seams. I turned my eyes to Mom, who gathered up her purse and reached for my hand.

She was crying by the time we got back to the truck. Karl was waiting for us, tipped back in his seat with his cowboy hat over his face.

"What happened?" he asked Mom when he saw her, and she told him the story between sniffles.

"Fuck it. That's it," Karl said, pounding the steering wheel with the palm of his hand. He slid from the cab, and Mom and I watched as he walked to the clinic and through the front door.

Ten minutes later, he jogged back to the truck.

"What happened?" Mom asked.

"Oh, not much," Karl said, popping the emergency brake and backing out of his parking spot. "Let's just say Mr. Asswipe might need to see a doctor of his own."

Mom stared at Karl for a moment, and then shook her head. "You're kidding. Please tell me you didn't hurt him."

"Damn straight. Nobody messes with my gals." He steered toward the street and hit the gas, causing the wheels to chirp against the pavement. "Now. What say we go and have a little fun."

KARL SAID HE HAD some stuff to take care of, so he dropped Mom and me off at a gigantic store that he said sold everything in the world. Through the front window, which was twice as high as our canvas tent back home, I could see smiling ladies putting money into big metal machines. Karl pulled his wallet from his back pocket and peeled off a few twenties.

"Now off you go," he said to Mom. "I'll pick you up in a few hours."

Mom and I walked into the store and stepped onto a moving staircase. I watched people passing on the way down, their eyes forward as they ignored everyone around them. I couldn't believe how different people dressed in the city. Ladies wore pants and jackets that matched, and men wore shirts that were open so low I could see the hair on their chests.

"I've got a surprise for you," Mom said as we cruised past racks of dresses. "I'm buying you a new pair of pants. And some underwear."

I gaped up at her. Mom had been promising me underwear for a while, but I hadn't actually believed it would happen. "Really?"

"Yes."

"Underwear!" I shouted, jumping up and down. "Hooray! Real underwear!" A few women stopped to stare at me, but only one of them smiled. I lowered my voice and grabbed Mom's hand with both of my own. "Thank you, thank you . . ."

"Okay. Just three pairs, though. We have to make sure we save enough money for your prescription. God knows how much that'll cost. And then there's lunch, and I need tampons, and— Cea?"

I didn't answer. Something had caught my eye that made even the exciting promise of new underwear fade in comparison. Before me was a low stage set up in the shape of a T. A small crowd was gathered around it, chatting as they watched the two women walking its length. One of the women had blond hair and the other had brown, but they were both tall and thin with bright white teeth. Their hair shone under the store lights, and their skin was as white as milk. From where I stood I could even see their fingernails, which didn't have a speck of dirt under them. They looked like women who had never tripped as they were walking or had food stuck in their teeth. Even more than that, they looked like women who had been grownups since the day they were born.

"Mom," I finally breathed. "Look. Barbie dolls. Real-life Barbie dolls."

Later, on the ride home, I sat thinking about my day. Besides that mean doctor, it had been the best one ever. In my lap were three new pairs of underwear, which Mom said I could wear just as soon as my pinworms went away. When I had told Karl about the real-life Barbie dolls, he said that I might even be pretty enough to be one myself someday. When we were nearly home, Mom and Karl were having a road toke when a cop pulled us over, but instead of busting us, he just asked Karl to clean off his license plate and then drove away. Mom was so happy about that, she rolled up another joint right then and there to celebrate.

IT WAS BECAUSE OF Kelly that I was playing beside the truck on the day it all went down. The dirt road wasn't a place I usually thought to go at all, but two days before we were supposed to leave Lake Minnewanka, I had woken up to find Kelly sitting outside our tent with a stray cat in her lap. I got out of bed and squatted down beside her, eager to pet it, but Kelly grabbed the cat's head and forced its face toward me.

"Look," she said. "I cut its whiskers off."

I backed away from her in horror. It was early enough for the adults to still be asleep, so I took off and wandered through the woods, trying to talk myself into believing that the cat hadn't felt any pain because it was probably just like getting a haircut.

After a while, I ended up at the dirt road near Karl's truck. There was a small pond just past it, so I walked close in the hope of finding a frog or two. There were none to be seen, but I did spot some tadpoles, the next best thing. I took off my sandals and stepped into the water. And I was here, stalking my prey with cupped hands, when I heard the car.

I stood up straight and looked along the road, shading my eyes against the morning sun with my hand. It was a police car. My stomach dropped. I leapt from the pond and sprinted into the trees toward home, not even feeling the rocks and twigs that stabbed at my bare feet. My mind was racing as fast as my legs: *cops—pot plants—slammer—*

When I was halfway back to camp, even before Mom could see me, I started waving my arms and screaming. "Mom!" I yelled. "The cops! The cops are here! Hide the pot plants!" I flew into camp and saw her standing in front of our tent, a look of confusion on her face. I ran full speed ahead until I slammed into her legs, and then threw my arms around her and sobbed.

"It's okay, sweetie, it's all right . . ." Mom said as she stroked my hair.

Karl came around the side of the tent, zipping up his fly as he walked. "What's going on?" he asked, looking around. "Did I hear you say—?" He stopped in mid-sentence, and I followed his eyes.

Two cops were moving toward us through the trees, pushing branches out of their way as they walked. I stared at their pants, spellbound by the yellow stripe running down each leg. They reached us and stood side by side, one with his hand over a black club stuck through his belt.

"Are you Karl Hofler?" he asked, and Karl nodded. "Then you're under arrest. Please place your hands behind your back."

"What the hell—"

"Just do it, sir," the cop said, and Karl turned around. The other man pulled out a walkie-talkie and said something into it. A voice crackled back at him, and he put it away again.

I started to cry, burying my face in Mom's belly. "What's going to happen?" I said to her. "Are they going to take you too—?"

"Shh . . ." Mom whispered. "It's okay."

I heard a metallic *click*, and pulled away from Mom to peek at Karl. He was standing turned away from us with silver handcuffs on his wrists.

"Now are you going to tell me what this is all about?" Karl asked angrily.

"Sure," said the cop with the club, taking Karl by the arm and turning him around. "You're under arrest for property theft. In a few minutes, we'll have two more officers here to recover the stolen property. You may want to take your child elsewhere, ma'am," he said to Mom. "They're going to be going through the contents of the tent and dismantling it. And you, my friend," he said to Karl, pulling on his arm, "are going to jail."

I watched in shock as the cops led Karl away from us. Moments later, I saw another pair of men walking toward us. Their mirrored glasses glinted in the sun. I broke away from Mom and ran into the tent, gathering up Suzie Doll, my Big Blue Book, my pink jewelry box and whatever else I could lay my hands on.

Mom came inside and watched me for a minute. Then she slumped down on my bed and started to cry.

SINCE I DIDN'T HAVE a backpack and had returned my borrowed one to Larry and Susanne, I piled all my belongings under a tree. Mom had done the same with her stuff, and was now running around looking for one of Karl's new duffel bags. I sat on the ground in front of my treasures to guard them. There was nothing to do now but wait. The cops were already inside our tent, looking over a list of typed words and checking things off as they found them. I knew there wouldn't be many checkmarks, as most of our stuff had been destroyed in the fire, but my main concern was the tent. With Karl gone, where would Mom and I live now?

Two hours later, my mother and I watched the policemen take our home down and roll it up like a big log. Then each of the men took an end in one hand, heaved a bag of loot over their shoulders with the other and started back toward their cars. Mom pulled me into her lap and held me as she cried. After a few minutes, Larry and Susanne sat down quietly beside us.

"You can stay with us," Susanne said to Mom, touching her shoulder. "Don't worry. We'll get him back."

Mom nodded through her tears, but her eyes told us what she really believed.

MOM INSISTED THAT LARRY and Susanne's tipi was already crowded enough with four bodies in it, so instead we borrowed a nylon tent to sleep in. Larry drove Mom into Calgary to try to get some information on Karl's arrest, but all the cops would tell them was that Karl had been assigned a lawyer and a bond of five thousand dollars. Mom came back to camp and went straight to our tent to cry. I sat in the tipi with Kelly, eating a bologna and mustard sandwich.

Larry said not to worry, because the Karl he knew always came out on top. "Bad luck hasn't been able to get the best of him yet, and I don't expect it ever will," he said to us with a wink.

But the days dragged on forever. Mom didn't seem to know what to do with herself other than fret and sit at the lakeshore, smoking Karl's last pack of cigarettes. I flapped around camp like a bird with a broken wing, unsure of what to do with myself for the first time in my life.

One day, I found her standing at the edge of the pot crop. "They're still too small," she said, rubbing a leaf between her fingers. "Nobody will buy them."

"What would happen if someone did?" I asked, stepping close to her.

"I don't know. We could use the money to get Karl back. Or buy a tipi, maybe."

"Oh. So are we . . . going to stay here now?"

She shook her head. "I don't know," she repeated. Then she lowered herself onto the ground and lit a joint, and she didn't even bother to blow me any smoke rings.

KARL WAS HARDLY A man of mystery, but when it came to revealing how he made bail for his release from jail, he had little to say to us. Ten days after the police took him away in handcuffs, he showed up back at our camp. His arrival was announced by a shriek from my mother, who was the first to see him coming through the trees. We all ran toward him for a big group hug. He looked tired and unshaven, but otherwise just like the same old Karl.

"Managed to hitch myself a ride," he said with a grin. "Nice old guy drove me all the way from Calgary. Did the speed limit the whole way, I nearly lost my mind." He reached into his pocket and pulled out a silk scarf. "Here, I got you a little something," he said to Mom, tying it in a bow around her neck.

Mom hugged him again and started laughing. "Is this real? Are you really here? Please tell me you don't have to go back there."

Karl put his arm around her shoulders as we walked toward camp. "Nah. My lawyer already stood before the judge, he gave me probation. No big deal. Hey, Small Fry—what say we have a little dinner and get ready for our big day tomorrow? It's about time for us to hit the road!"

I grinned and made a beeline for Larry and Susanne's tipi.

Later, when Mom tucked me into bed in our tent, she told me that Karl had a record now. I thought about this as I drifted off to sleep. A record? Those cops must really be dumb. Even if we did have a stereo to play it on, anyone with a brain could see that we didn't have electricity.

"MADMAN," LARRY SAID, GIVING Karl a hug. "It's been a slice. Let's do it again soon, huh?"

"You bet," Karl replied with a laugh, thumping his friend on the back. "Only next time maybe we'll try to give you a little more excitement."

In October of 1975, six months after we arrived in Lake Minnewanka, we hit the road again. It was a cold, rainy day, made just bearable by the odd patch of blue sky through the clouds. Larry and Susanne came to the truck to see us off, while Kelly dragged her heels behind them.

We piled into the cab and Karl started the engine. Benjamin gave us a gummy grin as we pulled away. I looked past Susanne at Kelly, but she was grinding a hole into the ground with her tennis shoe and didn't even bother to glance up. Her face looked pasty and mean in the flat light. I wondered why she hated me so much.

"Wow," Mom said, snapping pot seeds between her teeth as Karl drove. "That was some little adventure. Here's hoping for saner times ahead."

"You got it, babe, you got it. Gonna get me a real job, put some food on the table," Karl said, patting her thigh.

Knowing we had a long ride ahead of us, I pulled the map out of the glove compartment and studied it to pass time. After getting Mom to point out where we were, I traced a line along the roads with my fingertip, sounding out the names of the towns as I passed over them. Just past Lake Minnewanka, I found a place called Morley. The name looked familiar, but I couldn't think why. After a few minutes, I had it.

"Mommy, look!" I cried excitedly. "It's Morley! Didn't we used to live there? With Papa Dick and Grandma Jeanne?"

Mom took the map from me and stared at it with her jaw hanging open. "Jesus Christ, will you look at that." She shoved the map in front of Karl's face as he drove. "It's not forty miles from here. My *parents* aren't forty miles from here. They've been here the whole time! Did you know that?"

Karl cleared his throat and shrugged. "I . . . of course I did, yeah."

"Why didn't you say something?"

"What do I look like, Rand-fuckin'-McNally? You could have picked up the map and seen for yourself."

"You know I'm not good with maps."

"Yeah, well, I thought you knew. Where the hell did you *think* we were?"

"I don't know. Far away." She lifted her chin. "I got disoriented with all the driving back and forth, okay?"

"Still, you could have asked. It's not like I was trying to hide it. I thought you wanted your independence."

"Independence? *Independence?* For Christ's sake, I took Cea to live in the woods for a month! You think I wouldn't have gone home to them if I'd known? We could have hitchhiked there in an hour!" She folded the map up furiously and shoved it back in the glove box. "Take me there. Right now. I want to see them."

Karl opened his mouth, ready to protest, but then he saw Mom's face and changed his mind. He pulled onto the highway and headed east, the opposite direction from our destination. After just a few minutes we saw a sign: MORLEY 32. Mom sighed and crossed her arms huffily as we passed it. Half an hour later, we pulled off a familiar dirt road and parked. It had only been nine months since we'd left here, but it felt like a lifetime.

Ignoring the light rain, Mom started walking through the trees toward camp, and I followed. A minute or so later, I heard Karl's footsteps behind me.

Mom was the first to reach it. I found her standing at the edge of the clearing with her arms hanging limp at her sides. The clouds had parted to let a bit of sun peek through, but the scene it shone down on was a sad one. All that was left of my grandparents' camp was the wooden skeleton of a lean-to, along with three bare patches on the ground where their tipis had been. A scrap of torn canvas flapped from a tree branch.

Mom collapsed onto the ground in a sobbing heap, and after a moment I joined her. Maybe it was true; maybe my grandparents had never even existed. Anyway, it didn't matter now. They were gone, and God only knew where they were.

Chapter Fifteen

The most incredible thing about our cottage in Celista was that the morning after we arrived, I woke up to sunlight streaming through the window of my very own bedroom. The worst thing about it was that we weren't supposed to be there. The night before, Karl had walked right by the FOR RENT sign planted on the front lawn and broken into the cottage with his Slim Jim. Since he hadn't allowed us to turn any lights on, I had barely been able to see my surroundings, so opening my eyes to the sunlight was like discovering a new world.

I slid from between the sheets and pulled my clothes on. My breath puffed out into the freezing November air, but I barely noticed the cold. I was in the most beautiful room I had ever seen. The bed I had slept in—*my* bed, I thought to myself happily—was white wrought iron topped with a patchwork quilt. There was a matching blue dresser and night table, a braided rag rug, a lamp with a silk shade and, in the corner, a wicker chair holding a teddy bear. I picked it up and shoved it under the bed, then dug Suzie Doll out of my bag and seated her in the bear's place.

I stepped onto the landing and made my way down the narrow staircase. In the living room, a fireplace framed by a river-rock mantel reached all the way to the ceiling. I passed a bathroom with a claw-foot tub and a toilet. When I got to the kitchen, I stood in the doorway and caught my breath. It looked like a kitchen in a doll's house, just like Mom had said. The cabinets were painted a soft yellow, and pretty flowered paper lined the walls. I tested the taps—which worked!—and went through every drawer and cupboard. Then I opened and closed the fridge and turned the stove on and off, just to be certain they were real. Through the window over the sink, I could see the backyard sloping down to the lake. I threw my arms out and spun around on the linoleum floor. If I could just forget that we weren't supposed to be there, everything would be perfect.

Karl had given us the drill the night before. Our cottage was far enough away from its neighbor on each side to be private, he told us, but the lake was a problem. Boats still cruised the water even this late in the season, and word would spread fast if we were spotted. Besides parking the truck a quarter mile down the road, Karl had a full set of rules to keep our secret. There would be no lights, no music, no using the telephone or fireplace, no opening the curtains, no going into the backyard during the day, almost no use of the stove and hot water and no using the thermostat at all, so the owners wouldn't notice an unexplained hike in their utility bills. It was only for a little while, Karl promised, just long enough for him to land a job and get his first paycheck.

"After that we'll go legit. Pay our rent, get to know the neighbors, shit like that. Anyway," he added when he saw my mother's face, "it's a helluva lot better than camping in the truck for a month."

And to this, Mom and I could only agree.

True enough, Karl had no trouble finding work. Shortly after we arrived, he set off for the logging camp one morning and came home a little later an employed man. While he left each weekday before dawn, Mom passed the hours by sleeping in, organizing the kitchen cupboards and taking lukewarm baths with Joni Mitchell playing low in the background. I spent my time drawing pictures of my grandparents, sewing clothes for Suzie Doll and lying in bed playing with my new treasure: a snow globe that I had found in my closet. *J'aime Paris*, it said inside the plastic bubble in front of a tiny tower, and Mom told me that meant someone had brought it all the way back from a glamorous city across the ocean. I pictured myself in my grandparents' canoe, paddling until I reached the opposite shore.

"What does 'glamorous' mean?" I asked.

"It means fancy. Kind of . . . kind of like those models you saw that one time. They were pretty glamorous."

"Yeah," I agreed, and then I knew exactly what she meant.

I didn't go outside much, but when I did, Mom and I had a system. She would go up to my bedroom window, from which she could see the driveway, and holler to me that the coast was clear. Then she'd keep watch while I played. I would collect dried leaves or scoop dirt into a plastic bowl, but even with Mom watching I couldn't help looking over my shoulder every ten seconds. Eventually, I would get tired of the sick feeling in my tummy and go back inside.

The late fall days were short and chilly. By four o'clock we were lighting candles, and by five we were piling on socks and sweaters. We ate sandwiches and apples for dinner and spent our evenings playing the board games we found in the hall closet, sipping lukewarm tea and gazing longingly at the unlit fireplace.

One night, we were in the middle of a halfhearted game of Parcheesi when we heard footsteps outside. Karl blew out the candle and we all froze in place, listening to the sound of our breathing in the dark. The footsteps climbed to the front landing and stopped. I stared at the window in the door, certain that whoever was on the other side was peeking through it.

"It's a good thing there's a curtain," I whispered, and Mom clamped her hand over my mouth.

A minute later, we heard the footsteps leaving. After that, I stopped going outside altogether.

MOST OF KARL'S FIRST paycheck went to gas and food. We had already eaten our way through the supplies in the cottage kitchen, emptying the pantry of everything except a jar of cornmeal and a box of salt. Not wanting to draw attention to our family, Karl left Mom and me at home one Saturday and drove into town alone. He came back with a dozen bags of groceries and told us they would need to last us the month, so that his next paycheck could go to rent.

Later that night, I heard my mother and Karl talking as I lay in bed. I would be six years old in a few days, Mom was saying, and I should have started first grade three months ago. "Cea's smart," she said. "Not like me. She's got her father's brains." I heard a match strike, then Karl's low voice. Soon, he said to her. I couldn't very well show up at the local school without raising a few questions, but I could start just as soon as we went legit.

This seemed to satisfy Mom, but suddenly I was wide awake. School? The thought hadn't even crossed my mind. Mom had always told me she hated it, and that had been enough to make me pretty sure I'd never have to go.

On the morning of my birthday, Mom woke up and announced she was throwing the rules out the window. Then she cranked up the oven to bake me a money-cake. I sat inches from the stove, my face turning red from the heat as I watched her fold pennies into squares of wax paper and then tuck them into the batter. After sliding the cake into the oven, she put me into a hot bath and washed my hair, then made me a grilled cheese sandwich and soup for lunch. That night, I blew out six candles and wished to see my grandparents again and for Mom to never go to the slammer. Oh, and for Karl to make lots of money.

"Thank you, Mommy," I said later when she tucked me into bed with a kiss. "It was my best birthday ever."

And it was true.

MOM WAS COUNTING THE days until Karl's next paycheck. "Today's the day," she said to me on a Friday morning, tapping her astrology calendar. That afternoon, Karl came home and sat on the sofa with a new *Rolling Stone* magazine. When dinner passed and he still hadn't said anything, Mom got up from her chair and cleared his plate with a loud clatter. Then she leaned back against the sink and crossed her arms.

"So," she said, grabbing the phone off its cradle and holding it out to him, "I have the number from the sign memorized. 555-2680. All you have to do is call them up and say you'd like to rent their cottage." The dial tone buzzed loudly into the air.

Karl wiped his face with a paper towel and crumpled it into a ball. "Hey, babe, just relax, will ya? I've been giving it some thought. Everything is going so well here . . ." He smiled and patted his lap, but Mom didn't move. Karl shrugged and leaned back in his chair. "We've pulled it off so far. If we could hold out just a couple more weeks . . . I promise the next check will go to rent. But Christmas is coming up, you know? I'm sure you'd like to buy Small Fry a little something."

Mom dropped her hand a little.

"And listen, if we used this money to invest in our future, we could have a little extra. Maybe even take a holiday some—"

"What kind of investment?" Mom asked.

"Well, you know. If I bought some pot seedlings—"

"Pot plants! Not that again!" Mom slammed the phone back into its cradle and threw her hands up. "I've had it with your damn pot plants! Just where were you planning on growing them, in the yard we're never allowed to—"

"Actually, there's a guy I work with who'll rent me a plot of land. He can hook me up—"

"Fuck it! While you're at work all day I'm stuck here, a prisoner in my own home! No lights, no heat, always afraid the doorbell's going to ring! Trying to keep Cea occupied in the house all day long! Look at this supper—" She swept her hand toward my plate, which still held the crust of my cheese sandwich. "Cold food! Again! Made by the light of a candle. Again! When you said you were going to put food on the table, I didn't think you meant sandwiches every night! This is *bullshit*!" She wiped at her eyes furiously.

"Hey, hey, take it easy," Karl said, throwing his hands up like he was under arrest. "I'm not talking about forever here. Two weeks, that's all. You've been so great with it all so far, what's another few days? I promise I'll—"

Mom shook her head angrily and left the room before he could finish. Karl looked at me and shrugged, tapping his pack of smokes on the table. After a little while, he pulled out a cigarette and lit up.

I waited a minute longer so it didn't look like I was taking sides, then I followed Mom. I found her lying in her bed, turned away from me with her back shaking, her breath hitching in and out. I went to my own room and lay down, leaving the door open a little just in case she wanted to come in.

A FEW DAYS AFTER Mom and Karl's fight, Mom surprised me by being awake before I was. When I went downstairs, she was already at the kitchen table with my breakfast waiting. I sat down and began eating my cereal.

"So . . . listen," she said, clearing her throat. "I was wondering if you might be okay on your own for a couple of hours. I need to go somewhere, and I'm going to have to hitchhike. I'd rather go on my own. This is a small town, and people talk."

"Talk about what?"

She smiled and reached for my hand. "It's just for an hour or two, okay? I've left you a sandwich."

"But I want to go with you!"

"Trust me, it'll be really boring. You'll have way more fun here playing with Suzie Doll or drawing."

"Where are you going?"

"I just need to check something out. It's nothing for you to worry about."

I didn't respond, but when I saw that she was serious, I finally climbed the stairs to get my art bag.

"Good girl. Just stay inside, all right? I'll be back before you know it." Mom gave me a quick hug, and then she was gone.

The house settled around me. I knelt on a chair at the kitchen table and took out my crayons, clattering them loudly on the table to break the silence. Pressing a piece of paper to the table with my hand, I drew a jagged line across the center for mountains, a quarter-sun with long orange rays in the corner and a row of pink daisies at the bottom. A square topped with a triangle was our cottage, a rectangle was our door and a circle was Mom's smiling face at the window. I gazed at my masterpiece and then slid from my chair, wondering what to do next. I wasn't hungry yet, but I found my honey and butter sandwich in the fridge and ate it anyway, singing quietly to myself as I did.

I was halfway through eating when I heard the *thump*. I stopped chewing and held my breath. *Thump . . . thump . . . thump* . . . It was the sound of footsteps, I realized, and they were climbing the front stairs.

My body flooded with terror. I dropped my sandwich and bolted upstairs to my bedroom. Glancing around the room, I made a dash for the closet. I pushed backwards into my clothes, pulled the door shut behind me and crouched down in the darkness. Whoever was down there was knocking now, each rap as loud as thunder in the silence. My heart was beating so hard I could feel it in my throat. I was going to cry. I squeezed my eyes shut and took a long, shaky breath, waiting for the sound of a key in the lock and footsteps climbing the stairs to discover our secret.

NOT TOO MUCH LATER, I heard the front door open and close.

"Cea?" Mom called out, and I burst from the closet and hurled myself down the stairs and into her arms, bawling.

"Mommy! There was— I heard— There was someone— I had to hide—"

Shushing me quiet, she sat on the sofa and pulled me into her lap while I told my story. Even this long after the event, my heart was still thudding out of my chest. "What if they heard me? What if we get kicked out? What will we—?"

"Shh . . . It's okay. You did the right thing, sweetheart. I'm sure they didn't hear anything."

I nodded, still wiping away tears. Mom stared past me at the window, its curtains drawn tightly against the daylight. "In a way, it's good this happened. Maybe Karl will take our situation seriously now. Hmm?" She gave me a half smile and then shook her head. "Anyway. I have some good news. I found you a school! You start kindergarten tomorrow."

"Kindergarten?" I stared at her. A couple days before, Mom had tried to register me for first grade at the local elementary school, but had hurried me out the door again when the secretary asked for our address and phone number. After that, I thought I would be off the hook as far as school went. "But I thought—"

"I know, I know," she replied, waving a hand in the air. "It was the best I could do. So what if you're a year behind? I'm sure you can make it up later or something. They were very nice, very understanding—nothing at all like that other school. I told them we were staying with relatives for a while, and they said I could give them an address later. I even met a nice mother who said she would drive you to and from school. She has a daughter in your class. Who knows, maybe you'll even become friends with her."

She smiled at me, and I ducked my head under her chin. Given the choice between going to kindergarten the next morning or going back upstairs to my closet, I would happily have hidden in my dark little den for days on end.

I STOOD AT THE side of the road, holding Mom's hand. As usual, my pants were too short, ending an inch above my scuffed snowmobile boots. The zipper of my coat was broken, so I hugged it around me with my arm. I wished it wasn't so cold outside, so I could take it off.

Over the hill, a long yellow car appeared and stopped beside us. The driver had rollers in her hair and held a skinny cigarette between her fingertips. She leaned across the pretty girl beside her and rolled down the window.

"Climb in," the woman said to me, flicking her ash down the side of the door. "The back's all yours."

I nodded through the lump in my throat and got in. Mom shut the door behind me and tapped on the window. "I love you," she said through the glass, and I swallowed hard, staring straight ahead. The woman tilted the rearview mirror toward her face and twisted up a tube of lipstick, but I only had eyes for her daughter. Her hair was silky blond with a butterfly barrette on each side. She was wearing a pink wool coat, and on her feet were shiny black shoes with silver buckles.

"Tina," the woman said, tapping her daughter on the knee. "Why don't you say hello to your new friend. What was your name, honey? Cecilia?"

"Cea."

"Cea, yes. Say hello, Tina."

Tina turned around in her seat and peered at me from under her bangs. "I don't want to. She *smells* funny."

"Tina!"

"It's true," she said sulkily, and faced forward again.

I blinked, trying to stop the tears, and lifted my coat sleeve to sniff it. Tina was right. My clothes smelled like pot smoke. As her mother pulled back onto the road, I turned in my seat to see Mom through the back window. She was standing by the side of the road with a *go-get-'em* expression on her face, and I noticed that the hem of her coat was coming down on one side. She waved at me and blew me a kiss, and in that instant, I loved her and hated her more than I ever had in my life.

ON MY VERY FIRST day of school, I remember being lined up against the wall with the rest of the girls for a game of dodgeball.

"My goodness, are you ever tall," the teacher said, looking me up and down. "What on earth are your parents feeding you?"

I smiled, just happy she was talking to me. She'd barely said a word to me since I'd walked through the door, other than loudly announcing my full name to the classroom. "Well, my favorite is bear meat, but I haven't had any for a while. Mom says I'm just tall because my dad is. But I've never, um . . ." I stopped talking when I saw her expression. Her lips were stretched into a grin, but it looked more like Suzie Doll's smile than a real person's.

"You can go over there," she said, pointing to the line of boys against the opposite wall. "You're much too tall to play on the girls' team."

I ducked my head and walked across the room, feeling twenty pairs of eyes on me as I did. In that moment, any fragile hope I had of slipping into kindergarten unnoticed was shattered. I was a freak, and my height was just the start of it.

After our dodgeball game, the teacher sat us down for craft time. The noise of the other children jangled around me. Across the room, Tina whispered behind her hand to a girlfriend. The teacher walked over to them and looked down at their work.

"Good job, Tina," she said with a smile. "And Cindy, I love how you've put a dress on your snowman."

I glued my cotton balls onto construction paper, trying not to cry. Like a stuck merry-go-round, my mind kept circling around all the things that were weird about me. There was my name, my clothes, my secret home, my young (and different, though I still couldn't name exactly how) mother, my missing father, and my wilderness past. Then I started to think about the things I could change. I could get a different name, better clothes, make up a story about my past, and never let anyone meet my family or come over to my house. The idea was kind of exciting. For the first time in my life, I started to think that maybe I could turn myself into whoever I wanted to be.

MOM WAS EXPECTING KARL to blow a gasket when she told him the news that I had just had my first day of kindergarten, so she was surprised when he said almost nothing.

"Really," he said flatly, spearing an apple slice with his fork as we finished supper.

"Yes," Mom said, flicking her eyes nervously to mine. "Don't worry, though, nobody knows we're here. I didn't have to give them an address or anything. And her ride picks her up and drops her off half a mile up the road."

Karl kept his eyes on the table and didn't say anything. Then he lit a cigarette and left the table. A moment later, we heard the front door open and close again. Mom stared at his empty seat and shook her head sadly.

"Mommy, why did Karl go outside?"

"I don't know, sweetheart. This seems to be his new way of punishing me. Silence." She sighed. "I think I preferred the arguments."

"But he isn't yelling. Isn't that better?"

"Yeah, I guess so. It's just . . ."

"What?"

"Nothing."

"But what were you going to say?"

"It's just . . . I worry sometimes, that's all. We rely on Karl to support us. That means we need him to buy our food and keep a roof over our heads. I don't know where my parents are, and if Karl ever decided to leave us . . ."

A needle pricked at my belly. "What? If he ever decided to leave us then what?"

"Nothing." She got up from her chair and started clearing the table. I wasn't finished eating, but suddenly I wasn't hungry anymore. I picked up my plate and brought it to the sink.

"Mommy. I was thinking. Do you think I could change my name to Cindy?"

"Wha— Cindy? What are you talking about?"

I shrugged. "Just . . . I don't know. Cea is kind of . . . hard to say, that's all."

"No, it's not." She shook her head. "Anyway, you should be proud of your name. It's beautiful and different, just like you. And plus, your father chose it."

"Yeah, okay. It's just . . ." I shook my head, knowing this was a battle I probably wouldn't win. "Can I see a picture of him?"

She blinked at me in surprise. "Your father? Yes, of course." She left the kitchen and returned with a shoebox. She reached into it. "Here you go," she said, handing me their wedding picture.

It was a photo I had seen many times, the only one she had of the two of them together. They were standing by the side of the road in Reno, Greg holding a JUST MARRIED sign and my mother smiling so big she had dimples in her forehead. *Parents.* My *parents,* I thought, but the word sounded strange and warped in my head.

"No, the other one," I said. "The one of me and him."

She dug around some more, stopping to comment on a few of the pictures ("Look, here's your Uncle Dane. Wasn't he handsome before he lost all his teeth and went wacko?"), and finally pulled the right one from a yellowing envelope. I looked at it carefully: the only proof I had that I'd ever met my dad. There was me, two years old and screaming with my back arched, and there was my father, sideburned and horrified as he tried to hold me.

"Why was I so mad?" I asked Mom, pulling the picture close to my face.

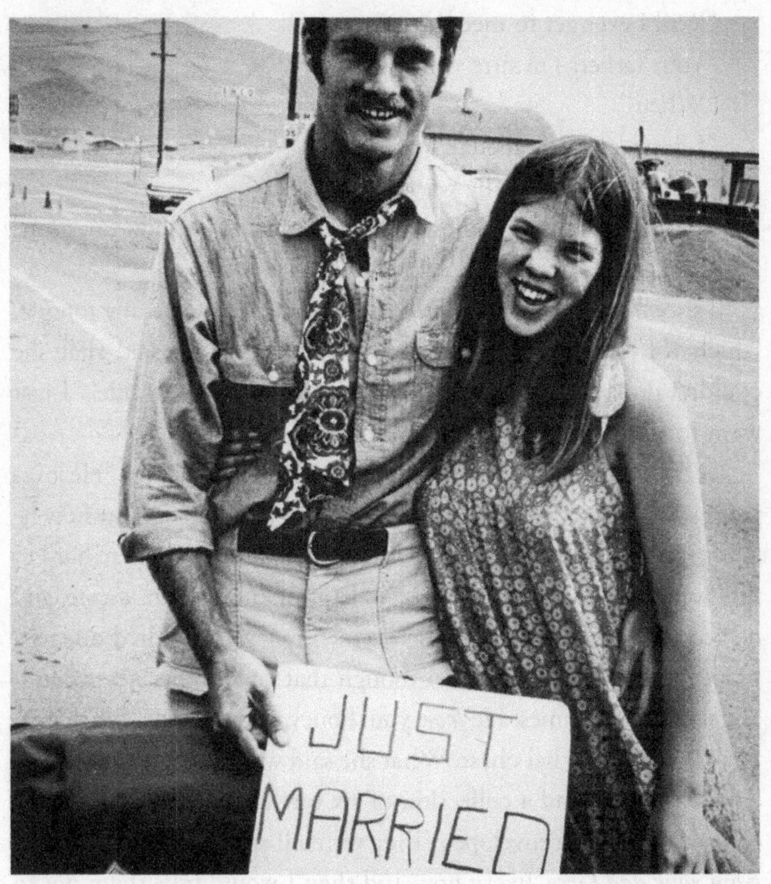

My parents on their wedding day in Reno, Nevada, in 1969. My mother was already several months pregnant with me.

"You weren't mad, you were just shy. You didn't really know him, so you were probably a little scared."

Scared? But he looked really nice. Why couldn't I have just been nice back to him? Then maybe he would have wanted Mom and me to stay in California with him. I pictured the three of us living in our same cottage, but surrounded by palm trees.

"Will I ever get to meet him?"

"Your father? I'm sure you will, honey."

"When?"

"I don't know. Someday."

"Good. 'Cause I really want to."

She smiled sadly. "I know. You must have a million questions for him . . ."

I shook my head and opened my mouth to show her my tongue, which I'd folded into the shape of a clover. Mom said that she couldn't do it, so I must have gotten it from my dad's side. "I just want to show him how I can do this."

"Oh, sweetheart . . ." She wrapped her arms around me. "He loves you," she said into my hair. "Don't ever doubt that. You know how he never misses sending you a birthday card? Even though we're hard to find sometimes? I send him letters to let him know where we are, and he keeps track of us. He even sends me money. A hundred dollars a month, never misses one, even though that's a lot of money for him and it's late sometimes. He *loves* you, honey, you must believe that."

I nodded into her chest. What she said was true; inside my pink ballerina box, I had a collection of six birthday cards with American stamps on the envelopes. They were all signed *With much love, from your dad Greg.* Every now and then I would take them out to look at, just repeating those last three words over and over again until they sounded a little more real.

"Well, that means he loves you. And now here you are, on your first day of kindergarten." Mom hugged me close. "I know he would be so proud."

IN MID-DECEMBER, A LITTLE while after I started school, my mother brought up a scary point to Karl: the owners of our cottage might decide to come back here for Christmas vacation. It was the push Karl needed. He got up from the table, crossed the kitchen and picked up the telephone. Then he dialed the owner's number and asked if he could rent their cottage—and just like that, we were free.

We drove to a neighbor's house and traded them an envelope full of cash for the key, and Mom was so happy that she promised Karl a blowjob when we got home.

Our being real home renters made me feel a little better about going to school, which I usually looked forward to about as much as a daily beating. I ran a brush through my hair each morning and tried to be nice to everyone, though the other kids still barely talked to me. Just before Christmas, the teacher called Mom in to discuss my "lack of social interaction." Mom came home in tears and hugged me so hard my ribs cracked.

"My little girl, lonely and friendless," she cried, shaking her head sadly. "It's just like school was for me. I'm so sorry, sweetie."

I hugged her back, feeling bad for her tears. I didn't really feel lonely and friendless, though, so much as I felt just plain weird.

That evening at the dinner table, Mom told Karl about her meeting. Karl slowly put his fork down, and then he asked me to go upstairs. From my bedroom, I could hear his muffled voice on the telephone.

The next day at school, one of the boys gave me his crayon when mine broke, Jenny Lund played with me at recess, and Sarah Parker gave me one of her cookies at snack time.

Years later, Mom told me that Karl had called the teacher up and read her the riot act, claiming to be a former bigwig at the education department who could have her fired faster than she could say her own name. Then he made a call to every single one of the children's parents and nicely asked them if they would please pull their goddamn heads out of their asses and teach their kids some manners. A few people hung up on him, but all in all, Karl's technique seemed to work pretty well.

THAT CHRISTMAS WAS THE best one ever. We built a fire in the fireplace and stoked it with so much wood that our faces turned red from the heat, ate cheese fondue for breakfast, and then opened presents.

Karl's gift to me was a bike. I knew it was stolen, but I hardly cared. It was purple, my third-favorite color, and it had silver streamers dangling from the handlebars. I spent the entire day rolling down the driveway until my feet found the pedals, and by that evening I had my balance. In the days afterward I rode up and down our road, pumping my legs furiously as the wind pulled at my hair. Now and then, just for fun, I would pretend the cops were chasing me so I could practice getting away from them. I was so fast that I could hear their sirens fading into the distance as I rode. But then I would remind myself that even if I got away, they would still catch Mom, so I would slow down again and just ride around like the other kids I sometimes saw pedaling down our street. I smiled at them shyly as they passed. I had a bicycle, a mother, and I lived in a real cottage where I could turn the thermostat up whenever I wanted to. Sometimes, I almost felt like a regular kid.

THE FOLLOWING MARCH, SOMETHING so exciting happened that it literally kept me awake for nights on end. Jenny Lund was turning six, and I had been invited to her birthday party.

When the day finally arrived, I dressed in my best outfit and waited on the front steps for Tina's mother to pick me up. The car pulled into the driveway, and I ran down the steps and threw myself into the back seat.

Tina looked at me over her shoulder. "Where's your present?" she sniffed. "It's Jenny's *birthday* party, you know."

My smile faded. To my horror, I saw that Tina had a pretty wrapped box resting in her lap. "Oops, I forgot it. Could you wait a minute?" I dashed back to the house and stormed through the front door. "Mom!" I yelled. "I need a present!"

Mom came out of the kitchen with a joint in her hand. "A present? Oh, my . . ."

I jumped back a little. "Mom, I don't want to smell like—"

"Oh, honey, you worry too much about what others think. Your real friends will accept you . . ." Her voice trailed away as she wandered upstairs to her bedroom.

I followed, and stood beside her hopping nervously from one foot to the other.

"Here. How about these?" she asked, holding up a pair of beaded feather earrings.

I shook my head.

She pawed through her drawers a little more and came up with a silk scarf printed with totem poles.

I shook my head again, tears gathering in my eyes, and then ran to my own bedroom and looked around wildly. I had no choice. I grabbed my snow globe and took the stairs back down to Mom.

"Good choice! I'm sure your little friend will love it," she said happily, holding out a gold bow left over from Christmas.

I stuck it on top of the globe and headed back to Tina's car. All the way to Jenny's house, I held my treasure in my coat pocket and tried not to cry. But when we walked through her front door, the magical scene before me was enough to make me forgot my sadness. The living room was filled with floating pink balloons, streamers and paper princesses. A giant cake in the shape of a ballerina sat on the table. The other birthday guests ran around me, their flouncy dresses swirling as they played. I glanced down at my own outfit: brown turtleneck, jeans and holey socks. I tucked my feet under my rear end and ran a hand through my hair.

"Why, hello there," said a voice, and I looked up. It was Jenny's mother, holding a pitcher of red liquid in one hand and a stack of paper cups in the other. "Would you like some Kool-Aid?"

I nodded shyly, accepted a cup and took a sip. It tasted too sweet. I gulped it down and then went to watch Jenny open her presents. She ripped open gift after gift, squealing with excitement, until there was nothing left except my snow globe sitting on the carpet. Jenny's mother picked it up and handed it to her.

"It looks like there's one more present here. Who is this from?" she asked in a singsong voice, glancing around the room.

I lifted my hand. Jenny took the globe, gave it a shake, and put it down again.

Her mother snatched it up and flashed me a smile. "Well, isn't this just lovely. Have you been to Paris, dear?"

I looked down at my hands and pretended not to hear, then got up to find the bathroom. I didn't have to go, but I wasn't sure what else to do with myself. Everyone seemed to be playing a game about ducks and geese, but I didn't know the rules.

As I walked down the hall, I passed Jenny's bedroom. I stopped and stared. Her bed was covered with a frilly white canopy, and painted on the wall was a picture of Rapunzel with her long blond hair flowing from a castle window. I checked behind me, and then stepped inside the room. There was a party dress draped across her bed. I touched it with my hand. It was pink satin, softer than a kitten's fur. Moving slowly, I picked it up and held it before me in the mirror. With my clothes hidden, I barely recognized myself.

I looked pretty, almost like Rapunzel. I glanced into the hallway. Nobody was there, and I could still hear shrieks coming from the living room. I took a deep breath, then I stripped off my clothes and slipped the dress over my head.

It was too small. The hem hung above my knees and the sleeves ended just below my elbows, but I didn't care. I felt like a real-life Barbie. I twirled in front of the mirror and let my hair fly out behind me.

Then I stopped cold. Over my shoulder, I could see the reflection of Tina standing in the doorway. She brought her hand up to her mouth and snickered, then she turned and ran back the way she had come. I felt like throwing up.

Seconds later, Jenny's mother rushed into the room.

"Oh dear," she said fretfully, "I should have closed Jenny's door. Her room is a frightful mess . . . Here, darling, just turn around and I'll get the zipper for you. It's just a tad too small, I see, but a nice color on you just the same . . ."

I nodded, fighting tears, and as soon as I could get my clothes on I went to hide in the bathroom.

When it was time to go home, I made sure nobody was watching, and then I picked up my snow globe and slipped it into my coat pocket. I would never be like the other girls, and I hadn't just been caught trying on someone else's dress. I had been caught trying to belong.

All I wanted to do was go home and forget about it, but Tina's mother had other plans.

"Tina, you've never met Cea's parents," she said as her car pulled into our driveway. "Why don't you go in and say hello?"

"Do I *have* to?" Tina asked, crossing her arms.

"Yes. It's the polite thing to do," her mother said, angling the rearview mirror at her face and twisting up her lipstick. "Now scoot."

Tina and I climbed the stairs in silence and stepped through the front door. "Mom!" I called loudly. "Tina from school is here! Wants to meet you!"

"Be right there!" my mother shouted back from the bathroom. I heard the toilet flush, the door open, and then Mom's footsteps coming down the hallway. She walked into the living room.

Beside me, Tina gasped and raised her hand to her mouth.

"Oh, hi there," Mom said, smiling at her. "I'm Cea's mom. Did you girls have fun?"

Tina stared at my mother in horror. For the second time that day, I wanted nothing more than to just disappear. I wasn't sure what was worse: the fact that Mom was standing before us with a joint in her hand, or the fact that she was doing it topless. I thought about Jenny's mother serving Kool-Aid in her flowered dress, and I had never felt like more of a freak.

DESPITE THE MISERY BROUGHT on by Jenny's birthday party and Mom's nudist, pot-smoking ways, by May of 1976 my life had settled into the closest thing to normal I'd ever known. The days passed, and there was nothing I wanted that I didn't have. At home, Mom cooked and kept the cottage clean while Karl got a raise and began to pull in enough money that we could even afford the occasional extra, like dinner in a restaurant or a new winter coat for me. I took baths and helped my mother with the laundry and went to school looking half decent. The other kids never liked me much, but they put up with me and even played with me sometimes. My wilderness years were beginning to fade in my mind. I thought about my grandparents less and less, and when I did, it was mostly to hope they wouldn't find us and take us back to the tipis. I was happy.

Then one day I came home from school to find my mother crying on the sofa.

Mom stood up and rushed toward me with open arms. She hugged me hard, pulled me into her lap and then started sobbing again. We weren't alone. Just across the room, a strange man sat in Karl's favorite chair.

"Why are you crying?" I asked Mom, fiddling with the roach clip that hung between her breasts. I had made it for her years before, and she had attached it to a string of leather to wear as a necklace.

She steadied herself with a deep breath and then told me the news: Karl had broken his back in a logging accident, and it was very bad. He was unconscious and had already been flown to a hospital in Nanaimo. We were to meet him there, but before we did, we were to pack our belongings and have the logging company ship them to our destination. We would not be returning to the cottage.

I jumped up. "No!" I yelled angrily. "I don't want to leave!"

"Cea, this isn't the time—"

"I said no! You can't make me!"

"Honey, please . . ." Mom tried to take my hand, but I kept it tucked stubbornly under my armpit. "Wait a minute," she said suddenly, as if realizing something. She turned to the man. "How could he tell you all this if he was unconscious? And Vancouver is closer than Nanaimo. Why didn't they take him there?"

"*Mommy!*" I howled.

"Just a *minute*—"

The man reached into his shirt pocket, took out an envelope and from that an unfolded a sheet of paper. "We have all our men fill out one of these forms in case of an accident. Family contacts, special instructions, what have you." He pointed halfway down the page. "See? It says right here. 'Pack all belongings . . . ship to my mother's house in Nanaimo'—"

"His *mother*?" Mom's jaw dropped to her chest. "His mother is dead! His whole family is. Except his brother, I think."

The man shrugged. "I can only tell you what it says here, ma'am."

"There must be some mistake. Anyway . . ." She looked around. "I don't know how he expects us to get there. I don't have any money—"

My heart leapt. No money, of course! That meant we couldn't go. But the man reached into the envelope again and pulled out a thin stack of cash.

"Karl put this aside for you. It should be enough to get you through."

"Oh . . ." Mom's hands fluttered to her lap. She looked around the room, slowly taking it in. "Well, I guess then . . . we better, um, get packing . . ."

I ran to my room and threw myself on the bed. Someday, I thought, I would buy a cottage just like this for Mom and me and my little baby girl to live in, and nobody in the world would be able to make us leave. But in the meantime, there was nothing left to do but cry. And I did, until my mother came upstairs an hour later and wrapped her weary body around my own.

"Here," she said quietly, holding an eyedropper in front of my mouth.

I shook my head and kept my lips clamped tightly shut. Mom thought Rescue Remedy was the miracle cure for everything, so I always acted like I felt a little better when she gave it to me. But tonight, I just didn't feel like pretending anymore.

Chapter Sixteen

Mom and I showed up at Mrs. Hofler's house on a bright day in May, squinting against the sunlight as we waited on her tidy front porch. Karl's mother was expecting us. The day before, after packing up the cottage and getting a man from the logging company to drive us to the Greyhound bus terminal, Mom had had a short phone call with her.

"The hospital already called her," Mom told me after she hung up. "Karl is awake. He let her know we were on our way."

"Was she . . . Did she sound nice?" I asked.

"It's hard to say. Strong Austrian accent, she was kind of hard to understand."

"Oh. Maybe you should call Karl and ask him why he made her dead."

"I already did." Mom shook her head. "He didn't want to talk about it. Just told me that his father had been a Nazi, and that he really did die a few years back."

"What's a Nazi?"

"I'm not exactly sure. Some crazy assholes who did a lot of bad stuff during the war."

"Like what kind of bad—?"

"Not now, honey, okay? Anyway, Karl wouldn't say why he lied."

Mom raised her hand to knock on Mrs. Hofler's door again, but just then it swung open. Before us was a woman holding a can of Lysol. Besides the smell of her, which made my nostrils burn, she looked like any of the old ladies I had seen on the ferry ride over here: shapeless dress, wrinkled face and short hair in tight silver curls.

She nodded at us unsmilingly. "Your room is downstairs."

I had never heard consonants pronounced the way Mrs. Hofler said them, as if they were almost too heavy for her tongue to push out. "It is up to you to keep it clean."

"Of course," Mom replied, smiling stiffly. "Thank you. I'm Michelle, by the way. And this is my daughter—"

"Yes, I assumed that to be the case." Mrs. Hofler opened the door wide enough to let us in. "Have the girl leave her boots here," she said to Mom without looking at me. "Then go into the bathroom and have her remove her clothing."

I shrank behind Mom's legs.

"Just do as she asked, sweetheart," Mom said softly. "I'll go with you."

I took off my snowmobile boots and walked through the house, looking behind me to make sure Mom was following. The smell of Lysol was everywhere. Every surface of Mrs. Hofler's home gleamed. I found the bathroom and took off my sweater, jeans and socks, then sat on the toilet to wait with Mom beside me. The door opened, and Mrs. Hofler came in with a plastic bag in one hand and a pair of tongs in the other.

"Underwear," she said, pointing.

I glanced at Mom, then slipped them off and put my hands over my crotch. Using the tongs, Mrs. Hofler picked up my clothes one piece at a time and put them in her bag. Then she handed Mom a bottle with a drawing of two screaming lice on it.

"Wash her hair three times with this shampoo."

Mom stared at the bottle. "But she's never had—"

"Just do it, please," Mrs. Hofler replied, and turned on her heel.

A minute later, we heard the washing machine starting up. After Mom washed my hair, she wrapped a towel around me, and we went downstairs to find our bedroom. Our backpacks were sitting outside the door with the zippers open.

"That's nice," Mom said with forced cheer. "It looks like she's done our laundry. Anyhow . . ." She looked around. "This is great. It should do just fine. Right, sweetheart?"

I nodded. My mother was right; it *was* fine. The room was small, but we each had our own bed, and there was a lamp and a large dresser to share. There was even a telephone and a small television set. Maybe everything would be okay, I thought. But that night, after a silent, boiled supper with Mrs. Hofler, the sick feeling in my stomach still hadn't gone away.

THE NEXT MORNING, MOM and I took the bus to visit Karl. As she and I passed through sleepy streets lined with cute houses and pretty rose gardens, I suddenly felt homesick for the wilderness. My grandparents, I thought. How would they ever find us now?

When we got to the hospital, Mom and I found Karl's room and walked cautiously through the door. He was asleep with his mouth open, and I barely recognized him. His entire torso, right arm and thigh had a hard white cast on them. His leg was slung up in a shiny metal pulley, and there was a bandage wrapped around his head. Mom put her hand on his arm, and he opened his eyes and slowly rolled his head toward us.

"Hey, pretty lady. Hey, Small Fry." He smiled weakly.

Mom took his hand. "Wow. You look pretty rough. How are you feeling?"

"Been better. Hanging in, though."

"Yeah. So what . . . what happened?"

Karl rubbed his good hand across his stubbly chin. "Managed to get myself on the business side of a falling tree. Didn't even see it coming."

"Wow," Mom said again. "How long will you have to be in here?"

"The doctors say at least three months."

She swallowed hard.

"Yeah, I know." He turned to look at the window. "How . . . how you doing at my mother's?"

"It's, uh . . . fine." She cleared her throat as if to continue, but Karl quickly nodded and changed the subject.

"Listen, you think you could bring me some real food next time you come?" he asked. "The meals in this place are killing me."

"Yeah, sure," Mom replied. "Whatever you want. Of course."

THE DAYS CRAWLED TO a stop at Mrs. Hofler's house. In the beginning, Mom spent most of her time at the hospital or sneaking out to the park to smoke a quick joint. I usually stayed behind in our room when she went to visit Karl, but I liked to go with her to the park. I would swing or climb the monkey bars while she puffed away in the trees, fanning the smoke with her hand to keep the busybody parents at bay.

On the way back to Mrs. Hofler's house, Mom often liked to talk about the wilderness days in a breathy, stoned voice. Somehow, it was these times that always made me feel a little better. As much as I wanted to be a part of the city, it also frightened me. Passing cars, crowds of people and loud noises made me jump. One time when Mom was talking about my grandparents, I stopped on the sidewalk and started to cry. Mom hugged me, then took out her pocketknife and cut some roses from the yard beside us. When we got back to our bedroom, Mom put the flowers in an empty jar. She said it was as close to bringing us back to the wilderness as she could manage here. I inhaled and tried to send myself back there, but it didn't work. The roses I remembered in the bush were loose and ragged-looking with petals that blew in the breeze, nothing at all like this perfectly shaped version from the city.

A BLACK AND WHITE cat ran after a yellow bird. The cat ran into a wall, slid onto the floor like a pancake, then shook himself back into a cat shape and walked away on two legs. I flipped the channel, searching for commercials. Mrs. Hofler had cable, which meant she even had a channel that played kids' shows until late. It was nine o'clock at night, and Mom was out again. She had promised to be home in time to tuck me into bed by ten, and so far she had always kept to her word.

Even though Mom still visited Karl at the hospital most days, she now spent many of her evenings out. When I asked her where she went, she said something about some new friends she had met through Karl's brother Marcus, who lived upstairs with Mrs. Hofler. A few times, I had wandered up to find Mrs. Hofler watching TV or drinking sherry at the kitchen table, but each time she had waved me back down the stairs without a word. The thought that she hated having me in her home touched me at a fearful place I couldn't quite understand, but I didn't need to.

My world was slowly shrinking to the shape of a ten-by-twelve-foot basement bedroom. I ate there, I read there, I sewed there and I played with Suzie Doll there. I turned on the TV in search of Breck Shampoo commercials, whose glamorous girls always made me feel hopeful, but mostly I just pretended here. Sometimes I imagined I was back at the cottage lying in my old bed, other times I was back in the wilderness with my grandparents. I named myself Cindy and made myself eighteen, an age that seemed both magical and ancient to me. As Cindy, I was a beautiful model who wore pretty dresses, and even though all the men wanted to have sex with me, I never did because I thought sex was gross and I never wanted to be pregnant because then everyone would know I'd done it just by looking at me. After a while, I would get tired of pretending and look up at the window, wondering when Karl would get out of the hospital so everything could go back to the way it used to be.

By the time we had been at Mrs. Hofler's for six weeks, each day felt like forever. Only Mom seemed happy—in fact, happier than I had seen her in a long time. She smiled a lot and swung my hand when we walked to the park. I didn't want to question her new good mood, but I couldn't help wishing that it hadn't come because she was spending so much time away from me.

ONE MORNING, I WAS in the kitchen grabbing an apple when I heard Mom and Mrs. Hofler talking. Their voices were low, so I crept closer.

". . . not her babysitter," Mrs. Hofler was saying. "Maybe you have a friend . . ."

". . . not an option," Mom replied. ". . . think of something . . . never meant to be a burden . . ."

"Perhaps you could stay home," Mrs. Hofler suggested, and she sounded mad. "Anyway, these are my rules. I trust you understand."

"Of course," Mom said.

I tiptoed back across the kitchen floor and hurried downstairs.

A few minutes later I heard Mom's footsteps, and then she was standing in the doorway to our bedroom.

"Well. Fuck a duck," she said.

"What's wrong?" I asked.

"Oh, just . . . I had a little disagreement with Karl's mother. Anyway, it looks like I'll be staying home at night from now on."

"But that's *good*!" I said happily.

"Yeah, I know. Only . . ." She shrugged. "Anyway, what do you say we go to the park? I just had a good idea."

THE PARK MOM LIKED to take me to had three parts to it: a playground, a picnic area and, on one side, the woods where Mom always hid to smoke her joints. The area wasn't big enough to get lost in and the trees weren't very thick, but no one other than Mom and I ever seemed to go in there. Sometimes we would walk in far enough that we could barely hear the sounds of the playing children and could see nothing but nature in every direction, but I still only felt as if I were in a fake forest in the middle of the city.

When we reached the park, Mom took me into the woods. "So last time we were here, I noticed something," she said, leading me over to a large spruce tree. "Look at this. Isn't this just a perfect little fort for you?" She lifted some of the bottom branches and crouched down.

I leaned forward beside her, hands on my knees, and looked inside. It *was* perfect, I thought excitedly. The branches formed a shelter big enough for me to stand up in. I ducked inside and sat with my back to the tree's trunk.

"Yeah. I could almost live in here!"

Mom smiled. "You see? It's just like being in the wilderness. I was even thinking I could bring some things in for you, maybe a blanket and some pots and pans, and you could make it into your little house to play in whenever you want. What do you think?"

"Groovy! Maybe even some real dishes and stuff?"

"Of course, darling. We'll find some at the thrift store."

True to her word, Mom took me on a shopping trip that very afternoon. We lugged everything back to the park, and then I ran around putting everything out while Mom smoked a joint on the ground beside me.

"Can we come back here tomorrow?" I asked just before we left.

"Sweetheart. We can come here *every* day!"

I DON'T THINK MOM introduced me to the tree fort with the intention of it becoming my babysitter, but that's the way it worked out. At first it was always the two of us, playing together and pretending it was our own little house. Then one day, she said she had to meet someone in the picnic area, and would I be okay playing on my own for a while?

"Meet who?" I asked.

"Just a friend. You don't know him."

Him. Of course. I nodded without looking up, knowing she would be within shouting distance. After a few minutes I barely noticed she was gone, and a little while later she was back again.

A few days after that, Mom sat beside me with her hands under her chin. "So I was thinking," she began. "I should go and visit Karl, and it'll probably be really boring for you. Wouldn't you rather stay here and play?"

"No," I said, throwing a handful of dirt into my pot.

"Are you sure? I won't be long. I just know you'll have way more fun here."

I didn't answer. The thought of going to the hospital or to Mrs. Hofler's house wasn't very exciting, but neither was the thought of being on my own. "How long will it take?" I asked finally.

"Not long, just an hour or so. I'll be back before you know it."

I shrugged.

"Okay," she said after a minute, and leaned in to give me a quick kiss on the cheek. "See you soon, my love."

I kept my head down while I stirred spruce needles into my pot. As long as I didn't see her feet walking away from me, I was pretty sure I wouldn't cry.

MY TREE FORT QUICKLY became the center of my new world. Every couple of days, Mom would bring me there and play for a few minutes, and then she would leave. I never watched her go. Instead I would kneel on the ground, decorating my mud cakes and mixing my leaf salads. I usually brought Suzie Doll for company, and I always had Papa Dick's roach clip in my pocket. After I finished cooking, I'd hang the roach clip from a branch and lie on my blanket looking up at it, pretending I was in the wilderness. The shrieks of the park's children floated to my ears, and sometimes I imagined them crashing through the trees, finding my secret place and taking it for themselves. It never happened, and Mom always came back to me. I never asked where she went. Somehow, I understood that she needed this time away from me.

But every day, I wondered when Karl would get better.

I SAT ON MY bed, watching my mother pace back and forth. Every few minutes she stopped and looked at the telephone, then began walking again. Outside our window, the last rays of sun had just given way to darkness.

"Why don't you go to bed, Mommy?" I asked finally.

She stopped and scratched at her arm. "I can't. I . . ."

"Why not?"

She tugged at her hair and then sat down beside me.

"Listen," she said, taking my hand. Her eyes looked funny, kind of like the eyes I had seen on a rabbit once just before Papa Dick shot it. "I need to go somewhere, but I can't leave you here. How would you feel about coming with me?"

"Where?"

"To a party."

"A party?" I shook my head firmly. "No. I don't want to."

"Sweetheart, it'll be fun. There'll be music, and food . . . just this once, okay? Please? It's not that far, we can even walk there."

I crossed my arms stubbornly. Mom fidgeted a little more, then she leaned down and scooped me up. When she set me on the sidewalk outside, I let my legs collapse and I crumpled to the ground, but when she started to walk away from me I stood up, dusted my knees off and followed. I thought she would have been happy that I came with her, but she still seemed nervous and jumpy.

Half an hour later, we arrived at a house with booming music. Even from the sidewalk, I could smell pot smoke. Mom took my hand and pulled me through the front door. It was packed. People yelled to be heard, the Eagles blared, drinks sloshed, food spilled, cigarettes glowed and pot smoke billowed. I looked around for other kids, but there weren't any. I clung to Mom's side while she circled the room. She led me to a table loaded with mismatched serving dishes.

"Are you hungry?" she shouted above the noise, plucking a tortilla chip from a platter of browning guacamole.

I shook my head. After a while, we made our way into the living room and sat beside a man on a torn sofa. He had tanned skin and a mustache that grew like a weed across his face. He smiled at me and mouthed some words, but I couldn't hear him. I climbed into Mom's lap and turned my face into her chest. I didn't like how her and the man's knees were touching, or how their shoulders were rubbing together.

"Cea," Mom yelled into my ear. "This is Sebastian. He wanted to meet you. Say hi."

I turned my head away. A minute later, I looked back and the man was still smiling at me. He had the whitest teeth I had ever seen, even brighter than the white shirt and matching bell-bottoms he was wearing. He leaned toward me and put his mouth by my ear. ". . . Michelle's daughter" was all I heard, but it wasn't what he said that caught my attention; it was how he smelled. It was the same smell I noticed on Mom when she picked me up from my tree fort. I glanced at the man's face again. I was pretty sure his eyes were brown, but they looked as if they were all pupils and no color.

He leaned in to me again. "Cea," he said, louder this time. "It's nice to meet you. You're a beautiful little girl, just like your mom said."

"Thanks," I said, feeling a little friendlier.

"Cea, do you know what?"

I shook my head, and he gave a little laugh.

"I am very, very stoned right now. I hope I remember this tomorrow."

He laughed even harder, so I turned away from him and put my arms around Mom's neck. The music was deafening. On the floor beside us, a woman was holding a wine cork behind her friend's earlobe and sticking a needle through it. Another woman in a yellow caftan came by with a piece of hash on a blackened butter knife. The man with the white teeth lit his lighter under the knife and took a long hit.

"Mommy," I said. "Can we go now?"

She looked disappointed. "You're not having fun?"

"No." I shook my head. "I want to go to bed."

"Not yet, sweetie, I still need to talk to Sebastian some more."

"But why can't I sleep here?"

She shrugged, and then shouted something into the man's ear. "Okay," she said to me. "Let's go find you a place to lie down."

The man trailed his fingers along her arm as she stood up, and Mom let him. She carried me through the crowd and down the stairs to a bedroom in the basement, where she plunked me on the bed and pulled the covers over me.

"I'll come back and check on you in an hour. Okay?"

"Mommy, who was that man?"

She smiled. "Sebastian? He's nice, isn't he?"

"I don't know." I looked at my hands, pulling the blanket under my chin.

I could feel her staring down at me, and then she bent and kissed my head.

"Just a friend. Sleep tight."

I rolled over to face the wall. The music still boomed down here, mixed with stoned laughter and chatter, but at least it was a little quieter. I slipped my hand into my pocket and brought out Papa Dick's roach clip, then curled it into my fist. Eventually, I slept.

PERHAPS MY MOTHER DID check in on me as promised, but I wasn't awake to remember it. What I do remember is waking up hours later to a still, quiet house. I looked around, trying to remember where I was, and after a moment it came to me. *Oh yes, the party. Mom. Where are you?*

I swung my feet onto the floor and switched on the bedside lamp. Light flooded a room containing mismatched bedding, a poster of Raquel Welch taped to the wall and a half-empty whisky bottle on a bookshelf. I stood up, walked to the door and turned the handle. It wouldn't budge.

At first, I was confused. I grabbed the handle with both hands and twisted it with all my might. And that's when the fear set in, because there was no mistaking it: I had been locked in.

Tears pricked at my eyes. Making a fist, I pounded on the door as hard as I could. "Mommy! *Mom!*" I waited, but there was nothing. I backed away and sat on the bed with rubbery legs. Outside the window, the sky was black. I cried until my tears turned to hiccups, and eventually lay back and fell asleep. When I woke up again, the sky was starting to lighten. I got up and tried the door again, then went back to bed and lay still, trying to calm the beating of my heart. What if she *never came back*?

I was half asleep when she finally did. There was the rattle of a key in the lock and then there she was, standing in the doorway like the dream I had had of her countless times that night. Her face was red and puffy from crying, and she looked so different that it took me a moment to recognize her. She walked over to me and stretched her body out beside mine.

"I'm sorry, I'm so sorry," she said into my back.

We lay there for a long time, not talking.

"Was this one of those times you couldn't be my mommy?" I finally whispered.

She didn't reply, but the tears soaking through my shirt told me the answer. I held her hand and stared at the wall, thinking that when I had my own little girl someday, I would never ever leave her alone even for a minute, for as long as I lived.

AFTER THE NIGHT MOM locked me in, she stopped leaving me when we went to the tree fort. Instead, she sat staring into the distance while I played. She put on a smile when I looked at her, but it seemed almost like my real mother was hiding behind some other lady's face. I wanted to ask her if she was going to see the man with the white teeth again, but I was afraid to remind her of him.

One day while we were playing, she picked up Suzie Doll and put her in her lap. "I have something to tell you," she said.

"Okay. What?"

"It's . . ." She glanced away, then took a deep breath and looked into my eyes. "Remember that time you asked me why I never get pregnant?"

"Yeah."

"Well, sometimes it happens even if you don't plan it."

"Oh. You mean like when you had me?"

"Um . . . yes." She smiled a little sadly. "Well . . . it's happened again. I'm going to have a baby."

My heart jumped. "You mean . . . I'm going to have a baby sister?"

"Or brother, yes."

I stared at her belly, which looked no different than it had the day before. "But there's no bump," I said, pointing.

"I know. It takes a while to stick out. And I'm only a few weeks along. I thought I was just late, but . . ."

"What about the diagram?"

She smiled again. "You mean diaphragm?"

"Yeah. Why didn't it keep the sperm out?"

"I just . . . sometimes I forget to use it." She rubbed her hand over her face, and I saw that there were tears in her eyes.

"Mommy, aren't you glad?"

"I'm . . . it's going to take me some time to get used to the idea, that's all."

I took Suzie Doll from her and fed her a bottle. "Is Karl going to be happy about it?"

Mom stayed quiet for a long time. "I don't know," she said after a while. "I guess we'll find out when I tell him. Until then, let's keep this to ourselves, okay? It'll be our little secret."

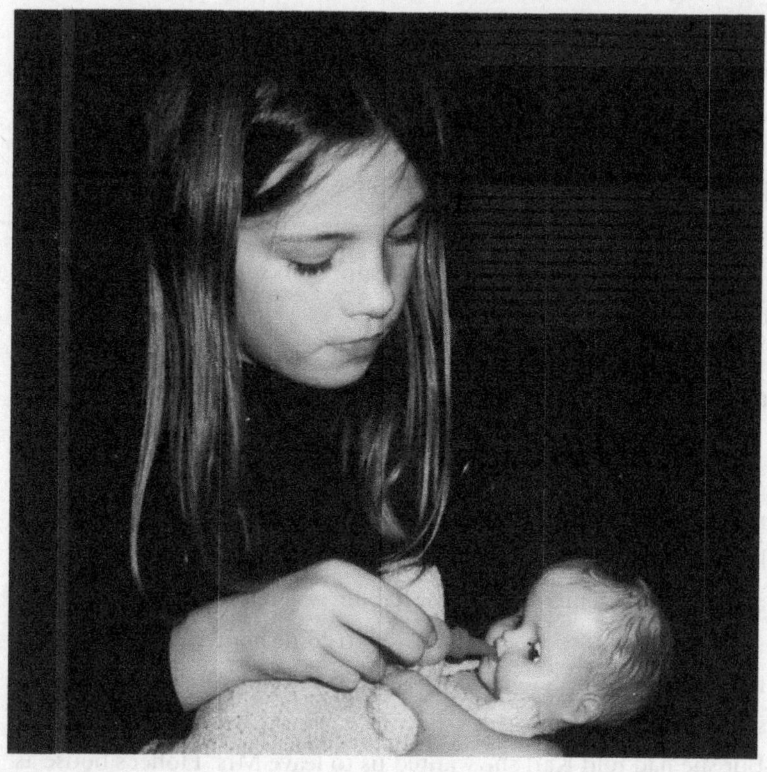

Me with my beloved Suzie Doll.

THINGS CHANGED AFTER MOM told me she was pregnant. We only went to the tree fort once or twice because she said she was too tired, and besides, she had lost her taste for pot. Instead, she started spending a lot of time in the bathroom throwing up. Her boobs were sore, she complained, and for the first time ever, I saw her wear a bra.

"Did you tell Karl yet?" I asked her every day when she came home from the hospital, but she always shook her head.

She never got the chance. One night, I was awoken by loud moaning. I turned on the lamp and walked to the bathroom, where the sound was coming from. Mom was sitting naked on the toilet with her head hanging between her legs.

"Mommy, what's wrong?"

She jerked her head up. "It's—there's a lot of blood. I think I'm having a miscarriage—"

"What's a miscarriage?"

She let her head hang down again. "I'm sorry, sweetie. I've lost the baby."

Mom put her face in her hands and cried, and I knew there was nothing in the world I could do to change any of it.

MY MOTHER WAS TWENTY-THREE when her second and last baby left her womb that night. Ten days later, and nearly four months after Karl first entered the hospital, he was released.

The day before he was supposed to come home, Mom had given me the lowdown. She hadn't bothered to tell Karl about the baby, she told me, because she was sure it would have just upset him. But she had told Karl she wanted us to leave Mrs. Hofler's house as soon as possible, and had even packed our bags. I nodded slowly, looking around our basement room. This had been my home for the past three months. A house filled with rooms I had barely set foot in, a perfect rose garden in the front yard, as normal as I ever could have hoped for. And yet my tree fort in the park had felt more like home than these four walls ever had.

Karl showed up in a taxicab the next day. Mom and I waited for him on the front porch, watched as he paid the driver. First his long legs swung out of the car, then his right hand, holding a cane. He planted the cane on the sidewalk and pulled himself to his feet, then walked up the front steps. Mom ran to hug him and dissolved into tears. After a few minutes, Karl pulled away from her and stood looking at us. Mom had lost weight, and she had dark circles under her eyes. I knew I looked pale and ragged from too many days spent in either a basement room or a tree fort worrying about my family. Karl patted Mom on the back and made his way to the front door, where Mrs. Hofler was hanging back.

"What is this, a horse show? I've never seen so many long faces in one place," Karl said, stepping inside. "Hello, Mother."

"Karl." She nodded curtly. "Lunch will be ready shortly. You can wash up in the bathroom."

Karl laughed and shook his head. "No, I think it's high time we blew the friendly Hotel Hofler." He pulled Mom toward him and thumped his cane on the floor. "Michelle, go and get yours and Cea's stuff. What this family needs is a vacation, and I've got the perfect place in mind."

Part Three

Pieces

Chapter Seventeen

Karl's idea of a vacation turned out to be seventy-five miles southeast of Nanaimo on one of the Gulf Islands, an area known as a haven for draft dodgers and grow-oppers. And in the beginning, it almost *did* feel like we were on holiday. Karl used his

Me at age seven. This was taken on the beach below the cottage that we lived in when we first arrived in the Gulf Islands.

workman's compensation funds to rent us a cottage nearly as wonderful as the one in Celista, and I spent my afternoons collecting clams and oysters from the beach below.

I started Grade One at the tiny island school and let Karl pretend to be Santa Claus on our roof that Christmas. I remember smiling a lot in those days, showing off my missing front teeth for Karl's new camera and standing on a stool to wash the dinner dishes while he and Mom smoked their evening joint. I remember the thrill of being invited to a classmate's pool party, even though I couldn't swim and spent most of the party playing with an inchworm on my fingertip. I recall inviting a girlfriend over to play for the very first time, and begging Mom not to smoke pot that day so my friend couldn't tell her parents on us. I spent hours in my bedroom, sewing tiny clothes for the Barbie I still dreamed of one day owning. I was happy, and life was as good as I'd ever known it to be.

I never knew what the last straw was, or who decided to end it. But just six months after we moved to the island, Mom and Karl called it quits. One rainy January day, I came home from school to find Mom sitting alone in the living room. She stubbed out her cigarette and opened her arms to me when I came through the door.

"We're moving," she said softly into my hair. "Just you and me."

And that was it, the quiet ending to Mom and Karl's chaotic two-year affair.

I remember that the room felt too cold when she told me the news, but I don't recall if I ever said goodbye to Karl. The next day, Mom and I moved in with a friend of hers, a single mother who lived with her two young sons in a one-room guesthouse. Mom and I slept on the floor and cooked our meals on the outdoor fire pit.

About a month later, I saw Karl standing at my school fence at recess one day. I walked over to him and grinned, lacing my fingers through the chain-metal between us. His face looked as familiar as the old snow boots I pulled on for school each day.

"Small Fry," he said, smiling down at me. "I just wanted to make sure you were doing okay here. You like your teacher?"

"Yeah. Mrs. Ross."

"Mrs. Ross, hmm. Well, you tell those other kids that if they ever bother you, they'll have me to deal with. You hear?"

"Yeah." I grinned back at him. "I will."

"Okay." He stuffed his hands into his coat pockets and stomped his feet. Even in February, the temperature didn't usually drop below freezing here, but there was a drizzle in the air today. "It's cold," Karl said, and I nodded. "How . . . how are things with your mom?"

"Okay, I guess. We're living with Sherrie. Mom says she's going to try to find Papa Dick and Grandma Jeanne again."

"Mm. Yeah, that'd probably be good for her."

"Yeah." I hesitated. "So, um, do you . . . are you and Mom ever going to live together again? Because I kind of liked it better before. When you did, I mean."

"I liked it too, Small Fry, I liked it too. It's just . . . I don't think your mom and I are the best match. I'm kind of like fire and she's kind of like water, you know what I mean?"

"Uh-huh." I pulled my hands into my cuffs and looked at the ground.

"Well. Maybe I could stop by here at lunch sometime and we could eat together. Over there on the grass or something. Would that be okay?"

"Yeah. I'll just have to let my teacher know."

"Of course, of course." He smiled brightly at me. "Well, I should be going. Until then, all right?"

"Yup. Okay."

Karl walked back to his truck and raised a hand to me, and I waved back.

After that, I couldn't help but look over at the fence for him each day at lunchtime, but he never came again.

IF MOM WAS UPSET over the breakup, she didn't let on. Karl had given her a bit of money, and even though it was surely running out, I never heard her mention looking for a job. Mostly she stayed up late with Sherrie, smoking joints and talking about men while I dozed at her feet in my sleeping bag. Mom said that her next boyfriend better be able to offer her more than just a charming smile and a hard dick, as she was sick of all the craziness that went down with guys the likes of Karl. As it turned out, it didn't take her long to find someone she thought fit the bill.

One evening, about a month after we'd moved in with Sherrie, I sat beside Mom as she held a mirror to her face and put makeup on. "I have a surprise for you," she said, smiling at me with hot-pink lips. "We're going out for dinner tonight."

"Oh, goody!" I clapped my hands excitedly, wondering how our luck had changed so quickly. Just yesterday, Mom had been wondering where she was going to find money for next week's groceries. "Can I get a milk shake?"

"Of course, sweetheart." She pulled me into her lap. "Do you remember that comic book I used to like, the one about Conan?"

"Yeah."

"Well. I've finally met someone just like him. He's everything I've ever dreamed of—sexy, manly, and he really knows how to treat a woman. He even has his *own* business. Things are going to change for us now, sweetie."

"Change how?"

"Just . . ." She fluttered her hands in the air. "Barry's really got it together, that's all. You're going to love him. He's going to be here in a few minutes, and I want you to be on your best behavior. Okay?" I didn't answer, so she poked me in the ribs and I started to giggle. "Okay?" she said again.

Just then, we heard a car honk outside. Mom took one last look in the mirror, then jumped up and walked me out the door.

My first thought when I saw Barry was that he looked like Luke from *The Dukes of Hazzard.* I had come across the show once at Mrs. Hofler's house, just long enough to see him vaulting over the door into the driver's seat of his topless car. Barry was sitting behind the wheel of a red El Ranchero, smoothing his mustache as he looked in the rearview mirror. It was early spring and the air was chilly, but he wore a sleeveless shirt that showed off his muscles.

"So," he said to Mom when we slid into the car beside him. "This is your little bush baby."

"Yes," Mom replied, smiling down at me. "Isn't she beautiful?"

"She doesn't look much like you," Barry replied, starting the ignition. Then he peeled out of Sherrie's driveway, leaving a trail of black screech marks behind us.

Barry did most of the talking at the restaurant. He sat back with his arm draped over Mom's shoulder, squeezing her boob whenever he thought I wasn't looking. He said "somewheres" instead of "somewhere." And when the bill came, instead of getting his wallet out, he went out to the car and came back with a crate of empty beer cans to pay for dinner.

"Wow," Mom said to me back in our bed at Sherrie's place, her cheeks flushed. "Isn't he just the best?"

I turned away from her, not sure what to say.

Four weeks later, we moved in with him.

BARRY LOVED TO TALK business. He owned the island's only hardware store, and in the days after I first met him, he would sit on Sherrie's couch using big, unfamiliar words like *partnership*, *profit margin* and *accounting* that never failed to make Mom's face go all dreamy-looking. But when it came to talking about where he lived, Barry was more mysterious. One day, he and Mom seemed to get into a bit of a fight about it, and Barry finally told her he was living with his mother. But it was only for now, he added, because he was actually building his own house.

"There, are you happy?" he asked Mom angrily. "You've ruined the surprise. The house is almost done, and I was going to ask you to move in with me."

"Oh, I'm sorry, babe . . ." Mom said, stroking his arm. "I didn't know—"

"Yeah, whatever," Barry said, lighting a cigarette. "I guess you can come see if it meets your high standards." He exhaled in a long, mad stream, and Mom said nothing.

A few days later, Barry drove Mom and me to see his house. The two of them had talked about it a little more since their tiff, and I had to admit it sounded pretty nice. Barry had described a view of the island, three bedrooms, a bathroom with a walk-in shower and a kitchen with brand-new appliances. Mom said it sounded just perfect. So when we turned onto the long, dusty road that wound up the hillside to the house, I wasn't at all concerned about what we would see at the top.

"There's just one more thing," Barry said to Mom casually, stroking her thigh. "It's not exactly *finished*, but I don't want you to worry about that. You won't believe how fast I'll be able to make it all come together. Just a few more weeks of work to do, a couple months tops. Okay?"

Mom nodded and smiled back at him. The engine whined as we climbed the hill, and Barry pulled into a clear-cut driveway.

At first, I thought we had to be at the wrong place. I climbed out of the car, blinking uncertainly at the structure before us. It was nothing more than a plywood frame. Plastic sheeting flapped at the window openings, and there weren't even any shingles on the roof. Barry lit a cigarette and led us through the cardboard front door. Inside was a single room with green tape on the floor to mark the walls, bundles of wires strung through two-by-fours and pink insulation stuffed here and there. There was no kitchen other than a refrigerator and hot plate, and no bathroom at all. "There's a Porta-Potty out back. And running water and electricity. And a phone," Barry said quickly when he saw Mom's face. Then he waved his hand as if it were all just unfinished details.

"Don't worry, babe, I'll have it done in no time," he said, and then he pulled Mom close and stuck his tongue in her ear.

Mom giggled and hugged him back, and our fate was sealed.

EVEN IF OUR HOME wasn't perfect—after all, Mom and I were used to living in offbeat shelters—one thing seemed certain: Mom was happier than I'd seen her in a long time. She opened the cardboard door each day with a smile when I came home from school, and stuck to Barry like a shadow whenever he was around, especially at bedtime.

Bed. That was the worst part. My own mattress was just feet from theirs, which meant I had to spend almost every night with my head under my pillow.

"Mom," I said to her shyly one morning. "Um . . ."

"Yes, my love? What is it?"

"Um . . . it's just a bit . . . loud. At night, I mean. I can't really sleep . . ."

"Oh, honey, I'm sorry. But you know," she added with a wink, "those are the sounds of a happy mama. You should be glad for me."

"But I—"

"Cea!" She turned on me and grabbed my arm. I looked down at her hand in shock. "This is just how it is. Okay? How it needs to be. Come on. You're my strong girl from the wilderness. You should know better than to complain about such things." Her eyes held mine until I looked away. I was pretty sure of what she was trying to tell me: that no matter what the situation might be, we needed this man to survive. It was like Karl, only different.

"And besides," she continued. "You have a mother who—"

"Loves me," I finished for her. "And that's more than a lot of kids in the world have." It was a statement I had heard countless times in my life, but however true it might have been, it never made me feel any better.

And I still dreaded the nighttime.

BARRY HAD NEVER REALLY shown any interest in me, so I was surprised when he suddenly seemed to notice me on a day in early summer. I had been invited to a classmate's costume party, and decided to wear a long pink nightgown and go as a princess. Mom made me a cardboard crown, draped some beads around my neck and curled my hair into ringlets.

"You need a little makeup," she said, bringing her kit out from under her bed.

A few minutes later, I looked in the mirror and barely recognized myself. My lips were pink and my eyes were rimmed with blue liner. I looked much older than seven, and best of all I felt pretty.

Mom stepped outside and hollered for Barry, who was sitting

on a stump smoking while he waited for us to get ready. He walked into the house and stopped abruptly when he saw me.

"Wow," he said.

I smiled shyly, plucking at my sash.

"Doesn't she look amazing? And look at this," Mom said, holding up my hand to hers. She had even painted my fingernails. "We have the same hands. See that curved pinkie? That means she's going to enjoy sex as much as I do one—"

"Mom!" I could feel my face turning red.

"What? It's nothing to be embarrassed about, sweetheart. A palm reader told me that."

I felt like crying. Mom was running around, gathering up her purse and jacket. I glanced over at Barry, and he winked at me.

"Ready?" Mom asked, pushing us out the door. "Let's get going, we're already late." She hurried out to the car, and Barry and I followed.

I sat in the open back of the Ranchero with my crown in my lap and my hair whipping in the wind. All the way to the party, I could see Barry's eyes flicking to mine in the rearview mirror.

BY EARLY JULY, BARRY's house may have looked exactly the same, but his behavior toward me had changed completely. He talked to me at the dinner table, and even built me a tire swing on the hillside.

"We should go to the lake today," he said to Mom and me one Saturday morning, and I ran to the cardboard box beside my mattress to get my swimsuit. Ever since school had ended a few weeks before, I had been dreaming of going to the place all my classmates talked about. The island's biggest lake, though filled with green scum and giant leeches, was always packed on the weekends.

"What are you, afraid of leeches?" Barry asked me when we got there, lighting a cigarette behind his cupped hand. I was sitting on my towel with my arms wrapped around my knees, watching the other swimmers longingly.

"No. I can't swim."

"Can't swim? What are you, seven now? We'll have to fix that."

I glanced at Mom, who was lying on her back reading her astrology book. Her skin glistened from the baby oil she had just had Barry apply. He had done it in long, slow strokes, which Mom had told me was a sign that their sex life was right on track. I wished she wouldn't say that word in front of me when Barry was around. I felt his eyes on me and tugged self-consciously on my bikini bottom. Compared to Mom, I felt like a stick figure.

"Mom said I'd just learn one day. Just jump in and start floating, you know?"

Barry ground his cigarette butt into the sand and stood up. "Come on, let's go. I'll give you a lesson." He held his hand out to me, and I tried not to look at his privates, which were right at my eye level. Barry's swimsuit was shiny and tiny.

"Mom," I said loudly. "We're going into the water. Do you want to come?"

"No, sweetheart, I'm fine." She lowered her book onto her chest and smiled happily. "But you two have fun, okay? I'm so glad to see you getting along so well."

Barry turned out to be a pretty good teacher. By my fourth lesson, I could jump off the wharf by myself, tread water and kick my legs enough to make it back to shore. What Barry wanted to work on next, he said, were my strokes.

"Let's do the breast stroke first," Barry said as I stood shoulder-deep in the water.

I blushed a little at the word *breast*, but he didn't seem to notice. Standing behind me, he held my wrists and pushed my arms back and forth. "Here, like this—" I glanced at the beach, searching for Mom. She was lying on her tummy, absorbed in her book. "And kick your legs at the same time. Okay?"

"Sure." I nodded, wishing he would let go of me. I always felt a little squeamish when Barry touched me, and that wasn't the only thing. Right now, I could feel something long and hard pushing against my lower back. "I think I got it," I said.

"Good," Barry replied, finally letting my arms drop. I waited for him to pull away, but instead he wrapped his arms around my waist under the water. "You're a good girl, you know that?" he said quietly into my ear. "And a very pretty one too. Someday, you're going to have a beautiful figure to go with that face."

I could feel my cheeks turning red. It wasn't that I didn't like Barry's nice words, it was just that they felt different from the ones Karl used to say to me. Karl's had made my tummy feel kind of warm, while Barry's made it feel kind of . . . sick.

ALTHOUGH MOM HAD SAID when she and Karl split up that she was planning on finding my grandparents, she hadn't brought it up again since we'd moved in with Barry. I asked her about it one day, and she just flapped her hands at me and said she didn't know where to begin. But I could see there was more to it than that.

By late fall, Barry was arriving home later and later from work and forgetting to kiss her when he did. For me, it was a trade-off. I hated that Mom was unhappy, but the quiet nights made it almost worth it. When my head wasn't filled with the sounds of sex, I could think about other things. I wondered about my grandparents. I thought about my dad, who still wrote sometimes. I could read his letters on my own now, but they were always addressed to Mom and mostly went on about his boring job and his new wife. I scanned the pages quickly, looking for sentences with my name in them, then gave them back to Mom.

I felt alone. It had just been Mom and me lots of times before, but now it was different because even when she was right beside me, she felt a million miles away.

I LAY ON MY back, counting colored lights as Mom snored lightly across the room. Red, blue, green, yellow, red, blue, green, yellow. It was just before Christmas, and Mom had strung the lights around the house's bare support beams. We were going to skip the Christmas tree this year, she said. "You're eight now, right? Probably feeling too old for all that Santa stuff."

I rolled over onto my side, hugging Suzie Doll into my chest. There was something about Mom's words that made me mad, but it wasn't the fact that she'd said I was too old. I knew that Barry had said no to a tree, and Mom always did what her boyfriends wanted, whether I liked it or not.

I heard the *creak* of mattress springs from Mom's bed and held my breath, praying it wasn't Barry rolling on top of her. There was nothing in the world that I hated more than the sound of them having sex. Footsteps shuffled toward me, and I turned over to look.

Barry was standing beside my bed. He was naked, his wiener sticking out straight at my head like an arrow. His face glowed red in the lights. "I'll buy you a present," he whispered, taking my hand. "Anything you want."

All it took was a few strokes, and it was over. The next day, I found her on my pillow when I came home from school: silky blond hair, strawberry red lips and chopstick legs, all wrapped up in a gauzy pink dress. Barbie.

I DON'T KNOW HOW long it went on, but it wasn't more than a few months. Sometimes Barry wanted me to touch him, but other times he just wanted to stare at me. He would shine a flashlight up and down my naked body, and somehow that was even worse than the other stuff. Across the room, my mother slept. I wondered how she could not know, and if I even wanted her to.

One day, when Barry knew she was going to be out for a while, he had me get her makeup kit out and do my face. The eye shadow looked painted on and the lipstick looked lopsided, but Barry told me I was beautiful. In the end, that made it all worth it.

And then suddenly, it stopped. Barry and Mom started having sex again, and even though I would lie waiting afterward, he never came.

I woke up one night, gripped by the question of why Barry didn't like me anymore, and I decided to find out. I walked over to Barry and Mom's bed and stood looking down at them. I lifted the blanket and felt my way over Barry's hip. My hand landed on Mom's fingers.

I jerked back as if I'd been burned, Barry snorted, and Mom rolled over to face me.

"Watch it, Cea," she said. "That's my spot."

SO SHE KNEW.

Day after day, I waited for her to bring it up, but she just kept on cooking and smiling and sweeping the plywood floor as if nothing had changed.

I was taking a bath one evening in the galvanized laundry tub when I felt Barry's eyes on me. A little later he slipped outside for a cigarette, so I stepped out of the tub and quickly wrapped myself in a towel. Mom pulled it off my body and began drying my hair with it.

"Mom!" I said, snatching it back and glancing at the door. "What's wrong with you?"

Without warning, my eyes welled up with tears. "It—it's Barry. It's just, you know, he looks at me . . ."

"Cea." She shook her head. "You have a beautiful body. You shouldn't be ashamed—"

"Mom! I mean . . . he *looks* at me! And other stuff—"

"Stop it, Cea, just stop it. You're being ridiculous. It's natural for you to have urges, you shouldn't be ashamed—"

"Urges? *Urges?* I—" In a moment of understanding, I shook my head helplessly. My mother would never see the world the way other parents did, and I was on my own.

But there was still one thing I could do.

"OPERATOR, HOW MAY I help you?"

"Police," I said, swallowing hard. "I'd like to talk to the police."

This was my chance. It was a Friday after school, the house was empty, and I knew exactly what I was going to say. Ten minutes later, the island's only cop, known to all as Constable Dave, pulled into our driveway. I stepped aside to let him in and smiled weakly. He was tall, his eyes were kind, and the moment I saw him I knew I wouldn't be able to go through with it.

"What seems to be the problem, young lady?" he asked, and I dissolved into tears. They wouldn't stop. They streamed down my cheeks and dripped off my chin. I held my arm across my face to hide my eyes.

"Well, hey now," Constable Dave said softly, glancing around at the two-by-fours, wires and pink insulation that made up my home. "It's all right, okay? You can tell me anything. Where's your mother?"

"She's . . . I don't know," I sniffled, rubbing at my eyes. "At the hardware store, I guess. Or getting groceries. Her friend Sherrie takes her. Mom can't drive . . ." I tried to think up a reason for having brought the police all the way up here.

"Okay," he said, smiling and nodding. "Now, why don't you tell me why you called."

I wiped my sleeve across my nose, buying time, and finally took a deep breath. "There's, um . . . there's a man who's been following me." Instantly, Constable Dave's face turned hard. I swallowed. "After school. He pulled over in his car and asked me if I would touch his . . . his thing. I said no."

"Give me a description," Constable Dave said, whipping out his notepad. "And then we'll go find him."

It took him one hour, six checked houses and three changed descriptions to figure me out. After the last regretful homeowner closed the door behind us, Constable Dave settled into his cruiser and sighed deeply.

I looked at him, certain of what was coming next. "I'm sorry," I said, staring down at my hands. "I just . . ." I shrugged. "I don't know."

"Mm," he replied, nodding slowly. I had expected him to be furious, but he seemed perfectly calm. "So, tell me. How are things at home?"

"Home? Um . . . fine, I guess."

"Yes? So, no problems with your mother? Or her husband—"

"Boyfriend."

"Okay, boyfriend. No problems with him?"

I shook my head, feeling Constable Dave's eyes on the side of my face. He watched me for a moment, and then he reached forward and started the ignition. "All right, then. Let's get you home."

Mom was waiting for us when we pulled into the driveway. She rushed at the car, pulling my door open before we had even stopped. "Cea! Thank God! What happened?"

I let her hug me, listening with dread as I heard Constable Dave's door open. He took my mother aside and said a few words to her, then he tipped his hat at us and drove away. Mom stood in front of me with her arms crossed over her chest.

"How could you do such a thing?" she asked angrily. "Why?"

I scuffed my toe on the ground and didn't answer.

"Was it because of Barry?" she asked finally. I didn't respond. She stepped close to me and stroked my hair. "Sweetheart. There's no need to call the police, or anyone else. Okay? I won't let anything terrible happen to you. Besides, remember. We need Barry." She reached out to hug me. "And you have a mother who loves you, right? That's more than a lot of kids in the world have."

I tried to nod my head, but it quickly turned into a shake back and forth, back and forth, and my eyes flooded with tears for the second time that day. My mother was crazy, and there was nothing I could do about it. When I could finally talk again, I looked away from her when I spoke.

"I want to go and meet my dad."

Chapter Eighteen

U.M. stood for Unaccompanied Minor, according to the smiling stewardess who placed the blue and white pin on my T-shirt before walking me to Security. She was the nicest person I'd met here at Vancouver International Airport. The man at Customs looked like he was mad at me even before I opened my mouth, and now a line of uniformed men and women were blocking my way. It was June of 1978, I was eight years old, and I was finally going to meet my father—if I could just get past these people.

"You can go now," the stewardess said, nudging me from behind.

I stepped forward through a metal archway, and it beeped loudly.

The woman on the other side held her hand up like a stop sign. "Empty your pockets, please."

My heart thumped. I knew what was in one of them, and I was pretty sure this lady wasn't going to be very happy about it. I looked back at the stewardess, but she was deep in conversation with a man in an outfit that looked a lot like hers.

I reached into my pocket and pulled out Papa Dick's roach clip. The security woman took it from me and held it up as if it were a live worm. "Wait here," she said, and walked over to another officer. I watched their lips move silently as they stared at it. The man brought it up to his nose and sniffed it. The woman jerked her thumb toward me, and then walked back over to me.

"Where did you get this?" she asked.

"I . . ." I swallowed hard. "I made it."

"You *made* it?"

"Yes. I got some beads in my Christmas stocking, so I made it for my grandfather . . ."

"In your Christmas stocking," the woman repeated. She looked at the roach clip again, then she stepped closer to me and lowered her voice. "Young lady, do you know what this is?"

I nodded.

"You do?"

"Yes." I nodded again. "It's a roach clip."

She stared back at me. "And you know what it's used for."

"Of course. But it's never been used for that. He just . . . wore it on his belt loop. Like a decoration."

She was looking at me as if I had two heads. "Like a decoration. Uh-huh. I guess that could be possible. But young lady, there's no way I can allow you to keep this. Any items of a drug paraphernalia nature must be confiscated immediately."

Panic gripped me. I didn't even know what *confiscated* meant, but I knew it wasn't good. "But—but it's— It's *Papa Dick's roach clip*! I—"

"I'm sorry," she said. "Please lower your voice."

I glanced around in desperation. My stewardess was now standing near the conveyor belt, looking at me with a tight smile. "Is everything all right?" she asked.

"Yes," said the security lady, slipping my roach clip into a zip-lock bag. "She's all yours."

The stewardess stepped forward and took my hand. "Are you okay, dear?" she asked quietly as we walked away.

I nodded back to her, hoping she wouldn't notice that my eyes were about to overflow with tears. All I could think of was that meeting my dad better be worth giving up Papa Dick's roach clip.

THE PLANE BANKED LEFT and I pressed my face to the glass, looking down at the tiny buildings, cars and patches of green below. San Francisco. This was a real city, with skyscrapers and an impossibly long bridge disappearing into the fog in the distance. I could feel sweat gathering in my armpits.

A whining sound came from below—just the landing gear, a stewardess said when she saw my face—and ten minutes later, the plane touched down and pulled up to the gate. My heart was thudding so hard I could feel my pulse in my neck. I gathered my new coloring book and crayons, and the stewardess walked me into the arrivals area. I scanned the faces behind the ropes, praying I would recognize him. And there he was. Standing with a boxy hat on his head, smiling at me with front teeth that looked just like mine, a gap in the middle. He walked around the rope and stood in front of me.

"I'm Greg. I'm your father," he said, and I smiled back at him for the first and last time that whole visit.

IT WAS THE LONGEST week of my life. My father, who I insisted on calling Greg, was smart, funny and kind. He started each morning by making breakfast for me, and then he and his wife Karen would take me out to the park or library or lunch. And I spent the entire time hiding, petrified of having a conversation with him.

What if he didn't like me? What if he asked me a bunch of questions about Mom, or Barry, or even Karl? I stuck close to

My father and me in San Francisco, 1978. This is the first time I actually remember *meeting him.*

Karen's side like a smaller shadow, placing her between my father and me as we walked, sliding into restaurant booths beside her, and tagging after her to the bathroom whenever she went. She didn't seem to mind, smiling at me and offering to trim my hair to look more like hers. "I wasn't sure if I'd like you, but I do," she said to me once, and I felt like I'd won the lottery. My dad's wife wore blouses that buttoned all the way to the top, she never said swear words, and she didn't seem to think I was weird. I would have let her do whatever she wanted, just as long as she didn't leave me alone with my dad.

One afternoon, after Greg suggested we go out to the park, I ran to the car and got into the back seat. He slid behind the steering wheel, then twisted around and smiled at me. I realized with horror that Karen wasn't coming with us.

"Cea," he said gently, patting the front seat beside him. "Why don't you ride up here with me?" I sank down and crossed my arms silently. "I don't bite, sweetie, I promise." I flicked my eyes to his uncertainly. "In fact . . ." He lowered his chin and launched into a perfect Donald Duck voice. "You might even like me, Minnie Mouse."

I smiled a little, but then caught myself and turned to stare out the window. After a moment, Greg started the engine. All the way to the playground, I thought about what my life might be like if I lived with my dad and his wife. No tipis or tents, no crazy road trips, no pot, no sex right in front of me, no stupid boyfriend telling me to touch his wiener.

And . . . no Mom. No matter how great I thought my father was, even the thought of life without my mother felt like a betrayal to her. And maybe, if my dad liked me too much, he would take me away from her forever.

When we got to the park, I launched myself from the car and bolted for the swing set. Greg came over and tried to push me, but I jumped off and ran away and headed over to the slide to play by myself.

CERTAINLY, MY FATHER TRIED his best with me. At the end of the week, after I bid Karen goodbye, Greg led me to the car and opened the passenger door with a hopeful smile. I hesitated, filled with dread, and then climbed in for the drive back to the airport. The whole way there, I leaned against my door, staring out the side window. Beside me, Greg chatted to the air for a while and then finally fell silent. Eventually I saw a sign for the airport, and relief swept over me.

"Well," Greg said, pulling off the highway. "I'm glad you came. And I . . . hope it wasn't too uncomfortable for you."

I shrugged. "Nah, it was fine."

"Good. I'm . . . not sure when we'll see each other again. If there's, you know, anything you wanted to ask me . . . or tell me . . . you can feel free to. What with all the stuff we had planned this week, we didn't get much of a chance to talk."

I kept my eyes on the passing scenery.

"Cea? Did you hear me, sweetie?"

"Yeah. There's nothing."

"Okay." He slid his hands up the steering wheel. "How . . . how are things with your mom?"

"Good."

"Okay. Well—"

"I like it here," I cut in, feeling like I needed to at least say something. "The city, I mean. I'd like to live in a city someday."

"Yes. Well, it suits you. Much more than the wilderness does, I think. It was always hard for me to picture you there."

"Yeah, well, we don't live there anymore. And I'm not sure if we will again. Mom . . . she's with Barry now."

I clamped my jaws shut, wishing I hadn't said his name, but I needn't have worried. We were already pulling into the airport parking lot, and Greg was leaning out his window to get a ticket from the machine.

Twenty minutes later, he placed my knapsack on my back and

gave me a hug goodbye. I waved at him as the stewardess led me away, and then wiped at my eyes as soon as he was out of sight. My dad was so nice and cool and perfect that I never wanted to see him again.

WHEN I GOT BACK from visiting my father in late June, Mom had some news for me: she and Barry were breaking up. When she told me, I sank down on my mattress and looked around the room. We had lived in this house for a year, and Barry hadn't worked on it for more than a handful of days. If anything, it was even worse now than when we had moved in. The refrigerator was broken, replaced by two plastic coolers, and the green tape on the floor that marked the walls had been scuffed away long ago. Even the Porta-Potty was gone, leaving us to do our business in the trees behind the house. All the same, it was home. All I wanted to know was where we would go.

Mom covered her face and started to cry. "I don't know," she said. "Barry said we could stay here until we figure something out."

I nodded, but when she reached to put her arms around me, I moved away from her.

Chapter Nineteen

Somehow, my mother and I always managed to land on our feet. Two weeks after I got back from visiting my dad, Mom came running into the house with a letter in her hand. She waved it at me, barely able to contain her excitement.

"It's from Mom and Dad! They've found us!" she cried, ripping it open.

I hurried to her side as a check floated to the ground. I read the number: *$150*. Mom opened the letter and ran her fingertip over Papa Dick's handwriting as she read.

". . . got a letter at our old P.O. Box in Morley. Phil Mesker still works there and forwarded it to us . . . I guess things didn't work out with Karl . . . living in the Yukon now, just east of Carcross . . . beautiful tipi site on Lake Tagish . . . not much money but hopefully enough to buy you two bus tickets north . . ."

Mom stopped and gazed into the distance.

"What? What is it?"

"Nothing, just . . . I didn't write to them. I wonder who . . ." Her voice trailed off. "'. . . things didn't work out with Karl.' Oh my God. Karl must have sent them a letter. I guess he just . . . took a chance and sent it to the old P.O. Box. I can't believe I never thought to try that. Too obvious, I guess." Carefully, she refolded the paper and tucked it into the envelope. "Okay," she said decisively. "We have a plan. I'll write and let them know we're coming, then we'll pack up and get out of here in a few days."

I jumped up and down excitedly. Suddenly, none of it mattered—Barry, my dad, or even Mom's weirdness. We were going home, wherever that was, and things were going to be okay. "Really? We're going to see Grandma Jeanne and Papa Dick?"

"Yes!" Mom laughed and hugged me, but then her smile faded. "One thing, though. That money they sent us? We're going to need it for food and stuff. We'll need to find another way to get up there."

My heart sank. "Like how?"

"Like . . ." She thought for a moment, then snapped her fingers. "Like hitchhiking! It's free and it's easy, and we can be on our own schedule. It'll be a fun adventure!"

Later that night, I read the letter in more detail. Papa Dick had written a lot of stuff about their new home—how they had discovered it on a canoe trip, the scenery surrounding their camp, the freezing winters, their recent purchase of a snow sled and two husky dogs, and even some history, like how the Yukon had once been home to gold prospectors but was now known more for its hard-drinking native population.

I read all the way to my grandfather's name at the end, and it was then that I realized he hadn't asked a single thing about where my mother and I had been for all these years. It was as if, in the time we had been away, we hadn't even existed.

THE MOON WAS IN Sagittarius on the day my mother and I left the island, which she said was perfect for travel and new beginnings. The last time I remember seeing Barry was the night before we left. He was sitting at the kitchen table, smoking a cigarette and listening to the Doobie Brothers on his ghetto blaster. Mom said he offered to drive us to the ferry, but then he left early for work the next morning and never came back to pick us up. She and I waited outside with our bags, and then she went back into the unfinished house one last time to call Sherrie for a lift.

After saying goodbye to Sherrie, Mom and I put our backpacks on and made our way to the ferry's passenger entrance. Just as we were about to board, I looked across the water and saw a familiar man sitting on a bench at the end of the pier. It was Karl. There was a woman beside him, and he was gazing down at a pink bundle in his arms.

"Look," I said, tugging on Mom's sleeve. "It's Karl."

"Wow," Mom said, inhaling sharply. "That must be his new wife."

"Wife?" I asked, shocked. It had never occurred to me that Karl might find another woman after Mom.

"Yeah. And they had a baby, I guess I forgot to tell you. That must be it right there. Looks like they had a girl."

Married? A baby girl? I felt a sharp stab of jealousy. "Should . . . should we say hi?" I asked.

Mom shook her head. "I don't think so. I don't think he wants anything to do with his past. Last I heard, he even changed his name."

As I stood staring at him, Karl suddenly looked up and saw us. He lifted his chin a little bit, and then his face broke into a smile.

Mom nudged me from behind. "Let's go," she said, her voice a whisper.

AFTER OUR FERRY DOCKED in Vancouver, Mom and I walked out to the highway to begin the sixteen-hundred-mile journey to

Carcross. Mom figured it would take two days, three tops, as there weren't many people who could pass by the sight of a mother and daughter standing at the side of the road.

The first half of the trip went without a hitch. As Mom had predicted, we caught rides easily with nice people who made small talk and shared their lunches with us. Other hitchhikers were kind. Competition for rides was sometimes fierce, but the other travelers were either backpack-laden young singles or couples, so they would happily wave us over in the direction of a braking car. At night, after snacking on our supply of fruit and granola, we would unroll our sleeping bags and sleep in the trees by the side of the road.

One time, on a particularly scorching day after we were dropped off, Mom decided to head to the town center in search of water. We trudged past gas stations and fast-food joints, but she still didn't stop.

"Mom, where are we going?" I asked, dragging my feet in the heat.

"Just follow me. You'll see." Several minutes later, she stopped in front of a tiny bookstore. I gazed in the window longingly at the display of children's books. "It's been a while since you've had a new book," she said, "and I know how you love to read."

"Really?"

"Yes." She smiled, taking my hand and pulling me inside. "Pick one out. Whatever you want."

I took forever, hemming and hawing as I flipped through each book and read the back covers, finally settling on a thick chapter book about a girl who travels to Alaska with her family. We walked back to the highway, and I sat down on the gravel shoulder to read while we waited for a ride. Mom rummaged through her knapsack and finally pulled out an apple and a plastic bag with a handful of crumbly granola in one corner.

"I'm hungry," I said offhandedly.

She blinked, and then held the food out to me. "Here you go, sweetie."

"Thanks." I took it and settled back on my pack. Beside me, my mother was still.

I understood then that she had spent her very last dollar on that book for me. I ate half the apple and then pretended to be full, handing it back to her along with the granola. Mom and I were in this together.

In the end, I didn't even like the book I picked out, but I forced myself to read it and tell her how much I loved it so she would know it had been worth the sacrifice.

ON THE THIRD DAY, our luck changed. Our ride dropped us off on a lonely strip of highway between Prince George and Dease Lake, where the evergreen-speckled landscape rolled out flat from the road to distant hills. Only two vehicles passed within an hour, each of their drivers shrugging apologetically as they gestured at their full back seats. Mom and I sat on our packs, reading our books and batting at tiny black flies as we waited.

I was the first to see the car coming. It was long and blue with a busted-out headlight, and it looked empty other than its driver. I grabbed Mom's arm and pointed.

"Let's hope for the best," she said, and stood up. She stuck out her thumb, but the car didn't stop.

I saw the driver's face turn toward us as he passed by, and I was suddenly glad he hadn't. He was very thin, with a receding hairline and a hooked nose. He looked like a vulture. I turned to say something to Mom about him, and then I saw his brake lights go on.

"He's stopping!" Mom said, grabbing her pack. "Let's go!"

I picked up my bag and followed her. Mom pulled open the passenger door and said something, then chucked her pack onto the back seat. "He's going our way," she said to me happily over her shoulder. "Come on, get in."

Mom slid in and waved at the back seat, but I squeezed in beside her instead. The man pulled back onto the highway and snapped the stereo on. Loud heavy metal music filled the car. "Do you mind?" Mom said to him with a smile, reaching out to adjust the volume. "Just a little."

The man shrugged and flipped his visor down, then took a joint out from behind an elastic band. "You up for a j?" he asked Mom, pushing the lighter into the dashboard.

I stared at the air freshener swinging from the rearview mirror, praying she would say no.

"Not just now," she said, smiling again. "But thanks. So do you . . . live around here?"

The man laughed, showing us a mouthful of yellow teeth. "Not exactly," he replied.

"Ah." Mom joined me in gazing at the air freshener.

The man lit his joint and inhaled.

"So. What's the likes of a gal like you doing out here on a lonely road?" he asked finally.

"Going to see my parents. They live in the Yukon."

"Is that so. Leaving your man, then, are you?" He laughed again, and Mom blushed.

"No, I just . . . I wanted to take my daughter to see them," she replied, waving a hand at me.

The man reached out and turned the music off. Telephone poles snapped by in a blur. I glanced sideways at him. He had a grin on his face but it didn't look the least bit friendly. Worse than that, I noticed something that made my stomach drop:

around his right calf was a leather strap with a knife handle sticking out of it.

The man let his right hand drop down to the seat, and then he slid it up Mom's thigh. Mom reached down and carefully removed it. He put it back on her leg again. She stared straight ahead. I swallowed hard.

"Gas ain't cheap, you know," the man said. "How about a little payback?"

"I, uh, that's not—"

"Come *on*, lady," he said forcefully. He was grabbing at her crotch now, rubbing it through her jeans. She looked scared.

"Look, my daughter is here, can't we just—"

"Get a room or something? No, I don't think so. Look around, lady, there's nothing around here for miles."

My stomach went liquid with fear. He was right. We hadn't even seen a gas station since long before our last ride had dropped us off, and that driver had told us we wouldn't for quite some time yet.

"Well no, just—"

"Mommy," I cut in loudly, "I have to go to the bathroom. Really bad. Number two."

"Listen," Mom said to the man. "Can we just . . . she can go in the bushes, okay? She's just a kid. I'm sure you don't want her to have an accident on your seat."

"Goddamn it," he said, hitting the brakes. "Make it fast."

"I will," I replied quickly, my tummy already settling a bit as the passing scenery began to slow down.

He pulled over to the side of the road, and I opened the door before the car had even stopped. "Be right back," I yelled. As I made a run for the bushes, I heard a noise behind me. I turned to look.

Mom was standing outside the car with the back door open, trying to haul our packs out. The man yelled something and hit the gas just as she pulled them clear. The car weaved away from us with the back door still hanging open. Mom slumped down by the side of the road, watching as it drove away.

I zipped up my pants and ran over to join her.

"Holy shit," she said breathlessly. "Holy *shit.* That was close."

"Why was that man so weird?" I looked down the highway, suddenly scared again. "He's not going to come back, is he?"

"No, honey, I don't think so." She put her head down on her arms and took a few deep breaths. "Thank God you had to go to the bathroom."

"Yeah. I had to go really bad."

Mom smiled up at me. "Your grandfather is going to love this story. He always did say how important poop was."

"Yeah," I chimed in boldly. "Saved from the asshole by the shit!"

Mom started to giggle and I joined in, and we didn't stop laughing until our stomachs hurt and tears were streaming down our faces.

My mother and I never knew how close we might have come to our end that day. Years later, this road would become known as the Highway of Tears, named for eighteen women who went missing from the area around the time we hitchhiked it.

Chapter Twenty

After years of longing for the sight of my grandparents and wondering where they might be, strangely enough I have no recollection of my reunion with them, other than walking up the trail to their tipi with a fluttery feeling in my chest.

My mother and me on the shore of Lake Tagish in the Yukon Territory, the location of my grandparents' third tipi camp.

Their new campsite was nothing like the ones in the Kootenay Plains or Morley. In the past we had lived peacefully side by side with the natives, but here my grandparents were squatting on Indian land and could only hope they wouldn't be discovered. Papa Dick had tried to meet with the tribe to obtain their blessing, but the chief told him that if they ever found a white man living on their territory, they'd torch his home to the ground with no questions asked. Papa Dick nodded understandingly and decided to say nothing about his intentions.

With the chief's warning in mind, my grandparents had picked a small, protected cove five miles by foot or canoe from the nearest road. Papa Dick continued to host the same courses as in the Kootenay Plains, kept the canoes out in plain sight, and even built a twenty-foot pier off their shore. Mom and I arrived in mid-August, so counting two of my grandfather's pupils, there were just six of us. When the pupils left, I assumed I would have my mother almost all to myself for an entire winter. It was a thought that filled me with both happiness and dread.

AS IT TURNED OUT, less than two weeks after we arrived at my grandparents' camp, Mom announced she would be leaving me. We were in the tipi, eating stewed prunes and yogurt beside the morning fire. My grandparents, forever busy with preparations for the upcoming winter, were outside chopping wood.

"I have to tell you something," she said, looking down at her bowl. "I, um . . . I have to go away for a while."

I dropped my spoon on the floor. When I bent to pick it up, it was covered in dried fir needles. "But . . . why? Where?"

"I'm going to the city. To Calgary," she said, finally meeting my eyes. "Mom and Dad have some friends there who've offered to put me up. I'll have a place to stay, and well . . . there's just no future for me in the wilderness, sweetheart. I love it here, but . . . hey, don't cry." She put her arm around me and pulled my head to her chest. "It's only for a little while. I've already talked to Mom and Dad about it, and they're going to drive you down to meet me when I'm ready. By then I'll have a job, and a place for us to live . . ."

"But why can't I just go with you now?"

"Because, honey, I just . . . I need to do this on my own. I don't have any money, and you would be miserable living in a new place with a broke mother, and no one to look after you while I work. You'll be safe here. Papa Dick and Grandma Jeanne . . . they'll take care of you."

"What about school?"

"I've already looked into it. You can do home schooling. Dad goes into town once a month anyway, so he can mail your assignments in." She shook her head, gazing into the distance. "It's just . . . you'll understand this when you're older, but there's no way for me to ever meet a man out here. And I'm the kind of woman who, I don't know, doesn't seem to do very well on her own."

I took a deep breath. "When will I see you again?"

"Next spring," she said quietly. "Less than a year."

I nodded resignedly. As much as I wanted to be enough for my mother, I knew I never would be.

IN THE BEGINNING, THINGS between my grandparents were as I remembered. They laughed together, dragged me along to folksy towns like Faro and Juneau for music festivals, and Papa Dick sometimes fondled his wife's naked breast as she sat washing dishes. Their familiar togetherness made my return to the wilderness feel effortless and comforting, much like the handmade moccasins Grandma

Jeanne slipped onto my feet when I arrived. Here, I was confident. I slept alone in a pup tent a hundred feet from my grandparents' tipi, and though I often heard animals thrashing nearby at night, I never ran to Papa Dick for help. I spotted bears regularly and was once rushed by a porcupine, but even they couldn't frighten me. My days were filled with the familiar routine of camp tasks. With my third-grade school lessons usually wrapped up before noon, I had plenty of time to fish with Papa Dick, work on target practice with his .22 rifle, shoot my bow and arrow at small game, haul water or ice and help Grandma Jeanne with the baking or cleaning.

But in the fall, I began to see a change between my grandparents. Their easy banter turned to long stretches of silence. Grandma Jeanne complained of migraines and spent hours lying inside the tipi. When she was up and about, she did her chores with deep frown lines between her eyes and avoided Papa Dick's gaze.

One weekend, she took me to a festival without him. I set up my own stand and sold earrings I'd made out of porcupine quills and beads, and used the money to buy molasses candies, my first taste of sugar in months. On our second night there, we sat on a sleeping bag listening to Valdy under the stars. Grandma Jeanne reached into her knapsack, pulled out a hard apple cider, took a swig and then handed it to me. I took a small sip and was surprised by its fizzy sweetness. I had never seen either of my grandparents drink alcohol before, because Papa Dick didn't approve of its high sugar content. But tonight, Grandma Jeanne didn't seem to care. While Valdy strummed "The Simple Life" on stage, she handed me her half-empty bottle and opened a new one. I tipped mine back and felt the liquid hit my belly, spreading warmly out to my limbs. Pot smoke wafted through the air. Long-haired, tie-dyed couples laughed in the darkness around me.

"Wow. Isn't this great?" Grandma Jeanne sighed to me happily. It was the most relaxed I had seen her in ages.

I emptied my bottle and put it on the ground beside me. My tummy felt funny, but not as funny as my head. My thoughts seemed to be coming in slow motion.

"Yeah," I said carefully around the fuzz in my brain. "But it would be even greater if Papa Dick were here. Right?"

Grandma Jeanne didn't respond, so I looked over at her. Her head was thrown back and her eyes were closed. I realized then that I didn't want her to answer.

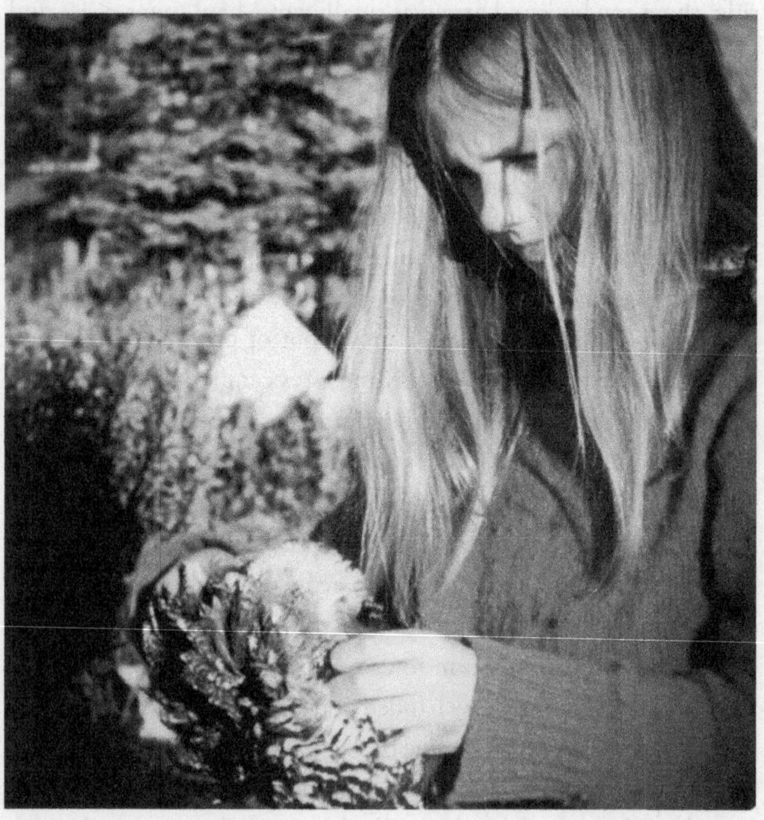

Me in the Yukon in 1978, skinning a grouse I'd killed with my bow and arrow.

Shortly afterward, I fell asleep. When I woke up, Grandma Jeanne was snoozing at my side. Bleary-eyed, I stumbled a few feet away from the sleeping bag and threw up. I cursed the burning in my throat, but as I lay back down, I couldn't help thinking about that pleasant, loose feeling I had had in my head.

DESPITE MY GRANDFATHER'S OUTSPOKEN condemnation of all things material and/or consumerist, he actually took his career very seriously. As he and Grandma Jeanne's relationship continued to deteriorate, he began going into town more and more often to promote his business. One time, he even came home with a small box of printed business cards: *Dick Person's Wild and Woolly Wilderness Thrival Courses*, it said above his P.O. Box address. Word about his enterprise was spreading, and he was even starting to get invitations from around North America to give lectures on his lifestyle. And the visitors, of course, kept coming. Papa Dick always told them in advance to get ready for their very first taste of the real world, and to leave their modesty at home along with their city shoes. For the most part, the visitors adhered to his wishes. Anyone who expected privacy at the shit pit, sugar in their morning coffee or to wear a swimsuit in the lake got over their illusions pretty quickly after a few days at our camp.

We had one visitor, a young man named Mark, who fascinated me simply because he came from New York City. He had long, shaggy hair and wore a hunting knife on his belt just like the other male visitors, but his banker's hands were clean and unscarred. I would tag after him relentlessly, peppering him with questions about his hometown, which might explain why one day he threw rocks into the bushes to try to convince me a bear was nearby. I knew better than to be afraid, but as the thrashing behind me increased and Mark screamed out that we were being chased, I gave in to my terror and tore down the mountainside into camp, screaming at the top of my lungs. When Papa Dick discovered what had happened, he nearly sent Mark packing on the spot. I had never seen my grandfather so angry. Such practical jokes might be funny in the big city, he said to Mark harshly, but allowing fear to overcome you out here in the wilderness could be your undoing.

"MUSH!" I YELLED, AND the dogs pulled. The husky in the rear nipped at his mate's heels, and the sled gained speed. The wind pulled at my parka and snowflakes stung my face. I could barely hear above the snow being crushed under the sled rails, but for this, my eyes were more important than my ears. Two hundred feet ahead of me, Papa Dick was breaking the trail with his snowshoes across the frozen lake. This was usually my job, but occasionally my grandfather let me run the sled, as he had on this trip into town today.

We rounded the point and headed toward the middle of the lake, which was basically a straight five-mile shot to Carcross.

I pulled my hood around my face and hunkered down behind the sled, trying to escape the wind. It was minus forty Celsius, and God only knew how much colder with the wind chill. I had three pairs of long underwear on under my ski pants, and four layers under my parka.

Up ahead, Papa Dick halted in his tracks, looking off to the shore on our right. "Stop!" he yelled, holding up a hand, and I hit the brake. He jogged over to the shore in his snowshoes, something I hadn't yet mastered, then motioned for me to follow with the sled. When I reached the treeline, I saw what had caught his attention. There, still alive but lying bleeding in the snow, was a female moose.

"Goddamn it," my grandfather said under his breath, reaching under the tarp for his rifle. "Damn it all to hell. Damn hunters." We walked over to the animal. She stared at us, her visible eye crazy with fear, and Papa Dick shook his head. "I'm sorry, dear lady," he said softly, and pulled the trigger. Blood splattered across the snow behind her. Papa Dick knelt down and touched his forehead to her shoulder, whispering something. Then he took out his hunting knife, slit her belly, let the blood drain into a cup and drank it. "Change of plans," he said to me, wiping his hand across his mouth. "You're going to have to help me get this back to camp. And quickly, before someone spots her and pins it on me."

I nodded and fetched the axe from the sled, mentally preparing for the grisly work ahead. The two dogs yelped and nipped at each other's heels, impatient to be on their way. I watched as Papa Dick skinned the hide off the moose. Once the animal was quartered, I helped him load the pieces, including the head, onto the sled. I knew that this was just the beginning of the long process of turning every part of the animal into something useful, and that Papa Dick would give most of the meat away. We had no need of this animal. After so many years in the bush, my grandparents were always well prepared for winter with plenty of food. But, just as my grandfather would never shoot a female animal or one out of season, he believed that letting one suffer or go to waste was just as bad. It was one of the many traits I admired about him, although my admiration competed fiercely with my frustrations with him.

If Papa Dick was the same man I had left behind three years before, I was a much different girl from the five-year-old he remembered. As he did with his pupils, he expected me to conform to his beliefs. So, to keep the peace around him, I pretended to hate the taste of sugar and disapprove of city life, and I kept my Barbie doll hidden. There *were* moments of genuine harmony between us, usually centered around a task that required focus, like hunting, or a cooperative effort toward survival. One time in the fall, he and I had returned late from a trip to town and got caught in a thunderstorm. The waves were high enough to crash into our canoe, rocking it so ferociously I could tell that even Papa Dick, so rarely rattled by the forces of nature, was nervous. I paddled with all my strength, ignoring the exhaustion and sharp pains in my back and shoulders, while he bailed water from the stern and shouted commands above the din of the storm. When we pulled the canoe up to the shore an hour later, weary and soaked through, I knew he was proud of me.

But my desire to please my grandfather was equaled by my growing modesty and annoyance at his preoccupation with people not showing or experiencing fear. One morning, I sat on a mat in my underwear, ready for the yoga routine he had insisted I join him for, when he came into the tipi and looked down at me disapprovingly.

"Cea. Don't you know that wearing clothing while doing yoga constricts your energy? Please. Take those things off."

"I'd rather not," I said.

He shook his head. "That makes me sad, Cea, very sad. You're living in fear of your own body. I guess all that time away in the city has corrupted your innocence."

Fear of my own body? All that time in city? Not only was he completely wrong on both points, I suddenly realized that he hadn't asked me once where I had been or what I had done during our years away. I waited until he had settled into lotus pose, and then I spoke.

"Papa Dick," I said quietly. "Don't you ever wonder where Mom and I were all those years?"

He didn't even open his eyes. "Peanut," he replied, using a nickname I hadn't heard since I was a toddler, "you know such things don't concern me. You're here right now, which means wherever you were doesn't really matter. You need to learn to move on from the past, Cea, and embrace the present instead. Any other choice is one made in fear. Now, please, take off that ridiculous underwear. Seeing you covered up like that just breaks my heart."

As I stood and slipped my underwear down my hips, all I could think about was Barry. Though my grandfather's intentions may have been nothing like his, the result wasn't any less humiliating. But I was beginning to understand that against my grandfather, there was simply no winning.

Chapter Twenty-One

Near the end of winter, my grandparents received a letter from my Uncle Dane. I was with Papa Dick when he pulled it out of the mailbox, his smile slipping as he read the return address. He tucked the envelope into his vest pocket, and didn't look at it again until hours later when we were back at the tipi. Meanwhile, my mind whirled with questions that I didn't dare ask: Was my uncle still in the mental hospital? How often did my grandparents hear from him? Would they ever let him visit here? I prayed not.

That evening, Papa Dick read the letter silently to himself and refolded it. Then he went outside for some wood and started stoking the fire in the stove.

"We should probably go see Dane," he said to Grandma Jeanne.

She stopped whistling, something she seemed to do more of when she was feeling blue than when she was happy, and put down the pot she was drying. "How come?"

Papa Dick held up the envelope. "Got a letter from him today. He's talking about reintegration again, and asking for money. I suppose we should drive down and talk to his doctors, see what the real story is. Leave before the next snow flies."

"It's February. That could be any day."

"Yes," Papa Dick said. "But it's clear right now. We best leave within the week."

THE DRIVE SOUTH TO see my Uncle Dane took two days, two nights, one Nancy Drew book, and six gas station stops to refill Grandma Jeanne's ice pack. I had never seen her so miserable. She lay in the makeshift bed at the back of the VW bus for almost the entire trip, complaining of a migraine, a cold pack draped across her forehead. Papa Dick was almost as silent, driving with a grim face and serving up mushy bananas and cold caribou meat for dinner. It was almost a relief when we pulled through the gates of the hospital.

Alberta's Ponoka mental health facility, my uncle's home for the past eight years, didn't look quite as scary as I had imagined. I had pictured ten-foot barbed wire fences and barred windows, much like a prison, but in actual fact it looked a lot like the hospital Karl had stayed at in Nanaimo. That all changed, though, when we passed through the front doors. We were greeted at the entrance by a security guard, who led us through a metal detector—just one more tool designed to control the population and force them to embrace the unnatural state of urban living, Papa Dick muttered as he removed his hunting knife from his belt. I watched the other patients roaming the hallways as we walked into the main building. A few of them looked like anyone you might see in town, but several were rambling on to themselves in loud voices, and one man was standing in a corner hiding something in his hand. He asked me as I walked by if I wanted to pet his mouse, but his hand was empty. A nurse quietly took him by the elbow and led him away. We reached Dane's room and crowded inside to wait for him.

It had been four years since I'd seen my uncle, but until he appeared before me that day, I had thought I could recall his face. I was wrong. He looked nothing like I remembered. He was about twenty pounds thinner, and looked to be about two inches shorter. Nearly all of his hair was gone, although from natural or intentional causes I couldn't tell. He had a set of aspirin-white dentures in his mouth that clacked together when he said hello. He entered the room and sat on his bed. Then he reached into his mouth, pulled out his dentures and placed them on his bedside table. His lips sank in, and he looked a little more familiar.

Papa Dick took his hat off and smoothed his hair down, staring out the window. Grandma Jeanne stepped forward and hugged her son. "Dane. It's so good to see you. Do you remember Cea? Your niece," she added, gesturing toward me. It was the most she had said in days.

Dane glanced up at me and shook his head. Relief swept over me.

"Don't remember," he replied, and switched his gaze to Papa Dick. "Did you talk to Dr. Rose? He'll tell you. Tell you I'm better."

"Not yet." My grandfather sat down in the room's only chair and placed his hat on his lap. "I wanted to talk to you first."

Dane smiled, causing his mouth to cave in even more. "I'm doin' good. Stayin' on my meds. When I hear the voices now, I tell them Dane's the boss. They have to go away and be quiet, because Dane's the boss. Dr. Rose—he said I had a breakthrough. Didn't want to talk, talk about anything, but now I do. Told him about little Dane. Little Dane who lived with his family, told jokes, went fishing, went to school, new one almost every year. And older Dane, afraid of aliens, naked in the snow, LSD, and Crazy Debbie, my first love who went to bed with my father."

Dane fell silent, his final statement hanging uncomfortably in the air. I had no idea what he was talking about, but Papa Dick seemed to. His face dropped a little, and he stole a sideways glance at Grandma Jeanne.

"All right, Dane." Papa Dick sighed heavily. "I'll have a word with your doctor. I can give you a little money, but not much. Not enough to live on."

"Doctor says I can get a job. Live in a shelter, go out in the day."

"I'll talk to him," Papa Dick said again.

I looked at my grandmother. She was sitting on the edge of the bed, wiping at her eyes.

Dane nodded and stood. With jerky movements, he walked to his closet and reached up to the top shelf. From there, he took down a photograph and studied it carefully.

"This girl, she reminds me of you," he said, and it took me a moment to register that he was speaking to me. "Can't remember her name." He held the picture out to me, and I took it.

It was of me, taken at the camp in Morley when I was about five. I was running toward the camera with my braids flying out behind me.

"Have you met her? It's such a sad story. Her real mother died, you know. She died in a fire."

BACK IN THE VAN, no one spoke. Grandma Jeanne lay down on her bed again, and Papa Dick started up the engine.

"Papa Dick," I said finally, after practicing the question in my mind several times. "Why doesn't Dane have any teeth?"

My grandfather tightened his grip on the steering wheel and stayed silent so long I wondered if he'd heard me. When he finally spoke, his voice was so quiet that I had to strain to hear it over the roar of the engine.

"He pulled them all out," he said.

Chapter Twenty-Two

During the year I lived with my grandparents, I heard from Mom about five times. Her letters were always full of clipped comic strips and Sagittarius horoscopes folded into notes she'd scribbled on grocery list paper, newsy bits and pieces about her life in the city: her new waitressing job at a health-food restaurant, a groovy party she'd gone to on the weekend, a cute guy who'd bought her a drink at a bar.

By April she was still living with friends, and I was beginning to get concerned. My grandparents were supposed to return me to her in just three months, and I wondered if she would be ready for me. The truth was, the thought of moving to the city scared me, even if I also didn't want to stay where I was. While comfort and familiarity lived in the wilderness, I knew that my future and my dreams—if I could make them happen—lived in the city.

So when Papa Dick returned from town one day in late spring with a letter from Mom, I snatched it from him eagerly, stuffed my Barbie doll into my pocket and went down to the lake by myself.

Stepping onto the ice, I ran a few steps and slid sideways, watching a cloud of mist plume into the air as I exhaled. The first signs of the warmer season were just emerging. Glancing up at the mountains surrounding our camp, I noticed a few patches of gray rock showing through the snow. We had yet to hear the loud cracking of the ice on the lake breaking up, but Papa Dick had warned me not to go too far out. "Everything could change in a day at this time of year," he often said to me.

Settling down on the ice, I unfolded the pages and began to read. Mom had a new job that paid a dollar an hour more, she wrote. She wanted to revamp her look a bit, so a friend had given her a home perm and a huge pile of old *Cosmopolitan* magazines. She had found us a place to live, a basement suite in someone's house.

Just as I was breathing a sigh of relief over this news, my gaze stopped on a word halfway down the page: *Barry*. My jaw dropped open. No. It couldn't be. But there it was, written in my mother's childish scrawl. He had driven to Calgary to find her, and they were back together. Could I possibly find it in my heart to be happy for her?

Tears sprang to my eyes. I crumpled the letter in my hand. Then I pulled my Barbie doll from my pocket and pressed her to my forehead. Barry. I wanted to scream. I pitched the letter furiously across the ice, and that's when I heard it crack.

Oh shit. I froze in place, gripped by panic. What had Papa Dick told me to do if this ever happened? Right, lie down flat and slide along the ice like a snake. I grabbed Barbie to stuff her back into my pocket, and that's when the ice broke. I plunged through knees first, the freezing water knocking the breath out of me. My head slipped below the surface and I kicked my legs until I reemerged, coughing wildly. Then I flailed my arms out, found a solid edge of ice and clawed my way forward, screaming for my grandparents. I waited, scanning the snowy shore, but I already knew it was hopeless. Papa Dick had chopped the ice and brought it up to the tipi that morning so Grandma Jeanne could heat it on the stove for water, so there was no reason for either of them to come down to the lake.

The current sucked at my legs. I had a sudden vision of myself being pulled under the ice, a dark shadow beneath the surface trying to break my way through. This had happened to Papa Dick once, and his friend had had to rescue him by chopping through the ice.

Maybe if I were lighter, I thought. Yes, I was too heavy with all these soaking-wet clothes on. Holding the ice shelf with one hand, I reached down into the water, pulled the laces on my Ski-Doo boots and kicked them off. Then I felt for my coat's zipper tab under my chin and worked it down until it was halfway open. The coat dropped around my hips and floated at my waist. I took a deep breath and threw myself forward once more. The ice held for a moment, and then crumbled beneath me again.

My body was turning numb. I knew I had to think, and think fast. But it was as if my brain were as frozen as my skin. How long had Papa Dick said it took for hypothermia to set in? For frostbite to begin? Until the body shut down completely? These were some of the facts he rambled on about every day, and now, when I needed them the most, I couldn't remember a thing.

I tried to focus. What had I been doing before the ice broke? Oh yes, the letter from Mom. Something about a new place to live and a home perm. And Barry. Barry, with his big reward to me for masturbating him. Of course.

I reached into the water with numb hands, and eventually managed to pull Barbie from the pocket of the parka floating at my waist. She was as soaked as I was, but her feet were bare and pointy. Sharp, almost like a pick. The problem was my hands, which were now too weak to form a grip. I thought for a moment, and then I stuck the fingers of my right hand into my mouth. Even my tongue was cold, but after exhaling forcefully many times, I felt my skin warm up a little. I put my hand under my armpit, which still held the slightest bit of warmth, and repeated the same with my left hand. Then I flexed my fingers, grasped my Barbie doll with both hands, reached my arms as far across the lake surface as I could, and plunged her feet first into the ice.

"LOOK AT ME, CEA!"

I opened my eyes. Frozen shards of hair were prickling at my neck. I turned my head, and they snapped off like dried spaghetti.

"*Cea!* Look at me."

Slowly, he came into focus. Wooly red cap, blue eyes and bushy beard. Papa Dick. He was on his belly inching toward me. My upper body was sprawled across the ice, but my legs still hung in the water behind me. I had tried hard, but Barbie hadn't been quite enough to save me.

"Look at me," Papa Dick said calmly. "I'm going to throw you a rope." It skated across the ice and snaked into the water beside me.

I reached out, touched it and felt nothing. My hands were paralyzed, making it impossible to form a grip.

"Grab the loop," he said. "Put it over your head."

Loop? Using my forearm, I lifted the rope from the water until it hung in front of me. Then I dropped it back onto the ice, picked it up between my wrists and slipped it over my head.

"Now, around your shoulders. Under your armpits. I'm going to pull you out. Keep your arms at your sides."

I felt the rope tighten against my back. I kept my arms down, pressing them against my sides to keep them from shaking. My hips slipped over the ice shelf. The ice broke and I plunged back into the water. I coughed and floundered. From far away, I could hear Papa Dick speaking to me. It was snowing now, hard flakes that pinged against my face even though I couldn't feel their cold sting.

"Cea! *Cea!* Listen to me! I'm reaching my hand out. Take it. Just take it."

I felt my wrists being gripped. Something was pulling at me.

Stop it, I said, but it was only in my head.

"Kick! Kick your legs!" He was screaming at me now.

I was being dragged forward, my chest and then my waist sliding across the ice, and then I was turning onto my back. Papa Dick was standing over me and stripping off his parka. Then the clouds and trees were moving; he was carrying me. We were so close to shore now that I could hear snow sliding from the branches in wet clumps. I looked back at my watery prison, the hole now six feet across from my attempts to rescue myself.

The last thing I saw before I closed my eyes was Barbie, lying facedown on the ice.

Part Four

Choice

Chapter Twenty-Three

I stood in front of the bathroom mirror, trying to imagine myself through a stranger's eyes. My Fancy Ass jeans were tight, the neckline of my sweatshirt plunged deeply, and my gold braided headband glittered under the lights. A pair of shoulder pads Velcroed to my bra straps completed the look. I looked super cool, and the best thing was that my outfit hadn't cost me a penny. This shoplifting thing was working out pretty well.

I turned in front of the mirror, examining my figure. Way too tall, of course, and no boobs yet, but my legs were long and thin and my waist was small. Not bad for an almost-thirteen-year-old. I picked up my Snickers bar from the back of the toilet and finished it off, then tore open another and devoured it greedily. Then I carefully buried the wrappers under the mass of tissues in the trash can. I ate four or five chocolate bars a day, but it wasn't because they were stolen that I hid them from Mom. Hash and pot were acceptable in our household, but white sugar was not.

Down the hall, I heard the front door open and close. I sighed, wishing I had had the foresight to leave the house before Mom came home. The dishes were still in the sink, and I hadn't done the grocery shopping yesterday. Once or twice a week, when her boyfriend could fake an out-of-town business trip to his wife, Mom would spend the night at a hotel with him. My mother's boyfriend was a married father. Their time together was precious, she said, so I should understand and help out with the chores as much as I could.

I leaned on the counter and waited quietly, knowing she would most likely go into her bedroom and spend the day catching up on her sleep. When I heard her door close, I reached behind the pipes under the sink and pulled out my cigarettes. Plucking one from the pack, I held it between my fingers and posed in front of the mirror with my chin lowered. With my lips slicked in frosty pink and my lashes coated with navy blue mascara, I looked about five years older than my actual age. And today, I had someone to impress. Papa Dick was due to arrive for a visit this afternoon. I hadn't seen him since I'd left the Yukon, and I wanted to be sure he saw exactly who I was now. One thing was for sure: I wasn't his little Peanut from the wilderness anymore.

Whoever I had been when I arrived in the city four years earlier was long gone. The shame and rejection I'd experienced since, along with my disgust at my naive bush-girl past, had made me do everything in my power to bury her. During my first few months in Calgary, everything had made me anxious: the bachelors who lived above our basement suite, the public bus, the twenty dollars in Mom's wallet that had to last us a full week. At school, I heard the other kids whispering about my thrift-store clothing, my ignorance about current TV shows—we didn't own a television—and my ridiculous height; though I was in fourth grade, I was taller by a long shot than any of the sixth-graders. One day when I was walking home, a gang of teenagers mistook me for a junior-high-schooler, tackled me to the ground and spray-painted my hair green. After that I would have feigned illness to avoid school, but the alternative was even worse: Barry. While Mom went off to her waitressing job

My mother and me in Calgary, just after I moved there in 1979.

each day, Barry stayed behind smoking pot and listening to the Doors on Mom's freezer-sized ghetto blaster. I refused to speak to him, and used every possible opportunity to cast him glares.

"What the hell is with you?" he asked me once, gripping my arm. Mom was in the shower.

"*You.* That's what's wrong with me," I replied boldly.

He released my arm and tapped a cigarette from its pack. "Is that right. Well, that's too bad, since I was planning on helping you guys out. With some money, I mean. Seems you ain't doing so well." He waved a hand around at our home. It was a single room, with a hot plate in one corner and red shag carpeting everywhere else. "But if *that's* your attitude, I guess I won't bother."

I stood up to my full height. "We don't need your help," I said, slitting my eyes at him. "Mom has a job now, and besides, I'm going to make lots of money someday."

He laughed and shook his head like I was the biggest joke he'd ever encountered, but a week later, I came home from school to find his red Ranchero gone from the curb. I unlocked our door slowly, knowing the scene that would greet me inside.

Mom was sitting beside the room's only window, tears on her cheeks as she blew pot smoke into the air. For once, I didn't go to comfort her.

IF GRANDMA JEANNE'S LETTER informing us of her separation from Papa Dick had come as a surprise to Mom, it hadn't to me. She left him just a few months after I arrived in Calgary, on New Year's Day of 1980—in honor of a new beginning, she wrote. Grandma Jeanne moved in with a friend while Papa Dick remained at the tipi. Shortly after that, we received a letter from my grandfather saying the Indians had discovered his camp and threatened to burn his tipi to the ground. He was looking for a new campsite, he said, and if Mom had time could she send him a batch of date cookies? He never even mentioned my grandmother, or the separation.

As for the rest of my family, I'd had little contact, but what I'd heard was more than enough. My Aunt Jessie had given birth to a mentally handicapped baby, who was removed from her care when my aunt called her social worker, worried the baby wasn't feeding properly. When help arrived, the screaming baby was trying to suck formula through a capped baby bottle. Despite my aunt's best intentions, she had failed both herself and her child. My Aunt Jan had disappeared once again into the world of hard drugs, and my Uncle Dane had finally been released from hospital, though his freedom had been fleeting. After only a few months, he was recommitted when his roommate found him trying to scale the outside wall under his window, shrieking that aliens were coming to turn his bones to liquid.

As for my father, his life seemed as happy as could be, but it was pretty clear that it didn't include me. He now had another child, a two-year-old daughter, who I could only imagine was the light of his life.

After Barry, there had been a parade of men through Mom's life. She brought them home from parties, from friends' houses, from work, and she had sex with them three feet from my bed. She called them "just a friend" and then slept with them the next night. She said she wasn't in love, and then cried when the phone didn't ring.

Eventually we moved from the basement suite into a more decent place, a duplex in a low-rent neighborhood that we afforded by sharing with an endless string of roommates, and that was when she had met her current boyfriend. Within days of starting a job as his secretary, the two of them began an affair. One year later, she was still spending her nights waiting for the sound of his key in the door and her days waiting for his phone calls, so oblivious to the rest of the world that she could barely remember what grade I was in. She didn't even work anymore, instead depending on her lover's sporadic handouts. When things were good between them, there was food in the fridge and a new silk blouse in my mother's closet. When they weren't, often because of my refusal to acknowledge him, Mom would start checking the classifieds or ask one of our roommates for a loan.

Our lives would be made so much easier, Mom said to me, if

I would only be nice to him. I stared back at her coldly, infuriated by her betrayal. Whenever her boyfriend got particularly impatient with me, he would threaten to send me to live with my father. Mom never did anything but sit silently by his side. I would threaten back, saying I'd tell his wife about their affair, even though I knew it probably didn't hold much water since I didn't really know who she was. Eventually my mother and I would turn furiously away from each other, adding yet another layer to the thickening wall of resentment between us.

In my family, there were no weddings or baby showers or anniversary parties. When my school friends moaned about being forced by their parents to attend this or that family event, all I felt was a raging jealousy. I would have given anything to have their complaints, and to exchange my crazy, self-centered relatives with theirs.

"PAPA DICK! OH MY God!" I said, pulling the front door open. Immediately, my cheeks reddened. I had been planning on playing it cool, letting my grandfather observe and wonder about the new Cea before him, but I was so happy to see him that I couldn't help myself.

"Peanut!" he exclaimed, smiling back at me. Then his eyes swept over my face. "What on earth are you wearing on your lips?" he frowned, swiping his fingers across my mouth and rubbing them together. "Don't you know what's in that stuff? Preservatives. Poisons. Carcinogens." He shook his head and pushed past me into the house. "Your mom around?"

"Yeah, she's—" Just then, Mom came around the corner. She had changed out of her skirt and blouse—her lover liked her looking like the lady she was, she had told me once—into a pair of jeans with a woven hippie belt and T-shirt with no bra. Her eyes were red from crying. More and more dates and phone calls with her boyfriend were resulting in tears these days, and I could only hope this meant that the end was near.

"Dad!" she said, throwing herself into his arms.

When they finished embracing, I followed them into the kitchen, trying to look casual.

"Cea," he said, smoothing his hand over his bushy gray hair. "I'm starving. How about whipping me up a little something to eat?"

"Oh . . . okay." I moved to the fridge, wondering what I could possibly make that wouldn't offend him, and started slicing an avocado.

The phone rang. Mom picked it up and walked with it, stretching the cord down the hallway. I rolled my eyes inwardly. "So," I said to Papa Dick as I buttered bread, "it's been so long since I've seen you. How are you? I mean . . . are you and Grandma Jeanne still in touch? I was really sad to hear the news. I mean I know it wasn't always easy for you guys, but after more than thirty years together—"

"Oh, Peanut, that's all in the past now," he said, waving a hand at me. "There's no need to dredge all that up. I want you to dig on what's happening in my life right now, and I have to tell you that I've met the most amazing woman. The first time I saw her—"

"Oh," I cut in, unable to help myself. "A new woman? Um, okay, well . . ."

"Yes. Truly, she's just the most unbelievable person you could ever meet. She's a little younger than me, and we have the most explosive sexual connection—"

I felt myself blanch. "Papa, um, that's kind of embarrassing for me—"

He looked at me levelly. "Remember, Peanut, embarrassment is just another form of fear. You need to open your mind a little. As I was saying . . ."

I tuned him out, though I managed to nod in all the right places. Finally, I set the sandwich in front of him and sat down again. He lifted the bread to examine the contents, grinned approvingly and took a bite. I waited until he was finished and then cleared my throat, wondering if he'd noticed yet how grown up I was.

"So . . . I got, like, ninety-two percent on this English paper I wrote last week. My *grade seven* English paper, that is. Do you want to see it? It's about bears. I was actually thinking about you when I wrote it." I smiled brightly. The truth was that I was also dying to show him some of the poetry I'd written recently. I spent hours scribbling down poems about forbidden passions, voiceless abused children, and the fall of nature to man's brutal hand—poems that I never let anyone read. But I felt like Papa Dick would appreciate them, especially the ones about man versus nature. I loved writing, and I knew I wasn't half bad at it. If modeling didn't pan out, I figured maybe a career as a novelist could be my fallback plan.

"Sure thing, Peanut, sure thing," Papa Dick responded. "All in good time. First I need to get a little exercise." He stood up and stretched, then walked to the bathroom. Five minutes later he entered the living room, stark naked, and settled down on his yoga mat with his palms turned up on his knees.

I quietly cleared his plate away, and then went into my bedroom and closed the door. Hot tears welled up in my eyes. There was a deep emptiness in my chest, almost as if my grandfather had died right before my eyes. It wasn't just that he hadn't observed and wondered about me as I had hoped and planned. It was that he hadn't even noticed me.

BY THE TIME PAPA Dick left us two days later, I thought that if I ever saw him again in my life it would probably be too soon. Not only had he not asked me a single question about myself—or my school project, for that matter—he had spent the entire time lecturing me on the evils of Cheerios, insisting I use sphagnum moss instead of maxi-pads for my period, and performing his embarrassing gut roll for my friends. He squatted on the toilet and left the door wide open when he pooped. He went on and on about the evil confinement of our walls and insisted on sleeping in a tent in the backyard to escape them. But at least he eventually left. Unlike Grandma Jeanne.

It was three months later that she came to live with us. Within a few weeks, she was spending most of her time in bed with her new lover, a stoner thirty years her junior who appeared to be homeless. He wore oven mitts around the house and brought her boxes of Tide with bows stuck on them.

Sometimes at night, I would sit in my bedroom thinking about my life. My family was crazy, and there wasn't a thing I could do to change it. I was twelve years old, and for at least the next six years, I would be their prisoner.

I WAS SITTING AT the kitchen table doing homework when the doorbell rang. Mom, at home on a rare weekend afternoon, got up to answer it. I heard a hoot and a holler, and then everyone was talking at once.

"Cea," Mom yelled, "there's someone here to see you. You'll never believe it."

I rose from the table, curious, and walked to the front door.

"Hey," a chubby teenager said to me, blowing a fat pink bubble with her gum. "Remember me?"

I blinked at her and started to shake my head, and then it came to me. *Kelly.* I shifted my eyes to the man behind her. Larry grinned at me and pulled a joint from behind his ear. "Well, well. Look who's all grown up."

I gave him a wan smile, and then turned back to Kelly. "Oh my God," I said to her. "You look so . . . different."

"Yeah," she said, letting the bubble collapse onto her face. "I'm all grown up now too. You got anything fun to do around here?"

"Um, well, there's the mall—"

"That'll do. Let's mosey."

"Okay, just let me—"

Larry pushed past me into the house, already lighting up. "Stay out of trouble," he said to Kelly, jabbing his joint at her. She smirked and held out her hand, and he pressed a five-dollar bill into it.

"Okay, I guess we're going to the mall," I said to Mom before following Kelly down the steps. I was still trying to match this teenager's appearance with the girl I'd known in the wilderness. Her face looked bloated and hard at the same time, plastered with orange makeup in a failed attempt to cover a bad case of acne. Never a skinny girl, she was now officially fat, with her exposed belly hanging down from a too-short KISS T-shirt.

"Um, wow," I said as we walked, "this is, like, really crazy. You don't still live—"

"In the bush? Hell, no. Thank God." She stopped on the sidewalk, digging through her fringed black purse and withdrawing a pack of cigarettes. She lit up and offered me one.

I hesitated, and then took it. My cigarettes under the sink at home were more for posing than anything, but I didn't want to look uncool in front of Kelly.

"So," she said, lighting my cigarette behind a cupped hand. I inhaled, willing myself not to cough. "You done any drugs yet?"

"No."

"Yeah, I figured. You always were Little Miss Perfect."

"Little Miss Perfect? What are you—?"

"Yeah, you know. Little Miss Purity. Never got in trouble, always everyone's favorite. Fuck, I hated it in the wilderness. Not like life in the city's much better." She snorted and spat up a green loogie on the pavement. "Me and my boyfriend, we do glue a lot. Or hash when we can get it. My old man keeps it in his underwear drawer, like he's being so goddamn sneaky or something." I stared at the sidewalk, certain that whatever I said would be wrong. Kelly snorted again and flicked her cigarette butt on the ground. "Fuckin' parents. All the drugs they've done, where the hell do they get off telling me I can't. I don't know. Hated it in the bush, but it sure was a lot easier than this shit. Don't you think?"

I nodded, realizing that in her own way, Kelly was trying to connect with me. I was the only person she knew outside her family who had lived through such craziness, and it had done its damage to her. She was sixteen years old, jaded and bitter beyond her years, and already far down a beaten path of self-destruction. In short, she was becoming her parents.

"Yeah," I replied agreeably, but mostly what I felt was relief. If there was one thing I was certain of, it was that I was nothing at all like Kelly.

I SLUMPED ACROSS THE sofa, reaching for my glass. I missed and tried again, giggling as it swam before my eyes. I was on drink number three, and there was a very low 7 Up–to-vodka ratio in my glass.

Someone sat down beside me. I turned my head slowly and saw dark hair, blue eyes and muscular arms. Chris Something. He reminded me a little of Karl. "Hey," he said, sliding his arm along the back of the couch. "How you doing there, pretty girl?"

"Good. I'm goooood," I answered, and then burst out laughing. Finally getting my hand around my glass, I tipped it back and took a long swallow. "Wow," I said, heaving myself into a sitting position. "It sure is noisy in here. Great party, huh?"

"Yeah. They always are."

I smiled up at him. Teenage boys were all too short, but this was a man, and he was even taller than me. "You're cute," I said, inching a little closer to him.

His arm dropped around my shoulders. "Um, I hate to ask this, but . . . how old are you?"

I threw my head back, hoping it made me look a little older. "Thirteen."

"Oh. Wow." He pulled his arm away just as someone cranked up the music.

"Barracuda" blasted from the cheap living room speakers, the bass thumping painfully against my eardrums. I looked up and saw Mom. She was dancing with one of her male friends, trailing a silk scarf around his neck with one hand and smoking a joint with the other. The one saving grace about Mom's parties was that she never invited her boyfriend, who disapproved of pot smoking and other such hippyish pursuits. Mom spotted me and released her victim, floating toward us.

"Cea! Are you having fun, darling?"

I slouched against Chris's shoulder. "Yeah, sure."

Mom looked down at us with a stoned smile. "Look at her, Chris. Isn't she just beautiful?"

"Sure is. A damn shame I'm almost twice her age."

"Yeah, I know. And she's got the sweetest little bush now. It's just—"

"Mom!" I launched myself into a sitting position, my face burning. "How could you—"

"Oh, Cea, just relax. It's natural for these things to happen to your body. After all, you're a teenager now." She smiled at me again and shook her head. "Thirteen. Same age I was when I—"

"—lost your virginity and smoked pot for the first time," I finished for her sarcastically, and then slumped against Chris's arm again.

"Yep," she said, lifting the joint to her lips.

I flicked my eyes up to hers, and suddenly, even through my fog, I knew what was coming next. She inhaled deeply, then blew smoke from her mouth and held the joint out to me.

I blinked at her. *"Mom!"*

"What?"

"Are you serious? Mom, you're offering me pot!"

She shrugged. "Yeah, well, you're drinking alcohol, and that's no better. I'd rather you did this, at least it's natural. Why don't you just try it? Maybe it'll help you . . . I don't know. Relax a little."

I jumped up from the sofa, suddenly sober. "What, you mean because I'm so uptight? Because I don't do drugs and screw random guys like you did at my age? Like you do *now*?" I turned my back on her and walked angrily into the kitchen. Pushing through the wall of bodies leaning against the counter, I reached for the vodka bottle and poured myself a long drink. As I slugged it back, I saw Chris weaving his way toward me through the crowd.

"Hey. Are you okay?" he asked when he reached me.

I stared at his mouth. Maybe my mother was right, I thought as I swayed from side to side. Maybe I just needed to go with the flow and be more like her. Stepping toward him, I slid my hands up his arms and planted my lips on his. We stood like that for a moment, but then the nausea hit. I broke away from him and stumbled to the bathroom. The last thing I heard before I slammed the door shut was Mom, laughing in that high-pitched, stoned voice that I knew so well.

Chapter Twenty-Four

I sat in my bedroom, tapping my pencil listlessly against my science textbook. I was supposed to be doing homework, but I couldn't focus. Mom was out with her married boyfriend, from across the hall I could hear my grandmother screwing her lover, and the house smelled like pot smoke. I lay back on my bed and gazed up at the ceiling.

The doorbell rang, and I reluctantly rose and walked down the hall. I knew it would be Tiffany from school. She was the only person I had let get a glimpse into my crazy world, but somehow I didn't even feel like seeing her today. I opened the door and smiled at her wanly.

"Hey. Come in."

She followed me down the hall, and I closed my bedroom door behind us. "Whoa," she said, sniffing the air. "Smells like your mom's been at it again."

"Nah. It's my grandma this time."

"Your *grandma*? Wow, I didn't know. She does it too?"

"Yeah."

"Wow. That's so cool. I wish my parents were more like yours."

"What do you mean?" I said irritably. "I don't have 'parents,' or hadn't you noticed?"

"Parents, mom. Same dif."

"No. It's not." I made a face and drew my legs under me on the bed. "And trust me, you don't want a family that's anything like mine."

Tiffany sat down and reached for my pink jewelry box. She opened the lid and tinkling music filled the air. Then she closed it, opened it, closed it—

"Do you mind?" I snapped. "That's kind of annoying."

"Hey. What's with you today?"

"Nothing!"

"Fine! Sorry for asking." We sat side by side in silence for a minute. "Hey," she said finally. "Want to go to the mall?"

I shook my head. *Go to the mall* was our code for shoplifting, which we did once or twice a week. But suddenly, the thought of it made me feel a little ill. "No. Look, I'm sorry. I just . . . I don't know. But do you ever think, What if I never get the life I want? Like, what if this is *it*?"

She shrugged again. "Dunno. I mean, what *do* you want?"

"I don't know. I just always had this weird sort of dream about having a life that was . . . *normal.* But sometimes . . . sometimes I wonder if this is it. Like, my mom and grandma smoke pot and screw all day, but we live in the city now at least, so this is as normal as it gets for me. It's hard to explain."

"Yeah, I get it," she said, but I could tell she didn't. She stood up and hooked her thumbs in her pockets. "Well, I should probably mosey. I'm supposed to be grounded. But hey, if I can get away this weekend, ya wanna hit Rod Johnson's keg party? His parents are away."

"Yeah, sure," I said distractedly. "Sounds like fun."

After Tiffany left, I walked back to my room and looked around. There was Suzie Doll on the shelf, right beside a stolen bottle of Fabergé perfume. My jewelry box, sitting on top of a stolen Stephen King book.

Shoplifting. Stocking up.

Booze. Pot.

I shook my head, and then I went to my closet and ripped every item of shoplifted clothing from its hanger and pitched it on the floor. Then I gathered it all up, walked down the hall and dropped it on Mom's bed.

When I got back to my room, I stood gazing at the collage over my bed. I had found the frame in our back alley, and spent hours pasting into it pictures of models cut from magazines. I took a deep breath and stood up tall. The idea that had been in my head for so many years now suddenly seemed a lifeline. There was one way to escape my crazy family, and all I had to do was grab hold of it.

I STEPPED INTO THE room and glanced around, then made my way to the receptionist's desk. "I heard there's, like, a modeling competition going on here?" I said, chewing my lip. "I, um, read about it in the newspaper?"

"Yes. Please fill this out, and the photographer will see you shortly." She handed me a form, and I took a seat.

The room was already filled with at least ten other modeling hopefuls, dressed to the nines and fully made up as if they had just stepped from the pages of a magazine. I had lost the cheap-looking makeup and let my hair go natural, but now I was regretting it. I felt like a child next to them.

I looked down at the form. *Minimum age to enter is 15*, it said in bold letters. I swallowed hard and wrote down my birthday, subtracting two from the year. Then I filled in my weight, eye color and hair color, passed in the form and sat back nervously to wait.

A door opened, and a slight man holding a massive camera stepped into the room. His eyes moved from face to face, and then stopped on mine.

"You," he said, beckoning with his finger.

I blinked back at him and glanced to either side of me. No, he was definitely talking to me. I stood up and followed him on rubbery legs. After closing the door behind him, he looked me up and down. I tried to read his expression, but my nerves were too frazzled to focus.

"I'm Wes," he said finally. "How old are you?"

"F-fifteen." My voice caught in my throat.

He nodded and waved me over to a white backdrop. "I'm going to take a few shots. Just be natural."

"Okay. Should I . . . put some makeup on maybe? I noticed the other girls—"

"No, no, you look great." He lifted the camera to his eye. "Let's begin."

This is it, I thought. I turned to one side and looked into the lens over my shoulder, smiling tentatively.

"Good," he said. "Perfect."

I turned to face him and dropped my chin.

"That's it. Eyes here. Beautiful."

Beautiful. I felt exhilarated, as if I had just been taken for a ride around a racetrack. Ten minutes later, Wes lowered his lens and grinned at me. "Wow," he said. "You're an absolute natural."

My heart leapt. "Really?"

"Really. You've got everything it takes. The only real question is, are you ready for this?"

"Yes!" I said, my voice embarrassingly eager. "I mean, totally."

He nodded. "And your family . . . Mom? Dad? Are they supportive?"

I almost laughed. Supportive? "Yeah," I said. "My mom . . . she's, like, good with whatever."

"All right," Wes said, nodding at me. "Then let's get you in to see the agency director. We have a scout coming from New York next week, and I have a feeling he's going to just love you."

One hour later, I walked out of the agency feeling like I had springs under my feet. I couldn't stop smiling as I stood at the bus stop to go home. *You are no longer looking at a too-tall, skinny teenager; you're looking at a future model*, I thought whenever someone

Me onstage during the modeling contest I entered when I was only thirteen.

met my eye. But I also knew I would never be able to explain my elation to an outsider. I was silently celebrating not just the beginning of a glamorous career, but also what I saw as my ticket to normal. Modeling was going to give me the money and freedom to escape my family and create the life I so desperately wanted.

There was just one thing standing in my way.

"HI, GREG? IT'S CEA. Your, um, daughter?"

There was a beat on the other end of the line, and then, "Why, Cea! How nice to hear from you! How are you, sweetie?"

"Pretty good. How's, um . . . the baby? Your new daughter, I mean. Not a baby anymore, I guess." I silently cursed myself, hating the obvious edge of jealously in my voice.

"Great," he said. "You know, *busy*! Growing too fast and running us ragged."

"That's good." I swallowed hard. No matter how much I tried not to be bitter, it still cut deeply each time I heard evidence of the charmed childhood my half sister seemed to be leading.

My dad cleared his throat. "So. It's been a while, huh? How's school?"

"It's okay. Well, I always get As in English. My teacher says I'm a good writer." I hesitated, then decided to go for it. "I, um . . . I wrote this story about getting drunk at a friend's party. I thought maybe she'd be mad or, like, report me to the principal or something, but she actually gave me a really good grade. Um . . ." My voice trailed off. Suddenly, I was embarrassed at my disclosure. It sounded pathetic to my ears, like I was begging him to notice that I was a teenager now.

"Is that right," Greg said in a measured tone. "And . . . how are you feeling about that? About getting drunk, I mean?"

"Feeling about it? Um, I'm not sure, I . . ." I gripped the phone hard, desperate to change the subject. "Anyway, that's not why I called. Actually, something amazing has happened. You'll never believe this, but I've been invited to go to New York. To . . . to model. With Elite—that's, like, a really big agency and stuff. This summer. Isn't that awesome?"

"Why yes, it certainly is. And I can't say as I'm surprised. You've certainly got the height and looks for it."

"Um . . . thanks. It's just . . . there's one problem. The agency . . . they're going to buy my plane ticket and give me a place to stay, of course I'll have to pay them back when I start working, but that shouldn't take long, at least Wes, that's the name of the photographer who discovered me, he said it shouldn't take long, he says I've got a classic look and that I move, like, really well in front of the camera, plus I look a lot older than thirteen so I'll probably get booked for magazines like *Seventeen* and stuff, and . . ." I realized I was rambling, but I didn't care. Anything was better than getting to the point that I needed to come to in this conversation. Maybe, if I went on long enough, he would figure out what I was getting at and just offer.

He cleared his throat again. "I see. So will you . . . have a chaperone? Your mom, maybe? I can't imagine you going to New York alone, sweetie."

I felt myself blanch. "I, uh . . . well, Mom can't really come with me, but I'm, like, really mature for my age, so you don't have to worry or anything."

"Well, of course I trust you. And I guess . . . if this is what you want, I can't really step in now and say no, right?"

"Yeah, not really, I guess . . ."

"Well. This certainly sounds exciting, sweetie," Greg said. "So, what's the problem?"

I took a deep breath. How badly I wanted to do this without my father's help. In my fantasy, this conversation would never happen. Instead, I would simply send him a magazine with my face on the cover in a few years with a short note: *Here's what I've been up to lately. Hope you and the family are well.* But it just wasn't possible. "I . . . I need a bit of money. Not a lot, just enough to buy food and subway tickets for, like, a month. Mom, she just doesn't have it, so I need maybe like a thousand dollars, tops, or if that's too much—"

"Of course, of course. That shouldn't be a problem."

My heart leapt. "Really?"

"Yes. I'm far from wealthy, as you know, but this seems important to you."

"It is. It really is. And when I make it big, I'll pay you back, I promise, and—"

"No, no, that's not necessary. Really."

"Wow. Well . . . thank you. I mean it." I swallowed hard, and then said something that pained me but that was undeniably true. "I couldn't do this without you."

He was quiet for a moment, and when he spoke again his voice sounded softer than I'd ever heard it. "It's the least I can do," he said. "The very least."

Chapter Twenty-Five

The air in the subway smelled like urine and tin. I emerged from the station into the bright sunlight, pushing my way through the throng on the street. Sweat dripped down my sides as I wiped at my face, fighting to keep the humidity at bay. A construction worker hissed and clicked his tongue at me, a sound that drove me wild with annoyance but that was slowly fading to the background of my daily life here in the city. I had only been in New York for two weeks, but I already knew the subway system by heart. I was fearless on the streets, holding my head high as I blew past the panhandlers and muttering weirdos, hunting out the cheapest delis and taking the subway to the Bronx to shoot one job on location.

My quick adaptation to the city was something even my agency commented on. "You're our youngest girl this summer, but you're also our bravest. It's like you were born here!" one of my bookers commented to me, and I smiled, thinking of the shock on her face if I were to tell her the truth of where I actually came from. But what she said was true. While girls three and four years older than me cried to their parents or boyfriends on the phone, cowered over cockroaches and blew their cash on taxis because they were either too afraid or too clueless to take the subway, I calmly did my go-sees, test shoots and very first bookings, returning weary each evening to the apartment on Lexington Avenue I currently called home.

But I was also learning that modeling was not a fairy tale. Hardly anyone got discovered and woke up six months later to find her face on the cover of *Vogue* and a limo waiting at her door to take her to the Concorde. The reality was that I lived in a cockroach-ridden, two-bedroom, one-bathroom apartment with nine other girls that first summer. We set the timer for showers, stored our

A frame from one of my first modeling shoots in New York. I was just fourteen.

clothing under our mattresses and wrote death threats on our labeled food. Every single girl in the apartment other than me smoked, filling the tiny space with toxic gray clouds as they sat chatting about coveted bookings, pimple remedies, grapefruit diets and boyfriends back home who just didn't understand. I deflected advances from photographers during the day and offers of drugs during the evenings, when we were expected to attend industry dinners.

But to me, it was all worth it. The fact was that I loved modeling, my actual time in front of the camera. My enjoyment was not driven by vanity—for it was actually rare to encounter a vain model, as picked on and insecure as we were about our looks—but creativity. It took no effort at all for me to morph into the photographer or client's vision: the innocent ingenue, the smiling teen, or the confident young woman. While the camera was clicking, I often felt like the luckiest girl alive. I was only fourteen years old, I had already found my life's calling, and with a little luck someday I would be paid generously for it.

But still, at night, I would sometimes think about Mom and cry softly into my pillow. I called her once, but she was rushing out the door to meet her boyfriend and promised to call me back. She never did.

"You're so young," one of my roommates said to me once. "Why isn't your mother here with you?"

"My mom? She, uh . . . just trusts me to do my own thing. I'm independent," I added, lifting my chin.

"But doesn't she, like, worry about you?"

"Actually . . ." I cleared my throat, and before I could stop them, the words were out of my mouth. "She doesn't live with me. She's kind of, like, an unfit parent."

"Oh." My roommate looked taken aback, but she didn't question me.

This was good, I thought; in this new world of mine, I could make myself into anyone I wanted to be. I knew what we fledgling models were known as: the summer girls. Only a small percentage of us would actually make a lasting career of modeling. At the end of the season we would all go back to school, most of us reabsorbed into our former lives with only a small collection of glossy ten-by-twelve photos as souvenirs of a short-lived dream. I couldn't help thinking that we were a lot like the summer visitors of my childhood. But I was sure that I would beat the odds. And when I left New York late that August, I told myself I was no longer Cea Sunrise Person, the weirdo from the wilderness with the crazy family. I was Cea the Model now, and I would never be that outcast little girl again.

I STOOD IN THE humid bathroom of the tiny Mauritius airport, sweat collecting on my brow as I pulled article after article of clothing from my carry-on bag. It was still too heavy, the woman at the check-in counter had told me. I held each garment up in front of me, deciding which I could live without. After I'd emptied half my bag, I threw my discards into a corner and walked briskly to my gate, trying not to think about the huge risk I was about to take—or the desperation that was driving it.

It was the summer of 1985, and I had just finished attending the finals of Elite's "Look of the Year" competition. It was my second attempt, after being disqualified the first time around for my age. This time, at fifteen, I had won the Canadian and then the North American semifinals, but yesterday that road had ended. Here, on the Indian Ocean island of Mauritius for the world finals, I had placed in the top twenty—just shy of winning a cash prize. I was devastated, not because I'd expected to win but because without the money I didn't know what to do next. As I had learned during my previous summer in New York, launching a modeling career took money. Elite wanted me to go to Paris for the rest of the summer, but I had less than twenty dollars in my wallet and no way to pay for a flight, much less anything else. I had lain awake nearly all the previous night, thinking about my mother. If I went home it would all be over. I would lose one precious year in an industry that prized youth, and what would I be trading it for? A job at the Dairy Queen, pointless walks to the mall with my only girlfriend, evenings spent at home alone while Mom swooned under the spell of her married lover. I finally fell asleep on a pillow wet with tears, more frightened of such a fate than anything a broke summer in Paris might hold for me.

The next morning, I had awoken with a plan. As luck would have it, the competition coordinators had flown me from Calgary to Mauritius on a route via Paris, which meant that technically speaking, I had a plane ticket back to Paris. All I had to do was get off the plane there and pray for bookings.

Twelve hours after ditching my clothes in the Mauritius bathroom, I emerged from Charles de Gaulle Airport into a dusky Paris evening with my pulse jumping. I had made it this far, but there was a major flaw in my plan: I had forgotten that the plane landed at night, and the agency wouldn't reopen until nine o'clock the next morning. I was exhausted with jet lag, in a strange city that spoke a foreign language, and I had no money for a cab or a place to sleep that night.

"Okay," I said to myself over and over again as I stood on the curb, trying to formulate my next move. "Okay. It's okay. Just stay calm, you'll figure it out." I had never talked to myself before and was on the verge of panic. My hands were trembling and I was about to cry. Compact cars with yellow headlights zoomed past me and people walked by, glancing at me curiously. I knew I appeared older than I was, but I probably still looked like a scared and lost teenager.

"*Avez-vous besoin d'aide?* Do you need some help?" one man asked, looking at me with concern.

I shook my head. "No, I, uh . . . just waiting for someone. Thanks."

"Okay," he said in his French accent, shrugging. "But if they do not show up, I have my car right here. You are going to Paris? I live near the Opera. It is no problem to give you a lift."

I tried to smile back at him, touched by his kindness. Very likely he was harmless, but I couldn't afford to take the risk. "N-no thanks, but thanks very much. Really, my friend will be here soon."

"Very well. As you wish." He lifted his hands and walked away.

"Okay," I muttered to myself again, back to near-panic. "Need to calm down. Calm down and figure this out." Out of nowhere, Papa Dick's face appeared in my head. I inhaled and squared my shoulders. This was it, I thought, my chance to prove to myself that I didn't need a family. After everything I had been through, a night alone in a vast, unknown foreign city wasn't about to bring me down.

Public transportation, I thought; there had to be some. Wasn't everyone always talking about how amazing the Parisian Metro system was? I headed back into the terminal and found an information desk. A woman pointed to an escalator. I walked down the moving steps, gaining confidence. I had a map in my hand and the address of the agency memorized. I could do this. I exchanged my pitiful handful of currency, bought a ticket, boarded a car and, as the train pulled away, sat down to work out the next part of my plan.

The way I saw it, there were two possible places I could sleep that night: the central station, where I could sit on a bench and try to stay awake for most of the night while pretending to wait for a train, or a city park, where I risked dozing among bums and/or being raped and murdered by morning. Too late, I realized I would have been better off staying at the airport, snoozing in a chair and hoping I didn't get kicked out. We were hurtling through the countryside now, and I almost wished I could get off and sleep in the trees somewhere, just like the good old days with Mom. My eyes flooded with tears, but I wiped them away impatiently. My wilderness days were over. I was in the city now, and it was time I developed some urban survival skills.

I checked my map again, matching it with the one in the passenger car to be certain I got off at the right stop. We were approaching the center of the city. It was completely dark outside, the cobbled roads narrowing as they became busier. There were still plenty of people roaming the streets at this hour, amid ornate architecture, quaint cafes and magazine kiosks. It looked just like the background in my snow globe, I realized with a small thrill as the train pulled into my stop. I exited into the night and walked until I found Rue Legendre.

The agency was in a small building with gray trim that seemed to house both offices and residences. Most of the windows were dark, but a few burned brightly. I tried the door, and unsurprisingly it was locked. I stood back on the sidewalk, thinking enviously about the people cozily ensconced in their homes for the night. Although I still didn't have a solid plan of what I was going to do, I was managing to hold myself together. But the darkness was starting to press into me, making me feel jumpy. A car sped by and tooted its horn. I looked up, and a man leaned out the passenger window and shouted something at me in French. I picked up my bag and moved closer to the entrance of the building. Just then, the door opened and a middle-aged woman came out with a small dog on a leash.

"*Voulez-vous venir à l'intérieur?*" she asked, holding the door open for me.

I stared back at her. I had no idea what she'd just said to me, but I could see the foyer just beyond her, beckoning like a mirage. "Uh . . . *merci*," I said, practically lunging over the threshold. I made my way up the staircase, found the door to the agency and leaned against it, grateful just to be inside. A wave of exhaustion washed over my body. The floor was carpeted, and I had taken the thin blue blanket from the airplane. To my left, I could see that the hallway turned a corner to an area that I hoped would be more private. I stumbled into the sheltered space, then sank down on the floor and slept.

When morning came, it was two female voices laughing and speaking in French that woke me. I turned over, my shoulder and hip aching from being pressed into the hard floor all night, and suddenly remembered where I was. I jumped up and peeked around the corner. One of the women was unlocking the door to the agency while her friend yammered on, apparently telling her a hilarious story. When they disappeared into the agency, I sprang into action. My bladder was bursting painfully, but there was something else even more pressing: I had to be sure I looked okay. I ran my hands over my hair, squeezed Visine into my eyes, popped a breath mint into my mouth and put on some lip gloss. Then I pulled my best outfit from my bag, a tight T-shirt with black leggings and ankle boots, and quickly changed my clothing. By then I had to pee so badly that I was starting to dance around, so I grabbed my bag, tried to look relaxed and walked into the agency.

The women looked up at me inquiringly, and then broke into a smile. "Cea," one of them said, rising to greet me, "you are even more beautiful than your photographs. Come in, come in."

"Thank you. It's so good to be here." I beamed. She moved toward me and kissed me once on each cheek, and I prayed I didn't smell bad. I stepped back a little and glanced around. "Um, you don't by any chance have a bathroom, do you? I'd just like to freshen up a little. Flew the red-eye in last night, you know how it is."

"Of course. Just beyond the booking table."

I smiled once more, and then walked as casually as I could toward the beckoning utopia of the wooden door. *I did it*, I thought to myself gleefully. Despite the hideous discomfort in my bladder, it was one of the best moments of my life. I was fifteen years old, I had chosen and created my own life, and now there would be no stopping me.

INDEED, MY PLAN WORKED. My agency set me up in an apartment with several other models in the grotty district of Pigalle, sent me around to go-sees, and within a week I was getting bookings. Within three weeks, I had made enough money to buy a ticket home and alleviate some of the stress of worrying about how I was going to eat.

One day, I was walking by a bus shelter when I caught sight of a picture of myself in an ad for a bank. I was lounging on a yacht in Corsica, presumably on a holiday paid for with all the money I'd saved by trusting this company with my finances. I stopped and stared, suddenly overcome by thoughts of Papa Dick. If ever there was a moment to horrify him, this was it. I had become everything he despised, a willing pawn in the urban consumer industry. As I sighed and moved forward, I realized I had no idea if the thought made me happy or sad. But then, I had little reason to care. Though

I'd written several postcards to my grandfather since I started modeling, I never heard anything back from him.

It wasn't until the end of summer that I finally set foot on the plaza of the Eiffel Tower. I'd observed it from afar as I traveled the city and seen it in the backdrop of many photos taken of me, but it was as if I feared that actually visiting the real-life landmark of my childhood snow globe could only bring disappointment. I exited the Metro station and approached the tower slowly. Of course, there was no denying its beauty. And as I gazed up at the famous crisscrossing architecture, I realized what the source of my reticence had been. I wanted Mom to share this moment with me, if not in person then at least in voice.

Smiling to myself, I made my way through the crowd of tourists until I found a phone booth. I picked up the receiver, inserted my telephone card and dialed her number, listening to the line buzz across five thousand miles.

"Hello?" Mom said sleepily, and my throat clicked closed. I had spoken to her only once since I'd arrived in Paris, just to tell her where I was, and I'd felt like she'd barely heard me. *Mom. What's wrong?* I had asked her, even though I didn't want to know. *Nothing. It's just . . . we had a fight. And it was so weird, because we had sex afterward and I couldn't have an orgasm—*

"Hello? Is anyone there?" Mom's voice pulled me back to the present.

In that moment, I realized that although I might return home for school and continue to share a roof with my mother, she would never be a parent to me. What's more, she didn't even deserve the label. I was fifteen years old, I was in Paris by myself, and she hardly cared. Since I had been here, a photographer had offered me cocaine and told me I would fail as a model if I didn't partake and offer him sex, and I had dealt with it. A gypsy boy had snatched my bag off my shoulder, leaving me penniless and without a passport, and I had dealt with it. A man on the Metro had masturbated into my hair, and I had dealt with it. Alone. I shook my head silently, tears flooding my eyes, and hung up the phone on the woman I had all but given up on.

But I was fine, absolutely fine, without her.

Part Five

Consequence

Chapter Twenty-Six

Looking back, I can see that it all started to fall apart with my first marriage. Until then, I had marveled to myself almost smugly at how unaffected I was by my crazy past and family. Even as my career took off in my late teens and early twenties, I fell into none of the typical pitfalls that many survivors of challenging childhoods did; I never did drugs, I had a healthy relationship with food, I didn't engage in casual sex and I only drank as much as my friends did. But for me, it was my craving for normal—that dangling carrot that seemed always just beyond my reach—that would be my undoing.

When my first boyfriend laid me on his bed and reached for a condom from his drawer, I never imagined I would one day marry him. I was sixteen, one year older than the girl I had been the summer before in Paris, and he took my virginity in his childhood bedroom while his mother was cooking a roast upstairs. For me, the moment was not driven by lust, but rather a desire to just get it over with. I was already an adult in so may ways—I had a career, I traveled on my own, I helped my mother pay the bills—that I saw this as the final step to bring me into womanhood.

Kevin was my little piece of sanity within the crazy, polarized world I inhabited. At home, things were terrible. Although I could have chosen to drop out of school and pursue my career full-time—after all, who was going to stop me?—the fact that Mom hadn't finished high school drove me to hang in and graduate. There wasn't a single thing I wanted to have in common with my mother. We were like black and white with no gray overlap between us, moving like strangers through each other's lives. While she continued her life as pot-smoking mistress to her married lover, I told her nothing about my mostly friendless existence at school, the hangovers I had after weekend parties, or the fact that I had stopped working on my one passion outside of modeling, writing, because my creative voice sounded to me more and more like a desperate whine. She knew little of my modeling life in New York, L.A. and Paris during the summers between school, the highs of landing national TV commercials and the lows of losing out on work to girls with straighter teeth or bigger breasts, the schmoozy parties that I detested but was forced to attend, the time a wealthy Los Angeles businessman bought me a new car (which I refused, dreading the strings attached) after meeting me once for coffee. I was lonely, and Kevin helped fill that gap, even though I refused to admit to myself how empty I still felt in his presence. I loved him mostly because he loved me, and because he had a family as predictable as the pecan pie they ate each Sunday after dinner. He and I stayed together for two years and then broke up when I graduated from high school, knowing we would be torn apart by the distance of our careers. My heart did not break. I moved to Paris and threw myself headlong into my work, and the truth was that I barely gave him a second thought.

But then a funny thing happened. Although I had initially seen modeling as my money train to a normal life, as time went on I found it harder and harder to maintain that vision. My constant need to adapt to new environments was taking its toll. I regularly worked in countries where I didn't know a soul, much less the language, and yet I would be out navigating the public transportation system on my first day there. I lived in grungy apartments with strangers one week and thousand-dollar-a-night hotel suites the next; ate cabbage for three days to fit into a swimsuit and then binged on chocolate bars for just as long after the job was done; made enough money to buy a car in ten days of work and then didn't get a booking for a month afterward, certain that my career was over.

By 1995 I was at the peak of my modeling career. This is from a shoot in Milan, Italy.

And though I loved my job, I hated the ugliness that went with it. I watched girls eat and then stick their fingers down their throat, fall off tables in nightclubs from too many drugs, and cry into their pillows because they were sixteen years old, stuck in a foreign country and didn't have enough money to go home. One time, at a pension in Milan, the elevator door slid open to reveal a model lying on her side with blood dripping down her arms; she had tried to kill herself after losing out on a big job to another girl.

And then there were the life stories. Family dysfunction seemed to run rampant in the fashion industry, and being constantly thrown together as temporary colleagues or roommates caused us to blurt out our pasts to each other in record time. Telling my own story a few times over too much wine, I forged quick and deep friendships with several girls, clinging to them as my real family fell further away. Though I sent postcards and gifts to Mom at her birthday and Christmas, I got almost nothing back. I didn't even know where my grandparents were anymore, and my father rarely called and never visited me. Somewhere along the line, my dream of normal had slowly morphed into a craving for mediocrity. I daydreamed about returning home and renting an apartment, getting a waitressing job, marrying whoever might have me.

And it was then, like a self-fulfilling prophecy, that I learned through an old friend that Kevin was living not a hundred miles from my current home of Hamburg. He had moved to Germany to pursue his career as a professional hockey player, she said, and had never stopped talking about me. I called him up, and we went out for dinner to catch up. As we talked, the feeling of nostalgic comfort that swept over me was irresistible. Kevin was my little scrap of home in a world as strange as the childhood one I had left behind.

When I was twenty-two, Kevin and I got married. Our wedding day was a snapshot of my new, perfect life that I wanted everyone to believe was real, complete with a white dress and trip down the aisle with my father, even though he felt like a stranger at my side. I invited my mother on the condition she wouldn't come stoned or bring her boyfriend, both of which promises she broke. I quelled my fury with too much wine. At the end of the evening, I observed my father grinning awkwardly while Mom waved a hand in front of his body, wondering aloud at the color of his aura, and I realized it was the first time in my life I could remember seeing my parents together in the same room. As I lay by my husband that night, I tried to tell myself it was exhaustion and too much booze that was killing my desire for him. I let him do his business on top of me, and then I lay awake for a long time afterward, knowing that I had made a huge mistake but also understanding that I was much too damaged to correct my wrongs. My past was catching up with me.

I cheated on my first husband with seven different men. When he and I finally split apart after two horrible years of marriage, I was so exhausted from my lies and guilt and confusion that all I wanted to do was drink my sorrows away. A nightly bottle or two of wine became my protection from the past that had hurt me, the present that disappointed me and the future that terrified me. I moved to Munich and embarked on a financially rewarding but creatively unfulfilling career as a catalog model, and spent my spare time partying.

Four years later, at the age of twenty-eight, I awoke one morning with a horrific case of alcohol poisoning and dried blood on my right hand. The night before, I had done so much coke and drunk so much booze that I had beat the crap out of my boyfriend. But it wasn't just the fact that I had lost control and unleashed a rage I didn't even know I had that horrified me; it was the *reason* for my fury. In my stupor, I had mistaken my boyfriend for Papa Dick. A man I hadn't spoken to in a decade, and yet it was he who I had struck out at in my darkest hour. I could no longer deny that I needed help.

Brutally hungover, I picked up the phone and dialed the number I hadn't called in months but still knew by heart: Mom's.

I ROSE FROM MY chair and stretched my arms, then walked slowly over to the bookshelf, perusing the collection of psychology and self-help books. Heather, my therapist, put down her pen and let an easy silence fill the room. She was used to my routine. I would often move around the room during our sessions, uncomfortable with her steady gaze upon my face and the constant expectation of disclosure. Sometimes I dreaded seeing her at all, afraid that my story would finally be told and I would have nothing left to say, forcing her to pronounce me either cured or hopeless. But still, I went.

"As you were saying," she said, her expression neutral as always. "You're thinking of leaving Munich? Where would you move to?"

"I don't know. Canada. I mean . . . *home,* I guess. Although it doesn't feel much like home anymore."

"Yes, and that's one of your challenges. But you've also been in Europe for over a decade, so you would have to expect an adjustment period."

"Yeah, I know. I think I'm ready for it." I glanced over my shoulder at her. "Thanks to you," I added, and it was true.

I had been lucky to find Heather, a British psychologist practicing in Munich. And after working together for six months, she had plenty of words to describe me: mother-attached, father-absent, male-abandoned, anger-suppressed, sexually-abused-and-overexposed, substance-for-love-replaced, parental-role-reversed, premature-responsibility-laden, innocence-deprived, guidance-deprived, role-model-lacking, hardship-enduring, stability-lacking, safety-yearning, and expectation-deficient. "Cool," I had said to her once. "I love that there are labels for all this stuff. All this time, I thought I was so freakishly unique."

Through Heather, I learned new things about myself. When I told her about Barry, I assured her that the damage probably hadn't been too deep because I'd almost thought of it as consensual. But that was the whole point, Heather said: it wasn't possible for an eight-year-old to consent to such a thing, and the very fact that I saw it that way revealed the scars it had left. And my relationship with my mother, surely the source of most of my afflictions, was cast in a new light. "You felt you owed your mother something for sticking with you through your childhood," Heather said to me once. "Did it ever occur to you that that was her duty and obligation?" I shook my head, shocked at my inability to see the obvious. As a child, I had held so much inside in an attempt to be strong that it would now take years of work for me to learn to express my true feelings safely. As a result, Heather had treatment suggestions for me beyond the usual talk therapy. Perhaps a staged rebirth would do the trick, she ventured, or an exercise in letter writing to all who had hurt me. But I declined, imagining my humiliation at both activities. I was fine, I told her. Thoughts of diving off Munich's Friedensengel, "Angel of Peace," statue in a moment of self-pity had passed, I'd sworn off drugs and casual sex, and I'd cut way back on drinking.

"How are things with your mother?" Heather asked me now. "You are still communicating?"

I nodded. When I called Mom on that dreadful morning, we'd made a pact: we'd agreed that our differences were probably insurmountable, but we would try to return to each other's lives. I'd taken her on a holiday to get reacquainted, and it had been mostly successful.

"Sure, yeah. Pretty good, I guess. I mean, she calls now, she seems to care and everything, so that's good. It's just . . ." Heather raised her eyebrows, waiting. "It's just sometimes I feel like if she really loved me, if she really wanted to make a fresh start of our relationship like she claims she does, she would act a little differently. You know, like not try to tell me about her sex life, which she knows I hate. Or smoke pot in front of me. And her boyfriend . . . I can't believe she's still with him. After all these years, and all the pain he's caused her . . . okay, so he finally divorced his wife, but my God . . . I mean, he basically stole my mother away from me when I needed her most, and he doesn't even care! And he hated me! He tried to push me out of their lives to go and live with my father, who I barely knew! How can she think it's okay to still be with him? How am I supposed to react to that? I feel like if I completely welcome her back into my life, I'm also welcoming all the pain and humiliation she caused me because of him."

"She will never be the mother you want. I don't think you're the only person in the world with that complaint. That doesn't mean she can't add value to your life."

"Yeah, I know. Anyway . . ." I turned back to the bookshelf and ran my hand over a row of spines. "I definitely feel more together. But I still feel . . . empty. Unfulfilled. I don't know, I hate how cliché that sounds, but I guess I thought this process would be more . . . dramatic."

"It doesn't happen overnight," Heather said. "You've been living with certain beliefs about yourself and your family for almost three decades. It's going to take time to undo that and see the truth."

"In other words, I have to get all the crap out before I can fit the good stuff in."

"Exactly."

I grinned. "Papa Dick would agree with that. When I was a kid, he always told me I had to get the poop out of my body before it could make room for nutrients. Man, that guy was obsessed with shit. This one time—" I stopped pacing, standing stock-still as I stared at a book with a yellow cover. Slowly, I pulled it from the shelf and held it before me. "Oh my God," I said quietly. "Oh. My God."

"What is it?" Heather asked, lowering her notepad.

I turned the cover toward her. "This book."

She pushed her glasses up her nose and peered at it. "Is the title familiar to you?"

"Not the title. The author." I dropped the book on the table. "It's my father."

Heather stared back at me, the shock on her face a contrast to her usual professional poise. "Your *father*? Truly?"

"Yes. He's studied childhood brain development for years, and I knew he had become an expert in his field. But I didn't realize he'd written a book. He probably told me at some point, but . . . I guess I pay about as much attention to his world as he pays to mine." I collapsed into a chair and put my head in my hands. "Well. How the fuck do you like that. Here I am, lamenting on about my childhood, while the man who was never a father to me is out there writing books about raising happy, well-adjusted kids. I wonder if he even sees the irony in that."

I lit a cigarette and let it burn between my fingers, untouched. I didn't really smoke anymore, but the feel of a cigarette in my hand somehow, stupidly, made me feel a little tougher. "You know, he and I have never even really talked about the past. He's never asked, beyond the superficial. And in the meantime, he's got these two other daughters at home who were raised with all the benefits of his knowledge. How could he write a book like this and not even show an interest in how it applied to his own child?"

"Maybe he's afraid to hear the truth. Afraid that you'll blame him for everything, and that the tenuous bond you share now will be broken forever."

"Yes, but still—"

"Don't mistake silence for lack of compassion, Cea. What he knows about your childhood probably hurts him deeply. And, being an expert in how his absence and your family's dysfunction must have affected your development, he probably lives with the guilt of it every day."

"Well. I hadn't thought of it that way."

She took the book from the table and looked at the cover. "I remember this. It impressed me." She set it aside and picked up her notepad again. "Listen. If it's any comfort, this is about you. Look at all you've been through, and yet here you are. Resilient, just like the title says. This may sound trite, but he would be proud."

"Yeah. Would be. I understand what you're saying, but hell, I speak to the man two or three times a year. I've seen him, like, three times in the past decade. Not once has he visited me here, not once in all the years I've been in Europe, even though I've invited him. He acts all concerned when he sees me, and then I don't hear from him for months. I guess that's just the story of my family, right? Out of sight, out of mind." I shook my head angrily, that old ripped-off feeling raging to the surface once more.

Heather looked at me sympathetically. "I understand that your father's behavior is frustrating to you. Clearly, you have some work to do with him. Do you think you'd feel comfortable discussing what we've talked about today with him?"

"I—I don't know." I was growing weary of the sound of my own complaining voice. "Really, I just want to move on. I've made it this long without him, I just want to . . ." I waved my hand. "Anyway, like I said, I'm done with Munich. I'm twenty-nine years old; it'll be another decade for me soon. I need a new start."

"That's a big decision. Will you be able to continue your career in Canada?"

"No. Not really, I mean. A little. I don't care. Anyway, I've saved up a lot of money. I need to do this."

"All right. But do me a favor, okay? Focus on your healing for a while. Don't jump into a relationship right away. Generally one chooses a partner after years of parental guidance and support, but you obviously haven't had the benefit of a proper role model. For the first time in your life, you have the tools to make a wise decision, but that doesn't mean you'll get it right the first time. Think of your next relationship as . . . kind of like your first one. Right out of— What do you Canadians call it—high school?" She smiled, and I grinned back at her.

"Don't worry. The last thing on my mind right now is finding a boyfriend."

Heather nodded. "Good. You're a very strong woman, Cea. I'm sure that whatever you do, you're going to do just fine."

Chapter Twenty-Seven

"Hey, look at this one," Mom said with a giggle, pulling a photo from the stack on her lap. "Look how *young* I was!"

"Yeah, you look about twelve. Hard to believe you were already a mother then."

"Isn't it? You would have been about the same age Avery is now."

I smiled down at my son, who was sitting at my feet with a toy truck in his hand. "Fruck!" he said, zooming it along the ground, and Mom and I burst out laughing. We were sitting on a park bench close to her house in Calgary, taking a photographic stroll down memory lane.

"Avery is amazing," Mom said, shaking her head. "I'm so glad you had him."

"Yeah, me too. Even if . . ."

"What?"

"Well, you know. Even if it doesn't work out with James. At least we have Avery."

"Mm. Things are that bad, huh?"

"Pretty much. I just . . ." I shrugged, wondering for the thousandth time how I had ended up in yet another miserable marriage that pinched at me like a pair of too-tight shoes that I was forced to put on each day.

Against Heather's advice, upon my return to Canada shortly before my thirtieth birthday, I had quickly latched on to the first man who had shown an interest in me, jumping in headlong and ignoring the many red flags that waved frantically at me from the beginning. Part of the draw was that James wasn't interested in having a family. *I don't want children*, I had said to him when we first met. *Ever. I need you to know that.* My childhood dream of having a baby girl had died long ago, when I realized how drained I was from the years of what felt like raising my own mother. Just the thought of a child, with its constant need for care and guidance, exhausted me.

But four years later, I had woken up one morning with Papa Dick on my mind. I rarely thought about him, but I was searching for a reason for the gloom that had hung over my head for as long as I could remember. That morning, I was thinking of the last time I had seen him. He had been passing through Vancouver for a Thrival gig, so I'd picked him up from the airport and driven him to James's and my place to spend the night. After talking briefly about Jan, Jessie and Dane—who were respectively missing, living in Calgary in a welfare walk-up, and still institutionalized—our conversation had turned to books. I told him about one I had just finished, and then he described an Eckhart Tolle he was reading. "It's such a shame," he said then, shaking his head sadly, "that no one in my family reads."

Confused, I cocked my head. "No one in your family? What about me?"

He blinked at me. "My kids, I mean. You know, my *real* family. Let's face it—you were always a bit too . . . *commercial* to be a Person."

I willed myself not to cry. Was he serious? Was he actually saying this? My grandfather, the closest thing I'd ever had to a father, didn't even consider me one of his tribe? I opened my mouth to speak, but he beat me to it.

"Say," he said brightly, glancing around my kitchen. "You don't have a basin around, do you? I just know I'm going to wake up having to pee tonight, and you know how I feel about modern toilets."

Ever since that conversation, something had niggled at me. It was no mystery that my grandfather and mother were part of the cause of my depression, but I also understood that I was thirty-three years old and it was time to stop laying blame—time to take responsibility for my own happiness. And if I didn't belong to my family of origin, perhaps it was time to start one of my own.

I had Avery when I was thirty-five, and from the moment he was born I understood everything I'd ever heard about the deepest love possible. But with his arrival, my desire to escape the unhappiness of my marriage was only heightened. I found myself thinking longingly about my own childhood, of the times it was just Mom and me, and actually wishing for the simplicity of life with an absent father. But I felt trapped by my son's right to an intact family, James's and my broken dreams, and my fear of striking out on my own. The cash I'd saved from modeling was long gone, blown away by bad business investments and lack of knowledge. How I'd ever thought I could handle any amount of money was beyond me, given my family's history with it.

So now here I was, seven years into my new life, standing in a playground with a young child, no money and escape on my mind. I sighed deeply and turned toward Mom. "I just don't want to get divorced again, you know?"

"Honey," she said. "It's not about how many times you get married or divorced, it's about finding happiness. Doing what you have to do to get to the right place. I mean, look at my parents. They went to great lengths to achieve their dreams, and they made it—"

"Mom, I know you think they were the most amazing couple ever, but even they ended up splitting when the dream turned sour." I laughed humorlessly. "There was Grandma Jeanne, doing all the cooking and mending Papa Dick's socks so he wouldn't have to be distracted from living his wilderness fantasy, and meanwhile, what was he doing? Cheating on her left and right. As soon as he realized she didn't idolize him anymore, he had to go out and recruit some new followers with his dick. It's no wonder she left him!"

"Cea, don't—"

"No, really! However you want to word it, that's how it went down."

"Honey, he's dead now, don't talk about him like that—"

"I know he's dead, and I'm sorry!"

I threw my hands to the sky, suddenly furious at the man who had let me down so completely in my adult years. He died of cancer just days before my last birthday, and although I had tried my best to cry for him, the tears just hadn't come. How ironic that a man who had devoted his life to avoiding pollution, tobacco, chemicals, alcohol and sugar had been tackled in the end by the big disease.

"I'm sorry I don't miss him the way you do. I loved him, I really did, but he was so narcissistic! He was the only real father figure I had, but it was like I didn't even exist after I left the wilderness! He never even wrote to me—"

Avery stood up, truck in hand, and turned toward me. "Mommy mad? Mommy sad? Av-wee kiss better?"

"Oh, honey, Mommy's fine . . ." I opened my arms and let him kiss me on the cheek, then placed him on the ground again. "And

I feel even better now. Thank you." I watched him toddle off to the sandbox before turning back to Mom.

"Anyway, I didn't mean to blow up. It's just . . . you and I are better now, I guess we've learned to accept each other's differences. Even though you're still with . . . him," I added quietly, unable to help myself. Mom's mouth tightened a little. It still made me furious that she had, after all these years, stayed with the man who had broken both of our hearts multiple times. It was like a hangover reminder to me of all the bad choices she'd made in men throughout my life.

"I'm sorry you feel that way," Mom said, and I nodded back at her curtly.

Really, there was nothing more to say on the matter. It was a conversation she and I had already had several times, and there was simply no resolution to it.

"Yeah, well. Anyway, it's just . . . I wish I could feel some sort of closure with my family. I mean, even Grandma Jeanne—"

"Mom? What do you mean?"

"I don't know. I'm her only grandchild, I've known her my whole life, and yet I feel like I don't really *know* her . . . She's so . . . *guarded*."

"Yes. But Dad told me that she wasn't always like that. It's like . . . as much as she spoke of living her life without guilt and regret, I think she actually has a lot."

"What from?"

"Us kids. Jessie's mental state, Jan's depression and drug problems, Dane's . . . *craziness*. And . . ." She glanced sideways at me.

"And what?"

"Well. There was a thing that happened to me, before you were born. It wasn't her fault, but I think she thought she should have been there to save me—"

"What are you talking about?"

"Just . . ." She hesitated again, and then cleared her throat. "Are you sure you want to hear this? It's kind of . . . awful."

"Yes," I said, although my mouth had suddenly gone dry. "Of course I want to hear it."

IT HAPPENED WHEN MOM was fifteen, she told me. The year before she got pregnant with me, when she was living in Los Gatos with her family. It was late October, and my mother was riding her bike home from school. During that spell in her life, she spent a lot of her time getting high. She passed many lunch breaks under the bleachers behind the gym, sitting alone in the shade having a little toke. And sometimes she did mushrooms, supplied by one of her male classmates who seemed to have a crush on her.

This was something she was noticing more and more lately: guys were paying attention to her, and though they never asked her out on dates, she had seen them staring at her boobs and bare legs as they passed her in the hallways. She liked to wear miniskirts, all the rage in late-sixties California, and even though she had been sent home once for wearing one too short, my grandfather had sent her back the next day with a note telling her teacher that if he insisted on living in fear of the female form, it was nobody's problem but his own.

Anyway, it didn't matter, because Mom wasn't really interested in other guys. She already had a boyfriend named Little Joe, the fourth guy she'd slept with since losing her virginity two years before. Little Joe's home life was rather sketchy, so lately he'd been living in the shed in her family's backyard. Mom brought his dinner out to him in the evenings, and sometimes she slept with him overnight if they smoked too much pot to bother getting up.

All the same, Mom's loyalties didn't extend to her not accepting other boys' gifts. And so it was that on this particular afternoon, Mom was high on mushrooms. The earth tilted slowly on its side, left and then right, as she pedaled down the street. Clouds swirled above her in gently rolling waves. She let go of the handlebars and spread her arms wide, enjoying the wind in her long hair. She was feeling good. The sun was warm on her face, and the mushrooms had given the passing world an appealing brightness she wouldn't normally have noticed. She grabbed the handlebars again and stuck her legs out to the sides like a child.

"Hey there," a male voice said to her out of nowhere, and she almost fell off her bike in surprise.

She looked to her left and saw a man on the sidewalk smoking a cigarette. She found the pedals again and braked, certain he looked familiar. It was Mr. Jackson, her math teacher from school. It seemed odd to see him here on the street, out of his regular context, but she smiled at him. Mr. Jackson had always been kind to my mother despite her failing grades and many missed classes, and she knew that his wife had died from cancer not too long ago.

"Where are you off to?" he asked Mom cheerfully.

"Home," she said, gesturing ahead. "Just up the next block."

"Ah. Well, I'm going your way. Mind if I walk with you?"

"Of course not." She started riding again, keeping her pace slow so he could walk along beside her.

"Lovely day," he remarked.

"Isn't it?"

He dropped his cigarette butt on the sidewalk and ground it out with his heel. "So, home, huh? Tell me who's there. Brothers and sisters?"

"Two sisters, yes. And a brother. And Mom and Dad, naturally."

He nodded. "Naturally. Bet they'll be glad to see you."

"No, well, I mean nobody's home right now. Mom and Dad had to go into the city today. My dad's a climbing instructor," she added proudly.

"Is that right? I do a bit of climbing myself."

"Wow. Really?"

They had reached my mother's house by then, so she got off her bike and walked it across the yard to the side gate. Mr. Jackson followed, chatting animatedly about his climbing days. She opened the gate and walked her bike through it, and that's when he grabbed her arm and twisted it behind her back.

"*Ow!*" she yelped, more surprised than hurt. "What are you doing?"

"Shut up! Just shut the hell up, or I swear I'll break it! Now get down on the grass!"

She craned her neck over her shoulder to see her teacher's face, shocked by the sudden change in his behavior. "But—but this is stupid, Mr. Jackson. What are you doing? I'll tell at school. And you're—you're *nice.* I don't want to get you in trouble."

The man snorted. "Mr. Jackson? Mr. *Jackson*? Who the hell is he?"

"Who—?" Oh God. Of course. This wasn't Mr. Jackson. Now that she was looking into this man's face, she could see that his eyes were brown, not blue like her teacher's. And Mr. Jackson's wife had died of lung cancer; he never would have touched a cigarette. How could she have made such a mistake? This man wasn't even tall like her teacher.

"Get down," the man commanded again. "Get *down*!"

Mom did as he told her, crumpling to the grass on her knees. The man pushed her head forward into the ground and reached under her skirt, ripping her underwear off with one vicious pull.

She needed to scream, she knew, but she couldn't. Her voice was frozen in her throat. Was this really happening? She felt so buzzed from the drugs, almost as if she weren't in her own body, that she couldn't be sure. Then she thought of something: Little Joe. He was almost always in the shed when she got home from school, and he was probably there right now.

"Joe! Hel—!" she managed to scream before the man's hand clamped over her mouth.

"Joe? Who the fuck is Joe? No, forget it," he said, tightening his grip. The man pinned her arms in place and pulled her back up to a sitting position. "Don't you dare scream," he said in a low voice. "I swear to God if you scream, I'll strangle you."

Behind her, my mother heard a fly being unzipped. She was scared now, really scared. She couldn't think straight as it was, and now she had to find a way out of this mess. Trying to fight back would be pointless, she was sure of that. She commanded herself to stop struggling, and the man's grip on her relaxed a little.

"Wait a minute," she said. "You—you don't have to force me, okay? I want to. It's just . . . I have my period. It's really heavy. How—how about if I give you a blowjob? I give really good blowjobs, guys tell me that a lot. And I—you won't regret it. I swallow and everything. Okay?"

He didn't respond at first, and then he jerked her around to face him and shoved her head down to his groin. "Okay, you've got yourself a deal. But this better be good. And if you bite me, I swear to God—"

"I won't, I promise," Mom said, her voice muffled against his crotch.

"Good. Get to it," he growled, and pulled his dick out of his pants and jammed it into her mouth.

Somehow, Mom got through it. The drugs helped, she said.

Instead of focusing on what was in her mouth, she focused on the sound of the birds chirping in the trees and the feel of the sunlight on her neck. She was almost able to convince herself that those were the things that were real, and the rest of it was all just happening in her imagination. She waited until he was finished, and then she held her breath and swallowed; she had come this far, and she didn't dare mess it up now.

It seemed a miracle when the man zipped up his pants and shoved her roughly to the ground one last time before he walked through the gate.

Mom wiped her hand over her mouth and struggled to her feet. She stumbled into the house through the back door, ran to the kitchen and washed her mouth out over and over again with hot water. She picked up the bottle of dish soap by the sink and squirted it into her mouth, then rinsed some more. She heard the screen door creak open and whirled around, terrified that her attacker had returned, but it was Little Joe. He was standing in the doorway, his grin coy and his hair disheveled from sleep.

"Hey, babe," he said, leaning lazily against the wall. "What's goin' on?"

BESIDE ME, MY MOTHER was dabbing at her eyes. "And you know what the worst part of it was?" she asked me, shaking her head sadly. "I didn't even break up with him. Little Joe. He didn't see what had happened, but when I told him, all he said was 'Wow, babe, that's a real bummer.' Like I had torn my favorite dress or something."

"Oh my God," I said, momentarily lost for words. "That's just . . . oh my God. I had no idea."

"Yeah. I never went to school again. I probably would have

dropped out anyway, my grades were awful, but I really couldn't go after that. I had this weird idea that even though Mr. Jackson had nothing to do with it, he would somehow know. Anyway, it didn't take anything to convince Mom and Dad. You know how they felt about schools and other such evil institutions." She gave me a weak smile.

"Yeah. Did . . . did you tell anyone?"

"Jeanne, of course. And Jan. They both helped me through it. That was the amazing thing about our family, we could always talk about anything without shame." She paused and took my hand. "You know, though, it's a funny thing. In a weird way, I'm almost glad it happened. Because if it hadn't, I don't know if I ever would have left Little Joe. I really didn't think I deserved any better than him. But I couldn't stand the fact that he knew. We never talked about it, of course, but that only seemed to make it worse. It's like he didn't even care, and it became this horrible sort of power he had over me. Looking at him made me remember it, day after day. So at one point, I made a decision. I decided I was going to find a better man, one who would treat me with respect.

"And then, just like that, your father came along. It was almost like a miracle. We were only together a few weeks when I got pregnant with you. And even though he didn't stick around, being with him was the one thing I did right, because you got his intelligence and his looks, and now you even have a decent relationship with him. I mean, imagine if Little Joe had been your father? Or Karl, or Barry?" She shook her head regretfully. "The sad thing is, though, my resolve didn't last. After Greg left me, I was so broken that all my good intentions to find the right man left me. I just took whatever I could get. And what I got was . . . not very good, for you or for me. And for that I'm sorry."

I nodded, trying to wrap my mind around this new information. There was a familiarity to one of my mother's statements that I couldn't get out of my head: *I just took whatever I could get.* And there it was: as divergent as my life may have been from my mother's, and as hard as I had tried to be completely different—*opposite,* even—from her, I had followed her pattern in love. Not once had I chosen a man based on his ability to meet my needs. Instead I had let them choose me, taking up with them at the slightest hint of interest regardless of our compatibility. It was an ugly admission, one that made me recognize the true standing of my self-esteem. But it was also very necessary.

I put my arm around my mother's shoulders and smiled at her. Her skin looked pale, I noticed, even though it was late summer.

"Hey, Mom. You feeling okay?"

"Sure, honey. Just tired, that's all. Just a bit tired."

Chapter Twenty-Eight

"Michelle Person's room, please," I said to the nurse at the reception desk.

She checked her computer screen and pointed down the hallway. "Number twelve."

I thanked her and moved forward, steeling myself for what I was about to see. "Now remember what I told you," I said to Avery, taking his hand. "Grandma Michelle isn't well, so she won't be able to play with you like she usually does."

"Okay," he said with all the present-mindedness of a two-and-a-half-year-old. "But when will she be better?"

"I don't know, sweetie," I said lightly, steering him to Mom's door before he could ask any more questions. I couldn't tell him the answer that was in my head: *Never.*

It was the day after my thirty-eighth birthday, and my mother was dying. Her cancer, a slow-moving breast tumor, had been curable with treatment, her oncologist had assured us. But Mom had refused both chemo and radiation, citing her belief in natural healing and leading to countless arguments between us. Not to be swayed, she had warded off the inevitable for a while with acupuncture and herbs before her decline. After that, it had all happened quickly. Two months ago, the last time I'd seen her, Mom had been well enough to cook a meal with me in her kitchen. Shortly after that, Grandma Jeanne had moved in with her to "help out a bit," and yesterday, when Mom hadn't called to wish me a happy birthday, I knew things must have gotten bad. My grandmother had finally called me late at night to inform me that Mom had been admitted not just to the hospital, but to the palliative care unit. I had boarded the first plane to Calgary that morning.

I entered the room, holding Avery close to my side. Mom was asleep, her face so still and lifeless that for a moment I thought I was already too late. Then her hand twitched, and I took it in my own.

"Mom," I whispered, and she slowly opened her eyes. "Avery is here. He wants to see you." I lifted him up to her face.

"Hi, Gamma 'Shell," he said.

"Avery. My angel." Her voice was a croak, but she smiled the tiniest bit before closing her eyes again.

So began my vigil. I spent my days at the hospital, alternating between sitting at Mom's bedside and playing with Avery in the visitors' lounge. As horrible as was my reason for being there, it was almost a welcome break from the wreck of my home life. Back in Vancouver, I had a husband I no longer loved, a mountain of bills that I couldn't pay and a failing business to contend with—several years before, I'd started my own line of swimwear, which, despite winning loyal fans and being embraced by celebrities, had proven too expensive and labor intensive for me to handle on my own. I watched my mother's face, cradled Avery in my lap, and refused to think of anything but her. People came to visit, even my Aunt Jan, who I hadn't seen in years. Grandma Jeanne stayed at her side almost constantly, rearranging pillows and fighting back tears. Nurses spoke in hushed voices, James flew out to pick up Avery, there was talk about stopping this machine or that, a minister even came. My mother's eyes turned yellow. When I ran my hand down her back, I could feel tumors bulging under her skin. Prepared for the inevitable, I mourned the loss of her before she actually passed. At night, I thought about my son's third birthday party that she wouldn't be in this world for, and cried into my pillow.

On the last day I saw my mother alive, the sun rose pink and orange in the sky as I sat beside her sleeping body. I placed my hand on the book in my lap. A nurse entered the room and pushed some buttons on the drip machine.

"How is she?" I asked quietly.

"A little worse. Any day now. She'll start to have fewer and fewer lucid moments."

I nodded, and she smiled sympathetically and left the room. *Okay*, I thought. *Okay*. I knew I couldn't afford to wait any longer.

As I grew up, my mother and I began to mend our relationship. Here we are during a bonding trip we took to Hawaii.

My mother's lucid moments were already down to one or two each day. Grandma Jeanne hadn't arrived at the hospital yet, so we were all alone. I stood up and moved to her side.

"Mom," I began. "There's a beautiful sunrise out there this morning." I looked out the window, but she didn't stir. I took her hand, staying quiet for a long time as the tears built behind my eyes. *At least you have a mother who loves you. That's more than a lot of kids have*, I heard her saying, and for once it didn't infuriate me. It was true. She had done the best she could. Memories of my childhood with her jostled with moments we shared during my teens and adulthood—watching her dance at one of her wild parties, slamming the phone down on her in anger, the two of us laughing together on the beach under a Hawaiian sun. I searched my soul for anything left unsaid. But after all these many years, our relationship was so complex, so filled with love and torment and everything in between, that it was hard to know where to begin or end. But perhaps that was the point. There didn't need to be an end, and as long as there was love, the rest could just fall away.

I swallowed hard. "I—I have something for you. I thought you might like it for your . . . journey." I picked up the Big Blue Book from my chair and placed it on my mother's chest, bracing for the dam to break behind my eyes. "Do you remember how you used to read this to me? And that time in the forest? The Brownie story was always my favorite. November, remember?" I squeezed her hand again, and she opened her eyes.

"Cea . . ."

"Yes. It's me. I love you."

"Love you too . . ." Her eyes were already closing again. "So much . . ."

I laid my head on her chest, choking back a sob. I saw her face in the dying light of the fire, smiling as she read to me. Yes.

Wherever we had been and whatever we had done, my mother had always built us "a fire of ruddy glow." And now, she was finally finding her home.

"Thank you," I whispered to her. "Thank you for being my mommy." It was all I could think of to say, and in that moment, I had never meant any words more truly.

CLOSING THE DOOR BEHIND me, I sank down onto my mother's guest bed and pressed my palms to my eyes. Tears spilled around my fingers, dripping down my cheeks and off my chin. I could hear the last of the guests leaving upstairs, and the lyrics to Van Morrison's "Into the Mystic" were still echoing in my head. It was the perfect send-off, I thought, for the woman with a true gypsy soul. My mother was dead, and her last party had just ended.

I found a tissue and blew my nose, thankful that at least James wasn't with me. The last thing my husband could offer me right now was comfort. Our marriage was holding on by a thread, and all that kept it from snapping was my fear of trying to raise my son with barely a penny to my name. Business ventures in recent years had been difficult for both James and me, and we now found ourselves in dire financial straits. I felt like a spider trapped in a drain; I was frightened, resigned to a life of misery, and just waiting for the water to come down and really mess things up. Only my love for my son kept me going.

A knock sounded at the door, startling me out of my self-pity. I blew my nose again and pulled the door open a crack. It was my Aunt Jan.

"Hey," she said, and I opened the door wide. If there was a sight sorrier than the photo of my mother's still-young face beside her urn of ashes upstairs, it was her sister Jan. Most of her teeth were missing, her hair was a matted mess and her skin looked ravaged from years of drug use.

"Hi," I said, wiping my eyes. "Sorry, I was just . . . having a moment."

"Yeah. This probably isn't a good time. Should I—?"

"No, no, come in. We're family, right? We need to lean on each other." I gave her a quick smile, hoping she hadn't caught the irony in my voice. Other than Grandma Jeanne, my aunt truly had nobody and nothing in this world.

"Tough day, huh?"

"Yeah." I sighed. "The toughest."

Jan entered the room and stood awkwardly. "Well," she said, giving me a little shrug. "Jessie wanted to be here today. She just . . . you know, has a hard time with social stuff."

"I know. How is she?"

"Okay. Getting by. She has a new husband."

I nodded, taking comfort in the fact that at least she had someone. Jessie's first husband had died many years before, and from what I understood, she almost never left her tiny apartment. I looked up to meet Jan's eyes.

"And what about you? How are you?"

"Oh, you know me. I just keep on keeping on."

I grinned back at her sadly. Both of us knew that after this brief resurfacing, she would disappear once more into the drug world. I wished there was something I could do to help her, but we were a useless team, because I lacked the funds and she lacked the willpower.

"Seriously, I'll be fine, I always am. Anyway, um . . ." She was fidgeting uncomfortably with the hem of her sweater.

"Yes?"

"It's just . . . you're leaving tonight, and I'm not sure when I'll see you again, so . . ."

"Uh-huh?" I smiled at her expectantly.

She sat down on the bed. "There's something I have to tell you. About your mother. She kind of . . . left a message for you. Before she died, I mean."

"Before she died?" I repeated. "Why didn't she just tell me herself?"

Jan tucked a strand of unkempt hair behind her ear, a gesture so like Mom's. "It was when she first went into the hospital. She didn't want to tell you herself because . . . she said she didn't want it to be your last memory of her."

"Oh. Okay," I said cautiously, lowering myself onto the bed beside my aunt.

"I don't know much about what went on when you were a kid. I know your mother had boyfriends, and that they weren't always the best kind of men—"

"Except Karl," I interjected. "I always liked him. He did some crazy things, but he was always nice to me, and he was funny, and in a weird way we were kind of happy when we were all together, so . . ." I shrugged and my voice trailed off. My aunt's eyes were darting around the room. I could tell that whatever she had to say, she just wanted to get it over with.

"I'm glad about that," she said with a nod. "But there was another one. Gary, I think?"

"Barry," I said robotically, and my stomach clenched. I could still see him, shining a flashlight up and down my naked eight-year-old body as I cringed inside. I could still feel my fingers, landing upon my mother's hand as they reached toward a place a child's hand should never go. The most shameful moments of my life.

"Yes, Barry," Jan replied. "Well, Michelle . . . she wasn't very coherent, she was already pretty bad, but she told me that she made a huge mistake. She said there was a time when he did something wrong to you. You knew that she knew about it, and . . . well. She's sorry. She's just so sorry."

I nodded slowly, my mind whirling.

"Are you okay?" Jan asked after a moment, touching my shoulder.

"Yes. I guess I should be grateful for the apology, but it's kind of just . . . another drop in the bucket of craziness that's been my life. Sometimes I feel like I'm defined by what I've survived, and I'm not sure if I like that."

My aunt grinned. "If it's any comfort to you, our family *is* nuts. Even I can see that."

"I know. But sometimes I just wonder why. Why there's so much love there, and yet also so much madness." I avoided my aunt's gaze, aware that I was including her in my statement, but she didn't flinch.

"Well. There was a lot that went on before you were born, especially with Dane. He and Dad . . . it was rough for them. Did you know that Dad used to seduce Dane's girlfriends away from him, right in front of Mom? It was pretty awful for everyone, even though my parents had an open marriage. Dane was really in love with this one girl Debbie, and he never got over it. Crazy Debbie, we used to call her, and when his mind went he became convinced she was your real mother, and . . . anyway, I've already told you that story."

"Yes. The night he stole me away from Mom, right? Yelling that she was an impostor." I shook my head. This piece of information about my grandfather wasn't really news to me, of course, as Dane had mentioned it during our visit to him in the hospital so many years before. All the same, it was an appalling fact. "I wonder if that's what pushed Dane over the edge," I ventured.

"I don't know," Jan responded, shrugging again. "And he's still in the hospital, so we probably never will."

"Right." I stood up and paced the room, suddenly angry. Although I could intellectually understand my family's strangeness, I still resented it. Why couldn't any of them just be normal? Why did my mother have to choose a course of useless herbs over readily available help for her disease, leaving her dead at fifty-four? And why did she wait so long to apologize to me?

"I wish Mom had said sorry in person," I said to Jan finally. "Now I'm just left with more questions. Like . . . here's an obvious one: why did she let it happen if she knew it was wrong?"

"Mm. I don't have the answer to that, of course, but . . . the sexual lines were very blurred in our family. Besides Dad taking Dane's girlfriends away, I mean. You do know about Michelle and Dane, don't you?"

Michelle and Dane. Only then did I realize how rarely I heard their names in the same sentence, so intent had my mother been on avoiding her brother my whole life. "No. What do you mean?"

"I mean . . . she never told you he molested her?"

The hair on my arms stood up. "*Molested* her? What are you talking about?" Jan looked away and shook her head. "No," I said. "You have to tell me."

"I thought you knew."

"No."

"All right. You see, Dane was . . . touching her. It started when she was thirteen. He always made her believe it was her problem, so she never told our parents. And when she finally had enough and told him to stop, that's when he stole you that night. She thinks that if she had just let it continue—"

"But she couldn't have," I said, horrified. "She *couldn't* have. It was so . . . so wrong."

"Yes, it was. But he was ill, and our parents, well . . ."

"Oh my God. Oh my God. That's just so awful."

"I know. But maybe this will help you understand her a little better."

I clasped my hands to my head amid a hurricane of emotions, overwrought from the events and revelations of the day. So that was it. My mother was a victim of sexual abuse, not only at the hands of a stranger mistaken for her teacher in her parents' backyard, but at the hands of her own brother as well. It really did explain a lot.

"Thank you," I said to Jan. "Thank you for telling me. I needed to know this."

She nodded and stood up, smoothing her bulky sweater down over her hips. "Well. It's been great seeing you, despite everything. I'm proud of you, kid. Somehow, you managed to escape it all. I mean, look at you. You got the beauty, the smarts, a glamorous career, a house, even a husband and kid. You turned out pretty good."

I smiled back at my aunt, wishing I could find some satisfaction in her words. The truth was, I had successfully created the *appearance* of my dream—beautiful from the outside, and perfectly hollow within. It was an illusion I knew would have to be completely shattered to be rebuilt in reality, but the idea of doing so was scarier than anything I'd ever faced. I thought about my mother, who, though she had made her share of mistakes with me, had refused to let her darkest experiences ruin her life. And in that way, her time on earth had perhaps been more successful than my own.

As I hugged my aunt goodbye, I made a decision: I had survived too much to let anything as mundane as financial stress and domestic discord stop me from achieving my dreams. I wasn't going to be the one to fail the legacy of my family. The Persons may have had their share of craziness and weaknesses, but they never lacked courage in their convictions or allowed themselves to be derailed by fear.

Chapter Twenty-Nine

I walked through the woods, singing a favorite old Fleetwood Mac song in my head to the sound of snapping twigs beneath my feet. "Future Games," with its poetic questions about what was to come, seemed perfectly fitting for where I was in my life now.

Sunlight filtered through the trees, dappling the stream that ran beside me with fluid shadows. It was a Tuesday morning, and the path was empty aside from a few chattering squirrels. Overhead, several crows screeched at a circling hawk. Having grown up in the bush, I'd always felt that city parks, no matter how vast and wild, were just cheap substitutes for the real thing. But Lynn Headwaters, a park at the edge of the city that included rivers, a lake and a small mountain range, was massive enough to swallow unprepared hikers for days at a time, occasionally never to be spat out again.

I crossed the suspension bridge, stopping to gaze down at the rushing waters a hundred feet below, then made my way down a hillside and continued along the river. It was almost noon. I found a log to rest on and took a sandwich out of my knapsack. As I ate, I tried to focus on nothing but the distant knock of a woodpecker, the rush of the water and the wind moving through the trees. The truth was that I should have been using this time to search for a job. Avery was with James today, as he and I had been sharing time with our son equally ever since we'd split up. Since leaving my second husband, my financial situation had become so desperate that I'd even had to pawn my wedding ring to put gas in my car (my *friend's* car, actually, as I had left my marriage without even a vehicle) and food in my fridge. But somehow, despite the daily stress of living under an umbrella of constant worry, I was happier than I had ever been. It was as if, for the first time as an adult, I was experiencing real freedom. I often thought about my grandparents, who had found their independence only when throwing all things material to the wind, and the irony of our parallel situations was not lost on me.

I finished eating, scanned the trees around me for birds, and then turned my gaze to the riverbank. What I saw there caused me to jump in surprise. Not thirty feet away, sitting against a tree trunk eating soup straight from the can, was a homeless man. Near his feet, I could see a backpack with a rolled tent attached to the bottom. I looked more closely. How had I not noticed him before? And *was* he actually homeless? I couldn't be sure. He looked to be about sixty, his face weathered and his long hair shaggy and tangled, but he didn't look the least bit drug-addled or unhealthy. Although certain parks in the city were a mecca for vagrants, this particular one wasn't.

I stood up and brushed off the seat of my jeans. I had meant to turn and walk away, but something held me to the spot. The man glanced up and gave me a friendly wave with his spoon.

"Lovely day," he called, revealing a mouthful of straight, white teeth.

"Yeah. Sure is." I hooked my thumbs into my back pockets, wondering why I, who so rarely had a word for strangers, was still standing here. I cleared my throat. "Looks like, uh . . . looks like you've pretty much got things figured out there."

"You got that right," he said with a smile. "Food, water, clothing and shelter. What more does anyone need?"

I blinked rapidly, hit by an unexpected wave of emotion. It wasn't just that the man reminded me of Papa Dick. It was as if I had entered a time warp. Suddenly I was four years old again, riding the shoulders of a summer visitor who had visions of the wilderness life that could be his, if he could just learn how to build that fire in the rain. It was 1975, and I was sitting in Karl's green pickup truck while he plundered a cottage for loot. I was eight years old, holding my mother's hand as we waited for someone's beat-up station wagon to show us its brake lights and give us a lift. And I was sitting inside my grandparents' tipi as the wind howled through another minus-fifty-degree Yukon night, unquestioning of my safety as I munched popcorn by the woodstove. This man before me was a throwback to what had once been so popular—a movement toward minimalism, emancipation and freedom that, for most, had ended with the turning of a decade, maturity, ambition or family obligations. Not so for Papa Dick, my grandfather of innovation and courage.

It had been two years since he died, and I'd finally made my peace with the way he'd failed me in my adult years. I realized that it was up to me to decide which man I wanted to remember: the deeply flawed one who had refused to acknowledge his shortcomings, or the father and grandfather who had given his family the ultimate gift of freedom, not to mention once saving my life. In a time and society obsessed with materialism and the pursuit of the American dream, he and my grandmother had created the ultimate sustainable lifestyle, embracing ideas that the rest of the world was just catching on to now. I saw him now, grinning at me beneath his battered felt cowboy hat as he recited a plethora of information about edible plants, bear poop, indigestion, porcupine soup, the

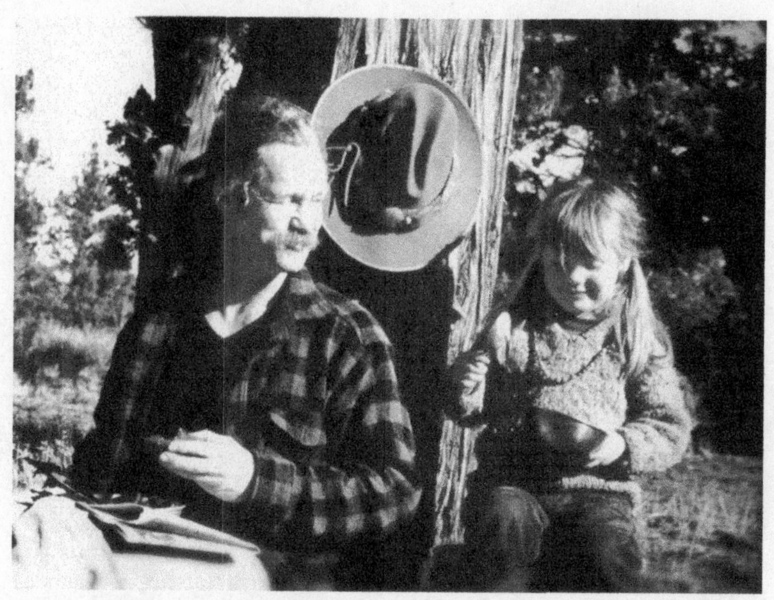

When I was little, Papa Dick was my favorite person in the whole world. On the tree is the same hat that I posed in as a baby; he was still wearing it the last time I saw him before his death.

evils of food preservatives, the benefits of marijuana and the craziness of the concrete jungle. *Papa Dick,* I thought with a smile, *you may not have been a hero to me, but you were to many. And I know I wouldn't be who I am today without you.*

"Funny, my grandfather used to say the exact same thing," I said to the man on the riverbank.

"Is that right? Sounds like a wise old soul."

"Yes, he certainly was. And he was right . . . except for one thing," I added, and the man looked back at me questioningly. "There's something he forgot. More than anything, everyone needs a family."

Epilogue

Parksville, B.C.
July 2012

They come running down to the shore, small feet slapping against the wooden walkway, and land on my beach blanket in a spray of sand. Both of them talking at once, filling me in on their adventures and pleading for snacks. My boys. I break out crackers, apples and juice, all of which they quickly devour.

"Watch this, Mommy!" Avery says, grabbing his skimboard and running toward an ankle-deep pool of water. Emerson follows, his chubby little legs pumping as he tries to keep up with his big brother. Avery throws the board across the water and jumps onto it, then loses his footing and crashes face first. Their laughter rings out into the air.

Parksville is my favorite place to come in the summer. Its beaches are only a ninety-minute ferry ride from my home of Vancouver, but it's a completely different world here. The sand flats are so expansive that you can walk a mile out to the ocean before stepping foot in it. Families converge on the sand, sculpting castles and tossing bocce balls by day and gathering around campfires with marshmallow sticks by night. Here, watching my kids from the shore, I can take a break from some of the daily tasks of motherhood. In fact, I am actually halfway through reading my first book of the year.

I'm about to open it again when a little girl in front of me catches my eye. She's piling sand dollars into a bucket and singing "Twinkle Twinkle, Little Star" in a high voice. Her features look similar to my own, as if she could be my own child.

"Katia," a woman wearing a tie-dyed caftan calls out. She holds up an orange for her daughter, but the girl shakes her head and goes back to her sand dollars. "Forget trying to get her to eat when she's playing," the woman says to me when she notices me smiling at her child.

"Yeah. She's adorable, though."

"Thank you." She starts to peel the orange, then stops and gazes out to the ocean. "It sure is pretty here, isn't it. Do you live in the area?"

"No, just on holiday. I live in West Vancouver."

"Ah. Nice." She nods, communicating none of the judgment I sometimes encounter on mention of my wealthy suburb. "Katia and I, we're just passing through, camping at the campground down the beach. She starts kindergarten next year, so I figured we should try to have a few adventures first. Just the two of us, you know?"

Her face disappears under her caftan as she removes it over her head, and I notice that there's no wedding ring on her hand. I think about Mom, who was similar to this woman in many ways, and of the short time I was a single mother myself. How drastically my life has changed since then.

I have been with my husband, Remy, for four years, and on this third attempt I have finally gotten marriage right. My realization that I was repeating my mother's patterns in love was a good starting point, but it meant tearing everything apart and going back to the beginning. Four months after splitting up with James, I typed my relationship wish list into an online dating profile like an employer's want ad. Three weeks later, I went on my first date with Remy, and by the time we left the restaurant my mind was spinning with disbelief at how perfect we seemed for each other. Not only was our connection immediate, he was everything I had ever hoped for: funny, successful, intelligent, affectionate, well traveled, tall and handsome. I thought about my mother, who had once promised herself she would find a good man and then promptly met my father. *Almost like a miracle*, she had said, and I felt exactly the same way about Remy.

In the beginning, when we talked about our past, I usually steered the conversation back to him. It wasn't for lack of my desire or his interest in discussing mine; it was more that I sensed that with this man, I would delve deeper than I had with anyone else, and I first needed to be certain our love was as real as I believed it was. I told him the basics: that I was a child of a hippie family, that I was twice divorced and currently flat broke, that I was looking for not just a life partner but an active stepfather for my son. He took it all in stride with humor and sensitivity. Then, three months into our relationship, I handed him a draft of the memoir I'd been working on for a couple of years and asked him not to call me until he'd finished it. I spent that day nervously cleaning my apartment, filled with paranoia as I imagined his horror and/or disgust at my past.

Seven hours later, he rang my doorbell and pulled me into his arms. He loved me even more for everything I had been through, he said, and his words were like warm water washing decades of dirt from my skin.

He drops down beside me on the blanket now and puts his hand on my thigh. "Hey, babe. Everything under control?"

"Yeah, sure." I turn to him and smile, still amazed by my attraction to him. "But I think Em needs more sunscreen on his face." I pass him the bottle, and he jogs over to the boys.

The woman beside me is having a discussion with her daughter about a pogo stick. The girl clearly wants one, but her mother doesn't mince words. Not only is she too small for a pogo stick, she tells her child pragmatically, but they can't afford to buy toys and eat too. My heart pinches a little.

I rise to join the boys. They're involved in a serious game of tag now, weaving crazily to evade each other's touch. As my husband passes by me, he brushes my lips with a kiss.

My children's laughter fills the air. Gulls circle overhead. I stand with sand beneath my feet and the sun warm on my head. There's rarely a moment of this life of mine that goes by unappreciated.

THE SUN IS GETTING lower in the sky. It's close to dinnertime, and the tide is coming in. Soon it will increase to a rush, flooding the beach to erase the day's sand shapes. I collect buckets, shovels, sand molds, granola bar wrappers and sunscreen bottles. I shove everything into my enormous beach bag and then pick up my blanket and shake off the sand. I've already called to Remy and the boys several times, but nobody seems anxious to go inside.

"Cea," a voice calls, and I look around. My father is holding Ayla, still sleepy from her nap, in his arms.

"Hi, Dad. Look who's finally up!" I take my baby daughter and kiss her cheeks. She smiles, blue eyes sparkling, and kicks her legs excitedly. "That was a long break. Thank you," I say to my father. "She did well with you. She obviously adores her grandpa."

"That makes me feel good," Dad says, and our eyes meet briefly.

I know we're both thinking of that moment frozen in time

forty years ago, me arching away from him while he grins gamely, but we no longer need to talk about it. Over the past few years, we've discussed everything there is to discuss and rehashed everything there is to rehash. And somewhere along the way, my father became one of my favorite people on earth. This development has helped me redefine my family, because the Persons are all gone from my life now. I've lost contact with my aunts, and two weeks before Emerson was born, Grandma Jeanne passed away in her sleep. I hold on to my last name, knowing that when I die, it will likely die with me. It's a thought that saddens me, and yet I'm proud to be the one carrying it to the grave.

The woman and child beside me are getting ready to leave. The little girl is pitching a fit, saying she wants to build one more sandcastle and that she hates their tent. The mother is trying to keep her own emotions in check, but her eyes look defeated. I want to say something to her, but I'm not sure what.

Since becoming a parent myself, I can relate to my mother's struggles so much better. Even if I may not always find forgiveness toward her in my heart, I do find understanding. I am forty-two years old, not just years but generations older than Mom was when she had me, and I truly wonder how she coped at such a young age. I know the sound of a baby who won't stop screaming for hours, of a toddler in the throes of a flailing tantrum, of a child who questions my every decision. But somehow she held it together, refusing to abandon me, and she gave me what she could. Not a stable home or routine mealtimes or princess-themed birthday parties, perhaps, but absolute acceptance and the gift of a parent who showed me how, despite her fear, to move quickly past obstacles and face whatever may be coming around the next bend. There is a unique strength born from a youth spent longing for something different. I think about my own children, knowing they will never wish for a home with walls that don't billow in the wind, a night in an abandoned farmhouse, a day free from pot smoke, or their mother's attention. And honestly, I'm not convinced that this is entirely a good thing.

My baby girl bears no resemblance to my mother. All the same, when I look at Ayla, I see Mom smiling at me, and I can't help believing that perhaps her spirit sent my daughter to me as atonement for her own wrongs as a mother. How poetic, in both its simplicity

My family and me today in Vancouver: Ayla, Remy, Emerson, myself, and Avery. PHOTO CREDIT: PAUL GAGNON

and complexity, if it were true. I kiss the top of Ayla's sun-warmed head, and suddenly I know what I want to say to the woman beside me. It isn't anything profound, but it's the truth, and sometimes that's enough to make a difference. I wait until her daughter calms down a little, and then I catch her eye.

"You're doing a fantastic job," I say to her directly. "My mom was young and single too, and you know what? I couldn't have had a more memorable childhood."

"Thank you," the woman says, and she sounds grateful.

I put Ayla over my shoulder, stand up and call to my boys. My family gathers around me, my husband and father and children, and my creation is complete.

This is my normal.

Acknowledgments

Having given birth to three children (and found the experience considerably less taxing than the nearly seven years it took me to write this memoir!), I can't help but compare the many people who helped me breathe life into *North of Normal* with the creation of human life.

The embryo of this book is my memories of the experiences I've wanted to share for as long as I can remember.

The bones are the many friends, family and enthusiastic acquaintances who offered support for my project and/or read versions of my manuscript: Aaron Greaves, Bernadette Burns, Bernadette Ruddy, Bruce Adams, Camilla and Magnus Nedfors, Cathleen Baenziger, Christian Benzing, Christine Haebler, Christopher Rummery, Cori Creed, the Gagnon family, Erik Hammerum, Jane Clark, Joel Iseman, Liisa Wagner, LucyAnne Botham, Lynn Schooler, Martin Wood, Meghan Black, Michelle Morgan, Monica Loeffler, Nick Captain, Roberta Burns, Romy Kozak, Rowena Gates, Sierra Perry, Sven Grueber, Tammy Lorence and Tisha Bryant; Linda Schneider, for her love and absolute faith in me; Megan Burns, for her open-mindedness to my history; Sharron Chatterton, for her dedication to my grandfather and advocacy of his story being told; my father-in-law, Rene, who helped me find many much-needed hours to work; Dianne Wood, for her invaluable help and remarkable history with my grandfather; my "Boat Club" gals, Amanda Tapping, Janet Allan and Jenny Drake, who all cheered for me so fiercely; my beautiful friends Amanda Lupis, Cynthia Merriman, Jennifer Park, Lisa Rose Snow, Susan Scarlett, Traci Hansen-Crivici and Tracy Comessotti, who supplied wine and encouragement at our countless chat sessions over the years; and of course, my longtime girls—Carleigh Kage for decades of loyalty and laughter, Heather Greaves for her steadfast belief in me and incredible spirit, Nicole Oliver for her allegiance and generosity, Shannon Nering for her inspiration and exemplary listening skills, Suzana Rummery for her humor, realness and admirable courage, and Wendy McDevitt for her warmth and shining light. I can't express how much your friendships have meant to me throughout this writing process.

The eyes of this book are Scott Steedman, whose input helped me immensely in my search for an agent. The lungs are my literary agent, Jackie Kaiser at Westwood Creative Artists, whose belief in me has been transformational . . . not to mention that she's also the loveliest woman on earth to work with. The skin are the teams at both HarperCollins Canada and HarperCollins USA, who created beautiful designs for my story. And the brains are my fantastic editors: Iris Tupholme, whose invaluable insight and attention to detail inspired me to create the best version of my manuscript possible; Claire Wachtel, whose enthusiasm for my story renewed my creative forces; and Noelle Zitzer, Doug Richmond, Hannah Wood and Allyson Latta, for their hard work and encouragement. I feel truly blessed to have had the honor of working with all of you.

It is my family who form the muscles and heart of *North of Normal*: my father, who had the strength to read my story, cry about it and then give me his blessing to release it to the world. My husband, Remy, whose unfailing love, support, humor and strength as a partner are something I never thought I would find in this lifetime; I can truthfully say that I could not have completed this project without him. And of course, my heart of hearts—my three amazing children, Avery, Emerson and Ayla, who often sat on me, around me or in me (and sometimes all three!) as I wrote.

The folks who crossed my family's path during my childhood and now find their place within these pages are the lifeblood of this book; thank you for sharing in our adventures.

If our bodies have spirits, and I believe that they do, the soul of this memoir would be the Persons: Mom, Papa Dick, Grandma Jeanne, my aunts and uncle. Thank you for giving me such an extraordinary story to tell.

I must also thank a woman I have never met: Jeannette Walls, whose incredible memoir *The Glass Castle* inspired me to finally tell my story, which had been living unwritten inside of me for most of my life.

You have all helped me create a body of work that I can be proud of. Welcome to the world, baby book!

Discussion Questions

1. Clearly Cea's conception of normal changed substantially from the time she was born to her teen years to adulthood. Describe how your own "normal" has changed since your childhood.
2. Do you think Grandma Jeanne was genuinely happy living in the wilderness, or was she just going along with her husband's wishes?
3. The Person family certainly had their share of tribulations. Aside from Dane and Jessie, do you think the rest of the family—Michelle, Jan, Papa Dick, and Grandma Jeanne—suffered from mental illness?
4. *North of Normal* is a story of resilience. Do you think Cea was born resilient, or did she become so out of necessity? What about our own children today—do you think they need a high dose of adversity to become resilient?
5. At one point in the book, Cea's paternal grandparents offer to raise Cea, but Michelle refuses. As unprepared for motherhood as she was, why do you think she refused? And why do you think Cea's father didn't try harder to "rescue" Cea from her circumstances? Do you think Cea would have been better off in foster care?
6. What do you think of Karl? Was he a danger-crazed narcissist,

or a man who genuinely cared for Cea and was doing the best he could to provide for her and Michelle?

7. Why do you think Cea felt so conflicted about being molested by Barry? Why didn't she see herself as the victim and him as the perpetrator?
8. What do you think of the way Michelle was raised by her parents? Was it a healthy, all-accepting environment or an overpermissive one?
9. Cea's view of Papa Dick changed significantly from childhood to adulthood. Describe the events that caused this change, and if you think her feelings were justified.
10. The theme of survival is multilayered in Cea's memoir. What do you think has been the most important survival lesson in your own life?
11. Which character in the book angered you the most? Whom did you feel had the best intentions?
12. What did you think about Papa Dick's philosophy of living without fear? Is it foolishness or something to strive for?
13. Cea often felt as if she didn't fit in. Name a time in your life when you either felt similarly or empathized with someone else who didn't fit in. If you noticed it, did you do anything about it?
14. Cea was lucky that she had the physical requirements for becoming a model. If she didn't, do you think she would have languished with her family, or found another way to escape them?
15. Why do you think that Cea didn't fall into any of the typical pitfalls of the modeling industry (e.g., drugs, alcohol, casual sex) in her teens? And why do you think she succumbed and struggled with all of them later, in her mid- and late twenties?

16. Why do you think Cea didn't try to repair relations with her family members, and vice versa, until her early thirties?
17. Of all the trials Cea went through, which do you think the most difficult was for her, and why?
18. Do you think Cea would have been more or less successful in her career had she been raised by a more conventional family?
19. What do you think about moving an entire family to the wilderness? Would you ever attempt an experiment like that, even for a short time?
20. What about this book resonated with you the most?

About the Author

Cea Sunrise Person, a happily married mother of three, supported herself from age thirteen to thirty-one as an international model, working primarily in Europe. She lives in Vancouver, British Columbia.